D0342272

Praise for
Jewish Megatrends:
Charting the Course of the American Jewish Future

"Schwarz combines remarkable institutional building experience, [an] extensive network of relationships with the best and the brightest in Jewish life, and keen knowledge of the American religious landscape to produce a must read for those concerned with the genuine challenges of the next era in American Jewish life.... The book is insightful and creative ... sober and hopeful, realistic and idealistic, temperate and optimistic, pragmatic and visionary. Brims with wisdom and confidence...."

—**Rabbi Irwin Kula**, president, Clal—The National Jewish Center for Learning and Leadership

"Provide[s] an invaluable framework for understanding the challenging dynamics of contemporary American Judaism [and] a blueprint for the future that will inspire and motivate leaders of our community. Anyone who wants to see American Judaism thrive in the twenty-first century should read this book!"

—**Rabbi Marla Feldman**, executive director, Women of Reform Judaism

"Face[s] difficult issues head-on. The faith we share in a creative Jewish future is due in large part to people like Schwarz and those visionaries he has gathered around him in these essays. Rabbis and other Jewish leaders should pay careful attention."

—**Arthur Green**, rector, Hebrew College Rabbinical School; author, *Ehyeh: A Kabbalah for Tomorrow* and *Radical Judaism*

"Throws down the gauntlet to Jewish community leaders seeking to engage the next generation in this perceptive book.... The result: a thoughtful road map for the future of the Jewish people in North America based on wisdom, justice, community and purpose.

—**Dr. Ron Wolfson**, author, *Relational Judaism: Using the Power of Relationships to Transform the Jewish Community*; Fingerhut Professor of Education, American Jewish University; co-founder, Synagogue 3000/Next *Dor*

"Spot-on in its analysis of the biggest changes in American Judaism.... Read this book to become informed, but more importantly, read it to become inspired to build the next vibrant chapter of Jewish life."

—**Rabbi Elie Kaunfer**, executive director, Mechon Hadar; author, *Empowered Judaism: What Independent Minyanim Can Teach Us about Building Vibrant Jewish Communities*

"A thought provoking, challenging and important book at this critical time of transition in Jewish life."

—**Rabbi Laura Geller**, senior rabbi, Temple Emanuel of Beverly Hills

"Delivers an excellent and well thought out set of assumptions ... combined with some of the best thinkers and doers in the American Jewish community. I recommend this book to anyone searching to learn more about the major trends and direction of our Jewish community."

—**David Cygielman**, founder and CEO, Moishe Houses

"Challenges us to do much-needed big picture thinking about the nature of American Judaism today.... By gathering and challenging major American Jewish thinkers in one volume, Sid Schwarz has given us the gift of a critical conversation wrapped into one important book."

—**Dr. Erica Brown**, scholar-in-residence, Jewish Federation of Greater Washington; author, *Inspired Jewish Leadership: Practical Approaches to Building Strong Communities* and *Spiritual Boredom: Rediscovering the Wonder of Judaism*

"A thoughtful work that challenges the traditional biases of decision makers in the Jewish community and empowers them to take risks and step into what could be a glorious future."

—**Rabbi Charles Simon**, executive director, Federation of Jewish Men's Clubs; author, *Building a Successful Volunteer Culture: Finding Meaning in Service in the Jewish Community*

"[A] compelling twenty-first-century case for a Judaism of four key value propositions—wisdom, social justice, community and sacred purpose—gains a fifth—honest conversation—through the voices of some of American Jewry's most creative leaders."

—**Shawn Landres**, co-founder, Jewish Jumpstart

"Wisely and skillfully offers a multi-dimensional platform for reinvigorating the Jewish experiences and charts a course for a future of Jewish relevance."

—**Rabbi Will Berkovitz**, senior vice president, Repair the World

"Brings ... many ... exciting developments [in modern Jewish life] into a focus that provides a fuller understanding of where we are and where we can go. It is a must read anyone thinking about the future of American Jewish life."

—**Esther Safran Foer**, director, Sixth & I

"Insightful and honest analysis [as well as] specific ideas for how we must evolve as a community.... Offer[s] innovative strategies for building a Jewish community so compelling that future generations will be inspired to connect."

—**Nancy Kaufman**, CEO, National Council of Jewish Women

"Offers us a roadmap to the unparalleled changes affecting the Jewish world today.... Uniquely lays out a new reality filled with challenges and opportunities that could not be more timely. After reading this book, one thing is for certain: the Jewish world of tomorrow cannot and will not look like the Jewish world of today."

—**David Bryfman**, The Jewish Education Project; co-designer, The Jewish Futures Conferences

"A must-read for anyone who cares about the future of the Jewish community.... Present[s] a realistic, yet hopeful view of how the Jewish world is changing and how those with leadership responsibilities in the community can respond."

—**Rabbi Laura Baum**, OurJewishCommunity.org and Congregation Beth Adam, Loveland, Ohio

"Engaging and spirited.... Calls for authenticity—a renewed focus on community, prayer, learning, social justice, Israel travel and cultural participation as ends in themselves, rather than as mere instruments to some other end. To get the best results, just do the right thing."

—**Professor Steven M. Cohen**, Hebrew Union College–Jewish Institute of Religion and Berman Jewish Policy Archive @ NYU Wagner

"If you want to understand the here-and-now of the Jewish community in the twenty-first century, then read this book today.... Helps us better understand the new narratives and urgent challenges of Jewish identity, engagement, and continuity."

—**Lori Weinstein**, CEO and executive director, Jewish Women International

"Schwarz's essay-as-premise and its responses reflect a Jewish world that is recalibrating and transitioning rather than floundering, and testify to the wealth of options for today's Jews to express Jewish identity and connect to core values, texts and tradition.

—**Esther D. Kustanowitz**, program coordinator, NextGen Engagement
Initiative, Jewish Federation of Greater Los Angeles

"Powerful … provid[es] a compelling and nuanced vision of what a meaningful Jewish future can look like and the change-agents who are working to realize this vision."

—**Rabbi Ari Weiss**, executive director, Uri L'Tzedek

"A tour de force… I encourage all committed Jewish professionals and lay leaders to absorb and process the vision in this book."

—**Jakir Manela**, executive director, Pearlstone Center, Baltimore, Maryland

"An impressive body of thought leaders offer their perspective on the key challenges of the twenty-first century, as well as their insights on how the community can respond with intelligence and creativity."

—**Rabbi Jason Kimelman-Block**, rabbi-in-residence, Bend the Arc:
A Jewish Partnership for Justice

"Gather[s] together an all-star cast of movers and shakers who have broken boundaries in their respective ways. Each contributes powerfully to a larger thesis that is important reading for all who take leadership seriously."

—**Rabbi Avraham (Avi) Weiss**, founder, Yeshivat Chovevei Torah and
Yeshivat Maharat; author, *Spiritual Activism: A Jewish Guide to
Leadership and Repairing the World*

Jewish Megatrends

Other Jewish Lights Books by Rabbi Sidney Schwarz

Finding a Spiritual Home:
    How a New Generation of Jews Can Transform
    the American Synagogue

Judaism and Justice:
    The Jewish Passion to Repair the World

Schwarz, Sid,
Jewish megatrends :
charting the course of t
2013.
33305228347963
ca   08/21/13

Jewish Megatrends

Charting the Course of the American Jewish Future

Rabbi Sidney Schwarz

Foreword by Ambassador Stuart E. Eizenstat

For People of All Faiths, All Backgrounds
JEWISH LIGHTS Publishing
Woodstock, Vermont

Jewish Megatrends:
Charting the Course of the American Jewish Future

2013 Hardcover Edition, First Printing
© 2013 by Sidney Schwarz
Foreword © 2013 by Stuart E. Eizenstat

All rights reserved. No part of this book may be reproduced or transmitted in any form or by any means, electronic or mechanical, including photocopying, recording, or by any information storage and retrieval system, without permission in writing from the publisher.

For information regarding permission to reprint material from this book, please mail or fax your request in writing to Jewish Lights Publishing, Permissions Department, at the address / fax number listed below, or e-mail your request to permissions@jewishlights.com.

Library of Congress Cataloging-in-Publication Data
Jewish megatrends : charting the course of the American Jewish future / [edited by] Rabbi Sidney Schwarz ; foreword by Ambassador Stuart E. Eizenstat.
      pages cm
   Includes bibliographical references and index.
   ISBN 978-1-58023-667-6
   1. Judaism—United States—History—21st century. 2. Jews—United States—Identity.
   3. Young adults—United States—Attitudes. I. Schwarz, Sid, editor of compilation.
   BM205.J495 2013
   296.0973'090501—dc23
                                            2012045819

10 9 8 7 6 5 4 3 2 1

Manufactured in the United States of America

Jacket Design: Tim Holtz

Published by Jewish Lights Publishing
A Division of LongHill Partners, Inc.
Sunset Farm Offices, Route 4, P.O. Box 237
Woodstock, VT 05091
Tel: (802) 457-4000 Fax: (802) 457-4004
www.jewishlights.com

To my children
Daniel, Joel, and Jennifer

"Fortunate is the generation in which the elders listen to the youth."
Talmud, *Rosh haShana* 25b

Contents

Contents

Part 3   The Way Forward

FOREWORD

Ambassador Stuart E. Eizenstat

Sidney Schwarz has written a critically important book. In addition to his insightful and important lead essay, he assembled thirteen of the most important American Jewish thinkers and practitioners to provide a dramatic challenge to the major institutions of the American Jewish community—from synagogues to Jewish community centers to Jewish Federations—and their leaders to adapt to the megatrends impacting American Jews, and particularly younger Jews who are no longer gravitating to the traditional organizations of the established Jewish community. The book offers a constructive way to deal with revolutionary changes impacting the world's largest Diaspora community.

For more than three decades, **Stuart E. Eizenstat** has served in senior positions with the United States government, including chief domestic adviser and chief White House policy advisor to President Jimmy Carter and in a variety of positions in the Clinton Administration, such as U.S. ambassador to the European Union and special representative to the president on Holocaust-era issues. He has received awards from the governments of France, Germany, Austria, Belgium, Israel, and the United States, and holds seven honorary doctorate degrees. He has also served in many leadership positions in the Jewish community, and is now co-chairman of the Jewish People Policy Institute in Jerusalem. He is the author of *The Future of the Jews: How Global Forces Are Impacting the Jewish People, Israel and Its Relationship with the United States* and *Imperfect Justice: Looted Assets, Slave Labor, and the Unfinished Business of World War II*.

No one is better positioned to provide this novel analysis and prescription than Sid Schwarz. Rabbi Sid, as he is affectionately called, has held senior positions in Jewish communal organizations and was a leader in organizing the Jewish demonstrations to help free Soviet Jews. He is the founding rabbi of an innovative and flourishing Reconstructionist synagogue and created a highly successful national institution, PANIM, which brings thousands of young American Jews to Washington and trains them—with a unique methodology using Judaism and Jewish values—to become change agents on the political and social issues facing our country and the world. Those who read the book will also see that he is a wonderful writer and a deep thinker.

Schwarz analyzes the dramatic drop in Jewish identification and affiliation in the United States against the backdrop of the successful integration of Jews into American society. He wrestles with the challenges that our atomized and individualistic society pose to a Jewish community that has always stressed collective responsibility, both toward other Jews and for the larger world.

Schwarz identifies a distinction between what he calls "tribal Jews" and "convenantal Jews." Tribal Jews see their identity in political and ethnic terms and are focused on threats to Jewish survival from enemies of the Jewish people and Israel and from rampant assimilation. Covenantal Jews, prevalent among next-generation Jews, have a weaker commitment to Jewish group identification even as they seek ways to live lives that are consistent with Jewish values, of which many may be unaware. Unless this younger generation is brought into the Jewish community, they could be permanently lost. Schwarz offers a novel four-point prescription for the Jewish community that needs to be taken seriously by the lay leaders and professionals who serve as the stewards of the American Jewish community.

Schwarz's analysis complements my own understanding of emerging trends in the world that I set forth in my new book *The Future of the Jews*. I look at how twenty-first-century global trends—the shift of power from the United States and Europe to nations of the East and South; globalization; the battle for the direction of the world's 1.6 billion Muslims; new security challenges, including the Iranian threat; a new form of anti-Semitism aimed at delegitimizing Israel as a Jewish state—all pose a risk to the status of the Jewish people in the world. I believe that we can successfully meet these new external challenges. However, it is critical that as we do, we not lose sight of the many internal threats to Jewish continuity, which may be even more difficult to overcome. This is where *Jewish Megatrends* has so much to teach us.

I see the American Jewish community of five million as being like an enterprise with two, roughly equal divisions: one healthy and engaged in all aspects of Jewish life—religious, cultural, political; the other division is near bankruptcy and challenges the health of the overall American Jewish venture. This second division is underscored by soaring intermarriage rates with low rates of conversion by the non-Jewish spouse, birth rates below replacement levels, and a dramatic decline in Jewish philanthropy for Jewish causes and membership in major Jewish organizations.

We need to strengthen the healthy division, creating a massive Jewish educational endowment to lower the increasingly unaffordable costs of Jewish day schools, reach out to intermarried couples, and dramatically increase support for Hillels on campus and for Birthright Israel. The State of Israel must realize that strengthening the American Jewish community in ways that *Jewish Megatrends* suggests is in its national security interest.

Jewish Megatrends offers a vision for a community that can simultaneously strengthen the institutions that serve those who seek greater Jewish identification and attract younger Jews, many of whom are currently outside of the orbit of Jewish communal life. Schwarz and his collaborators provide an exciting path, building on proven examples, that we ignore at our peril.

PREFACE

The nineteenth-century Danish theologian Søren Kierkegaard was quoted as saying that life is lived forward but only understood backward. I think of that saying when reflecting on the trajectory of my own life and career serving the Jewish people and the Jewish community. Nothing that I've done was part of a grand plan. Yet in reflecting back on my career, I now see that, time and again, I was more inclined to forge my own path, create new institutions, and invent new programs rather than fit into more conventional career boxes.

My first book, *Finding a Spiritual Home: How a New Generation of Jews Can Transform the American Synagogue* (Jewish Lights), was a result of twenty-five years of thinking about how to do synagogues differently. It started with a course I was invited to teach at the Reconstructionist Rabbinical College by Ira Silverman (*z"l*) soon after I was ordained. Some ten years later, as the founding rabbi of Adat Shalom Reconstructionist Congregation in Bethesda, Maryland, I had the great privilege of working with a community that was open to risk taking and thinking outside of the box. Adat Shalom became an ideal laboratory for me to experiment freely in the realms of religious worship, social action, life-cycle events, and community life. When I decided to step down from that pulpit, I wanted to better document how and why the congregation was as successful as it was in attracting Jews who would not otherwise be inclined to affiliate with a synagogue. I undertook a study of three other congregations, one from each of the major denominations of American Jewish life, to create a composite of new paradigm synagogues that had the ability to attract next-generation Jews. I called the new paradigm the "synagogue-community."

Ever since the publication of *Finding a Spiritual Home* I have worked with dozens of synagogues and hundreds of rabbis to help transform synagogues into places that challenge the minds and touch the hearts of Jews.

In *Judaism and Justice: The Jewish Passion to Repair the World* (Jewish Lights), I set out to articulate the history, theology, and sociology of the Jewish engagement with justice, service, and social responsibility. My laboratory for this work was PANIM: The Institute for Jewish Leadership and Values. I founded PANIM in 1988 to bridge the gap between the fields of Jewish education and Jewish public affairs. Over the course of more than twenty years, PANIM became a training ground for young people, educators, and rabbis to inspire activism, leadership, and service in the context of both the Jewish community and the larger world. Our tools were Jewish texts, Jewish values, and the role model of Jews who came before us and played leadership roles in many of the progressive social causes of the twentieth century. It became clear to me that PANIM was creating a new framework for contemporary Jewish identity, one that integrated serious Jewish learning with a commitment to heal a broken world.

I am not unaware of how many Jews seem uninterested in Jewish life, nor do I take lightly the studies that show rising rates of assimilation and intermarriage. Yet I served as the rabbi of two different congregations for eight years each and I worked with thousands of young people through PANIM programs. Week in and week out I was able to see how Judaism could excite the passion of Jews. Judaism was neither seen as irrelevant nor as a burden but rather as a framework to make life more meaningful and a source of wisdom that helped people navigate the most challenging issues in their personal lives and in society.

In *Jewish Megatrends* I build on my previous two books, *Finding a Spiritual Home: How a New Generation of Jews Can Transform the American Synagogue* and *Judaism and Justice: The Jewish Passion to Repair the World*. I attempt to paint a picture of the challenges that the Jewish community faces as it tries to adapt to a new social landscape and a new generation that comes with a very different set of assumptions and expectations than any generation that came before it. I have taken that which I found "works" and shaped it into a four-part prescription of what

I think needs to be the new playbook for any Jewish institution that hopes to speak to the next generation of American Jews.

I then reached out to some of the top leaders of different sectors of American Jewish life and asked them to react to my prescription. Does it sound right to you? What are you seeing in your particular sector of Jewish life? To what extent is your sector adapting to the dramatic changes taking place in American society? What are the most exciting innovations that you are trying, and what makes them work? What emerges is not only a portrait of a community in transition but also some clear patterns of how we can effectively engage the next generation of American Jews.

It is true that some established institutions are stuck in old paradigms and are becoming increasingly irrelevant. But a handful of established institutions are taking bold risks to reinvent themselves. And then there is an amazing array of relatively new organizations and initiatives, many led by and aimed at the next generation. They are not only worth watching, but they are also worth our investment of time, attention, and financial resources. I believe that over the course of the next decade there is a unique opportunity for cross-fertilization between the established institutions of the American Jewish community and the robust innovation sector of American Jewish life. If each side recognizes the value of the other and commits to a program of collaboration, I believe that we are on the verge of a renaissance of American Jewish life. I hope that this book contributes to that conversation and that collaboration.

I am grateful to my thirteen contributors for being willing to engage in this dialogue with me. Each, in his or her own right, has been a pioneer, rising to the top of their respective fields not by being conventional but by being risk takers. In the process of developing each essay I learned much from them. More than once I returned to my original lead essay and made revisions based on the conversations I had with the book's contributors and the observations that they made about the Jewish community. I want to particularly thank Rabbi Joy Levitt, Nigel Savage, and Dr. Jonathan S. Woocher, who took the time to give me very helpful comments and feedback to later versions of my lead essay. The book also benefitted from the feedback of several other cherished colleagues, including Dr. Erica Brown, David Bryfman, Rabbi Elie Kaunfer, Rabbi Jason Kimelman-Block, and

Shawn Landres. I am grateful to Rabbis Irwin Kula and Brad Hirschfield, who welcomed me into the Clal family of thinkers and communal leaders after I stepped down from the presidency of PANIM. I feel privileged to be able to continue my work in training the next generation of rabbis under the auspices of Clal—The National Jewish Center for Learning and Leadership. I am also grateful to Emily Wichland and Stuart M. Matlins of Jewish Lights, who guided this book from concept to publication.

I dedicated my first book to my parents, Allan and Judy Schwarz, and my second book to my wife, Sandy Perlstein. I am fortunate to still have my parents in my life. And I can't imagine my life without Sandy, who is a constant source of encouragement and love. It can only be considered *b'shert* (fated) that my third book is about the future. Thus it is appropriate to dedicate this book to my three children, Danny, Joel, and Jennifer. They are now young adults making their way in the world, and I could not be more proud of them.

Some people say that parenting is the hardest job they ever had, but, for me, it has been a source of great joy. To the extent that I hope that this book helps make the Jewish community an ever more vibrant and creative place, my fondest wish is that my children, and theirs, find it to be a place that gives them both roots, to know where they came from and who they are, and wings, so they can become who they are destined to be.

Part 1

The Changing Face of Jewish Identity in America

Jewish Megatrends

Charting the Course of the American Jewish Future

Rabbi Sidney Schwarz

The Jewish community is in a time of transition. Those who are active in the community certainly know this. Many of the institutions that have been the backbone of the organized Jewish community—synagogues, JCCs, Federations, membership organizations—have been losing market share for more than two decades. This is a decline that cannot be attributed to bad leadership or a bad economy. The decline is deep and systemic, and it will require dramatic rethinking on the part of those who are the stewards of the Jewish world.

This essay offers a framework to help us better understand the dramatic changes taking place within American Jewry and how those in a position of leadership in the community—Jewish communal professionals, rabbis,

Rabbi Sidney Schwarz founded and for twenty-one years led PANIM: The Institute for Jewish Leadership and Values, an organization that is dedicated to inspiring, training, and empowering Jewish youth to a life of leadership, activism, and service. He is also the founding rabbi of Adat Shalom Reconstructionist Congregation in Bethesda, Maryland, where he continues to teach and lead services. A PhD in Jewish history, Rabbi Schwarz is currently a senior fellow at Clal—The National Jewish Center for Learning and Leadership and a consultant to Jewish organizations. He is the author of *Finding a Spiritual Home: How a New Generation of Jews Can Transform the American Synagogue* and *Judaism and Justice: The Jewish Passion to Repair the World*.

lay leaders, and foundations—might be able to address the challenges that face the major institutions that compose the organized Jewish community. It reframes the conversation away from more typical hand-wringing and doom and gloom expressions, which are hardly constructive, toward a clearer understanding of the challenge that we need to collectively confront.

From Generation to Generation

I begin with a personal narrative. My parents typify the Shoah (Holocaust) generation. Both their families came from Poland and emigrated from the poor backwaters of the Polish shtetl to the more cosmopolitan Berlin in the 1930s, where the families came to know each other. My maternal grandmother sensed the dangers of Nazism and prevailed upon my grandfather to move to the *Yishuv*, pre-state Palestine, where my mother was raised. Financial hardships in the Holy Land then brought them to Baltimore and, after that, to New York.

Most of my father's family perished in the camps, but two siblings survived. At age fourteen my aunt went on Youth Aliyah to Israel, where she raised a family and lived her whole life. My father was ransomed out of Germany by relatives in the United States when that was still possible. Just two weeks before *Kristallnacht* (the Night of Broken Glass, which launched the physical assault on Jewish people and property in Germany in 1938), he came to New York at age sixteen without his family. He was a passenger on the last successful voyage of the *St. Louis*, a boat whose next voyage would be termed "the voyage of the damned," because it was forced to return to Europe when the ship was not allowed to disembark the Jewish refugees aboard even though the ship was within sight of Miami. Half of the passengers of that ship subsequently lost their lives in the Shoah.

As were hundreds of thousands of other Jews who came to these shores, my parents were deeply scarred by the Holocaust, in awe at the founding of the State of Israel, and eternally grateful to the United States of America, which allowed them to build a new life. Their lives revolved around their synagogue, the events of the Jewish community, and the fate of the State of Israel, where dozens of their family now lived. As immigrants, they could not imagine navigating American society without the intermediary agencies represented by the Jewish community.

YOUR GUEST NUMBER IS
50

IN-N-OUT BURGER MORGAN HILL
198 3 362 3126

Cashier: KENNETH JA
Check : 50

Db1Db1	3.85
> GR L T only	
FF	1.75

Counter-Eat In	5.60
TAX 9.00%	.50
Amount Due	$6.10

| Visa Tender | $6.10 |
| Change | $.00 |

CHARGE DETAIL

SALE
Card Type: Visa
Account: ***********4394 C
Auth Code: 408228
Trans #:   3126
Auth Ref: 1440407885
AUTH AMT: $6.10
THANK YOU!
Questions/Comments: Call 800-786-1000

2017-05-02   L1 T3   3:52 PM

I was born in 1953. My most powerful childhood memories include the anxiety in my household in the weeks leading up to the Six-Day War. My parents felt certain that Jews were about to face another holocaust if Israel were to be overrun by invading Arab armies. The subsequent Israeli victory was seen as a miracle—David slaying Goliath.

Nine years later, in 1976, I was on a public bus on a crowded street in Israel when all traffic stopped. The bus driver turned up the radio, and we heard the news bulletin that an Israeli commando team had succeeded in flying twenty-five hundred miles to an airport in Entebbe, Uganda, to rescue more than one hundred Jewish passengers who were being held hostage by terrorists and the soldiers of dictator Idi Amin. The rescue symbolized that Israel was an international protector of Jews; Jews would no longer be victims. As the newsflash ended on the bus, everyone stood up, as if on cue, and sang "Hatikvah," Israel's national anthem.

Fast-forward: December 6, 1987. The Jewish community decided to organize a rally in solidarity with Soviet Jewry to coincide with the visit of Russian premier Mikhail Gorbachev to meet with President Ronald Reagan in Washington, D.C. The Summit Rally for Soviet Jewry was not without its risks. Until then, the largest Soviet Jewry rally was a few years earlier and held across from the United Nations when then premier Leonid Brezhnev came to New York. The crowd then was estimated at ten to twelve thousand people. On the huge expanse of the mall behind the U.S. Capitol, ten thousand people would have spelled "failure."

David Harris, now the head of the American Jewish Committee, was then the director of the AJC's Washington office. He coordinated all of the plans for the rally. I was then the executive director of the Jewish Community Relations Council of Greater Washington, D.C., and I served as one of David's lieutenants. On the permit we filed for the rally with the National Park Service, we had to provide an estimate for the crowd we expected. We put down fifty thousand, though no one in any position of leadership thought that was possible, including us. Not during the winter. Not in Washington, D.C., where the Jewish population was a fraction of what it was in New York. More prudently, we planned on setting up shuttles from airport and railway terminals for twenty-five thousand people coming in from out of town.

I was privileged to be on the speaker's podium that day behind the Capitol along with then vice president George Bush, Elie Wiesel, newly freed Jewish refusenik Anatoly (soon to be Natan) Sharansky, and Peter, Paul and Mary, who sang. The windchill factor was about zero. But people came. Not 25,000. Not 50,000. But 250,000. The next morning President Reagan started his meeting with Premier Gorbachev by showing him the front pages of the *New York Times* and the *Washington Post*, both of which featured photos and stories about the rally. He stated that there would be no increased trade, no progress on arms reduction, and no warming of relations between the United States and the USSR until Gorbachev changed his policy of repression against Soviet Jews.

Within a year of that Summit Rally the gates of emigration opened for Jews. Close to one million Jews left the Soviet Union, most of them moving to Israel. The Soviet Jewry movement, a cause that had fully engaged me for twenty-five years, since my first visit to Russia as a high school student with United Synagogue Youth (USY, the Conservative Jewish national youth movement), could claim victory. The movement has been cited as a turning point in the history of human rights, because it gave evidence of the power and effectiveness of international citizen activism against a totalitarian regime.

I begin with these personal stories because they help explain why the Jewish community today is struggling to engage the next generation of Jews. In the course of my life I have been exposed to events and people that reflect both the tragedy and the triumph of Jewish history. My parents and their families were directly affected by the Holocaust and the birth of the State of Israel. I have firsthand memories of several glorious chapters in Israel's history, including its victory in the 1967 Six-Day War and its dramatic rescue of Jewish hostages at the airport in Entebbe. Meeting with Jewish refuseniks, who had the courage to practice Judaism and fight for immigration rights despite the dangers that entailed, gave me a deep sense of pride in my own Jewish heritage and subsequently shaped the course of my life and my career.

My generation now fills the ranks of the professionals and lay leaders who run the organized Jewish community. It is a generation that came of age in the 1960s, and we have a hard time imagining that we are now on the other side of a generation gap. We believe that we invented the generation gap and thus are immune from the blind spots that affect those on the older side of the divide. Yet the Jewish community has lost major market share among generation X (born 1965–81), and it seems that we are poised to do even worse with engaging the millennials (born 1982–2000) as they mature into adulthood.

I want to focus on three factors that have contributed to the weakening of Jewish identity and affiliation in America: Israel and its ongoing challenges, the end of the ethnic era of American Jewry, and overarching trends in American society. I will then look at trends in American culture and society that require thoughtful and strategic responses. Finally, I will suggest four propositions that point to areas of activity that can and should serve as the focus of the American Jewish future. I think that these areas are ripe for significant investment on the part of philanthropists and intensive programmatic efforts on the part of synagogues and Jewish organizations. Despite some of the current indicators of communal deterioration, I see something very different. On the margins of the community there are stirrings of Jewish revival. It looks a lot different than the Jewish community of the last generation, but if properly nurtured, it has the potential to grow into a great renaissance of American Jewish life.

> Despite some of the current indicators of communal deterioration, I see something very different. On the margins of the community there are stirrings of Jewish revival. It looks a lot different than the Jewish community of the last generation, but if properly nurtured, it has the potential to grow into a great renaissance of American Jewish life.

The Israel Variable

Gen X came to maturity as the optimism about the Olso peace process focused on the Middle East came to a crashing halt with the onset of the Second Intifada in September 2000. An epidemic of suicide bombings throughout Israel over the next few years effectively ended the peace process. The UN World Conference against Racism in Durban, South Africa, in September 2001 highlighted that, in a post-apartheid world, Israel—a democracy—was the new pariah nation of the international community. That, even though dozens of countries that had never known a fair and free election had far worse records on a range of civil liberty and human rights issues.

Notwithstanding the double standard, Israel bears more than a little responsibility for changing the way younger Jews started to think about their Jewish identity. Even as America remained Israel's strongest ally, a succession of Israeli governments continued to build Jewish settlements in the territories that were captured in the 1967 war despite strenuous objections of U.S. officials. Because Israel is a democracy, human rights organizations operate freely in the country, and they have found much to report on in terms of Israel's treatment of Palestinians under their control. Similarly, Israel's vigorous free press reported story after story that took the gleam off Israel's reputation as a country to be admired and emulated.

Israel became a badly tarnished brand. No PR efforts on the part of the Israeli government or by the resourceful and well-funded array of American Jewish organizations could counter the impression that Jewish youth received from the mainstream American media. After the Six-Day War, Israel was no longer the struggling democracy in a hostile Arab neighborhood trying to make the desert bloom. The miracle of *kibbutz galuyot*, the way a young and struggling nation spared no effort or expense to gather in oppressed Jews from the four corners of the world during its first decade of statehood, was now something for the history books. Instead, Israel was portrayed as the preeminent military power in the Middle East. It was also a country that was part of a select group of nations that possessed nuclear weapons (though Israel has never publically acknowledged this). If sympathy for a people decimated by the Holocaust helped create the international will to establish a Jewish homeland in the State of Israel, then international sympathy in the post-1967 period was firmly on the side of the Palestinians. Despite evidence that Palestinians were cynically used as pawns by Arab leaders, Israel was the nation seen as standing in the way of Palestinian well-being and political self-determination.

Even Israel's concessions for peace seemed to fuel Israel's diplomatic isolation and approbation in the international community. Soon after "experimenting" with ceding a piece of captured territory—the Gaza strip—to the Palestinian Authority in 2005, the area was taken over by the terrorist organization Hamas in free elections. It wasn't long before Gaza became a base for regular shelling of Israeli civilians and a safe harbor for Islamic extremists bent on Israel's destruction. When Israel decided to act in her own defense by invading Gaza in early 2009, accusations of disproportionate retaliation filled the international media. A subsequent UN report from a commission headed up by respected international jurist (and a committed Jew) Richard Goldstone said that both Hamas and Israel were likely guilty of war crimes and that further investigations were warranted.

In the course of forty years Israel went from being a darling of the Western world and the impetus for a revival of Jewish pride and identity to something very morally complex. It is true that thousands of Jewish college students have been mobilized into Israel advocacy organizations and campaigns to defend Israel against unfair accusations in the court of world opinion. But the far greater majority of young Jews have distanced themselves from Israel. The result is that today Israel is anything but the unifying force in American Jewish life that it once was.[1]

One 2010 study compared attachment to Israel by age cohort. Asked if the destruction of Israel would be a personal tragedy, 80 percent of Jews over sixty-five said "yes," while only 48 percent of Jews under thirty-five said "yes." Forty percent of the older cohort considered themselves "very emotionally attached to Israel," while only 22 percent of the younger cohort did. In a third question, 83 percent of the older cohort was "comfortable with the idea of a Jewish state," while only 53 percent of the younger cohort was. The authors of the study, Steven M. Cohen and Ari Y. Kelman, who have tracked these questions over time, note two significant variables. One was that attitudes among younger American Jews strongly correlated with the marital status of their parents. The offspring of the intermarried were far less attached to Israel than those from in-married families, suggesting that if the intermarriage rate continues to rise, the attachment to Israel may become even more tenuous. But the authors also note that over time, large sections of younger Jews were moving from "disengaged" with Israel to "alienated" from Israel.[2]

The single most significant intervention that might change the trajectory of the trends cited above is Birthright Israel. Promoted by philanthropists Charles Bronfman and Michael Steinhardt and launched in December 1999 as a partnership between the Jewish Federations of North America and the government of Israel, Birthright has sent close to three hundred thousand young adults to Israel on free ten-day trips. Participants have come from sixty different countries and more than one thousand North American colleges and universities. The most recent study of alumni who had participated in the program five to ten years earlier suggests that the impact of the trip on Jewish identity has staying power. As compared to a peer group that did not participate in the program, Birthright alumni were 42 percent more likely to feel very committed to Israel and 45 percent more likely to marry other Jews.[3] Assuming that funding for the program remains stable, Birthright has the ability to significantly impact the attitudes and behaviors of next-generation Jews on matters related to Jewish identity and ties to the State of Israel.

Tribal Jews and Covenantal Jews

Tracking the changing relationship of Jews to Israel is important because for more than a century, American Jewish identity has been driven more by ethnic affinity and a concern for survival than it has by faith and religious observance. To a community so shaped by tragedy and persecution, Israel became, in the words of one scholar, "the civil religion of American Jewry."[4]

But there are other generational differences between the younger American Jews and their elders that are not related to Israel. In my 2000 book *Finding a Spiritual Home: How a New Generation of Jews Can Transform the American Synagogue*, I identified several characteristics of what I called the "new American Jew":[5]

- They do not respond emotionally to appeals based on the Holocaust or the State of Israel.
- They do not derive their sense of place from their Jewish connections.
- While aware of historical anti-Semitism and ongoing anti-Israel animus in the world, they do not share the persecution phobias of earlier Jewish generations.

These observations paralleled the findings of a major study of Jewish identity by Steven M. Cohen and Arnold M. Eisen that came out the same year in the book *The Jew Within.*[6] Cohen and Eisen coined the term "the sovereign self" to describe a generation that was radically individualistic and less and less inclined to identify with the public institutions of Jewish life.

More recently I have described the growing polarization in the Jewish world in terms of the difference between tribal and covenantal identity. Tribal Jews see their identity in political and ethnic terms. They are very concerned about threats to Jewish survival, both from enemies of Israel and the Jewish people and from the rampant assimilation within the Jewish community. They do not apologize for investing their time and resources in advancing group self-interest, and they have created an array of Jewish organizations to support their work. Tribal Jews have a strong affinity for the State of Israel because it is the most public manifestation and validation of the Jewish people's existence and survival.

In contrast to tribal Jews, covenantal Jews see their identity less as a matter of group solidarity than as a spiritual legacy. I use the term "covenantal" to distinguish behaviors that align with core teachings of Judaism even if those behaviors are not attached to overt forms of affiliation with the group. If covenantal Jews feel an affinity to Judaism it is because of the ethics and values that Judaism has brought into the world, such as justice (*tzedek*), compassion (*chesed*), human dignity (*tzelem elohim*), and the protection of those who are most vulnerable (*ahavat ger*). Most covenantal Jews could not name these values in Hebrew or identify the source of these concepts in Judaism's sacred texts, but they are aware that these are ideas that Judaism brought into the world via the Bible and they are very proud of it. In addition, despite the fact that the term "covenant" (*brit* in Hebrew) is closely tied to the Jewish people's encounter with God in Exodus chapter 19, in the way I am using the term "covenantal Jew" here, theology has little to do with it.

Covenantal Jews feel pride when Jews in various fields of endeavor make contributions to the world, yet they resist the Jewish community's emphasis on group survival as the highest priority. Motivated by what they see as the higher mandate of Judaism, their loyalties are decidedly more

11

global and universal. Covenantal Jews would not respond well to the classic Jewish teaching that requires supporting Jews before supporting non-Jews. Nor are they sympathetic to appeals that might come from parents or Jewish authority figures that they should marry other Jews. All such claims that privilege Jews over other human beings strike covenantal Jews as ethically objectionable. If Israel is accused of human rights violations, covenantal Jews are as inclined to voice their criticism about it as they are about any other country. Perhaps they are even more inclined to do so because it proves their commitment to principle over their own people.[7]

I hasten to add that the gap between tribal Jews and covenantal Jews is not exclusively a generation gap. There are younger Jews who strongly identify as tribal Jews and older Jews who identify as covenantal Jews. A stronger indicator is denominational affiliation and observance. Orthodox Jews skew heavily toward tribalism, whereas liberal/progressive Jews skew strongly toward covenantal attitudes and behaviors. But even here, there are exceptions. In fact, most Jews alternate between the categories depending on circumstances. Nonetheless, the categories are helpful to understand how the attitudes that determine Jewish behavior are changing.

What is important to note is that the institutions of American Jewish life (e.g., synagogues, JCCs, Jewish Federations, Jewish educational institutions) speak the language of tribal Jews and program accordingly. They do that even as they recognize their wholesale failure to attract and engage younger American Jews whose biases are decidedly post-tribal. Thousands of these "covenantal" Jews play leading roles in the fields of human rights, global peace, worker justice, gender and LGBT equality, education, domestic poverty relief, and international development efforts. A 2012 study found that one in six American Jews identified as "Jewishly engaged and congregationally unaffiliated." Labeling them "cultural Jews," the study found that their commitment to economic justice (52 percent) and spirituality (56 percent) was significantly higher than for comparable samples of synagogue-affiliated Jews. Despite avoiding any formal affiliation with Jewish institutions, many of these covenantal Jews (or cultural Jews) will identify with the Jewish historical narrative and ethical legacy as a source of inspiration and an important component of their formative personal identity.[8]

Here we enter the realm of what sociologist Herbert Gans calls "symbolic ethnicity." Many Jews, with no identifiable patterns of Jewish affiliation or behavior, nonetheless define their motivation in the world in the context of their Jewish heritage. But given the way that the Jewish community currently functions, such Jews, who might otherwise be open to Jewish community initiatives or programs when such endeavors align with their universal and liberal values, are defined out of the tribe and driven away by implicit communal institutional messages.

Rabbis and the organized Jewish community are notoriously bad at understanding and validating covenantal Jewish identity. Drawing hard and fast lines on who does and who does not belong to the Jewish community becomes even more difficult and complicated because the Jewish identity of covenantal Jews is soft and highly ambivalent.

In my work with teenage, college, and young adult Jews over several decades, I have seen how impressionable they can be. Imagine a twenty-year-old, raised in a non-Orthodox synagogue-affiliated family whose Jewish education stopped after Bat or Bar Mitzvah. Let's call him Bill. Like many who came before him, the totality of Bill's involvement in the Jewish community may be attending High Holy Day services with no intention of any further involvement with Jewish life. Still, Bill may be proud of his Jewish identity and not at all reticent to be counted as one. However, if Bill gets engaged to a non-Jew and the one call he places to his childhood rabbi goes unreturned or the response to his call makes Bill feel rejected, there is a good chance that Bill will opt out of any ties to the Jewish community at all.

> Rabbis and the organized Jewish community are notoriously bad at understanding and validating covenantal Jewish identity. Drawing hard and fast lines on who does and who does not belong to the Jewish community becomes even more difficult and complicated because the Jewish identity of covenantal Jews is soft and highly ambivalent.

But here is an alternate scenario. Bill signs up for a Jewish-sponsored alternative spring-break trip to Central America. He isn't motivated by the fact that it is sponsored by a Jewish organization, but he likes the destination, the price is better than two other trips he checked out, and the dates work for him. On the trip there is a fabulous Jewish educator, and in the context of living and working with people poorer than middle-class Bill could ever have imagined, suddenly the wisdom and ethical dictates of Judaism come alive. Bill comes back and becomes campus super-Jew, changes his major to Jewish studies, and is destined to become a pillar of the Jewish community for the rest of his life.

The story is not fabricated. It is a composite. I have seen a thousand variations of this story. I can offer a dozen examples of experiences that will turn Bill off to his Jewish identity for the foreseeable future, and I can offer the same number of experiences that will spark his Jewish identity. This is what I mean when I call covenantal Jewish identity soft and ambivalent. Bill's Jewish identity is up for grabs.

Covenantal Jews represent a growing pool of the Jewish market of the future. The future vibrancy of the Jewish community depends on leaders of the Jewish community reaching out to this constituency and finding ways to reach them, even as it will challenge many long-standing assumptions of what the Jewish community should look like.

The American Context

Thus far, our analysis has mostly focused on the Jewish community. However, a strategy to better reach and engage the next generation requires us to also understand the larger social context in which young American Jews operate.

The Jewish community is not alone in facing declining interest on the part of gen X and millennials in the organizations that were created to reinforce and perpetuate religious identity. Robert Putnam and David Campbell's recent study of religion in America, *American Grace*, provides important data in this regard.[9] The data for the book comes from a 2006 national survey called Faith Matters. Putnam and Campbell track what they call "religious inheritance," which is the extent to which religious faith and affiliation gets handed down to the next generation. They found that fewer than two-thirds of Americans simply inherited their parents' religion in terms of both affiliation and observance patterns. Because religious inheritance is much stronger among blacks and Latinos, it actually skews the data. Among white Americans, 40 to 45 percent switched away from the religion of their parents during their lifetimes or allowed their faith to lapse.

Mormons and evangelical Protestants were two exceptions to this trend and were far more likely to successfully transmit religious loyalty to their children. More than 50 percent in each of those communities reported continuing to observe and affiliate with the religion of their parents. In contrast, fewer than 30 percent of Jews reported staying connected to the religion of their parents, a figure 9 percent lower than mainline Protestants, a sector of America's religious landscape that has suffered terrible attrition over the past forty years.[10] The single strongest indicator for religious retention is whether a person's family was religiously homogeneous (no intermarriage) and whether or not that household was religiously observant.

A second telling data point from the Putnam and Campbell study is what they call "the rise of the 'nones.'" Historically, Americans have been very loyal to their religious affiliations. Even as American society was seen by many as more and more secular (if not godless), Americans saw themselves as faithful to their houses of worship. In the 1950s, in response to the question "What is your religious preference?" 95 to 97 percent of Americans named a specific denomination (e.g., Baptist, Methodist) or a religious tradition (e.g., Christian, Jewish). This data means that only 3 to 5 percent of Americans checked the box that said "none" when asked about their religious affiliation. But by the year 2000 that number skyrocketed to 25 percent. Not surprisingly, the highest incidence of "nones" was among the young, a trend confirmed by comparing the Faith Matters data with comparable data from an annual survey of college freshman.[11]

The authors cite two large social trends as mainly responsible for this flight from religious affiliation. One was the aftereffects of the cultural revolution of the 1960s. That "revolution" was characterized by the liberal politics of President Johnson's Great Society programs, the civil rights movement, permissiveness in the realm of sexual mores and drug use, and changing gender roles and norms. To many Americans, these were indicators of a growing moral decay in American society. In reaction to these dramatic changes in American society came the growth of evangelical Christianity and the rise of the religious Right. Millions of Americans were drawn to the reassertion of certitudes around God and country that the 1960s had undermined. Ironically, the very trend that raised the commitment of so many to religion was also what later alienated so many Americans and drove them into the "none" camp. Many students of American religion now assume that because so many of the "nones" come from the middle and left of the political spectrum, their rejection of religion is a backlash against the marriage between religion and conservative politics that became a major force in American life over the past thirty years.[12]

The findings of Putnam and Campbell correlate closely with a 2010 study by the Pew Forum on Religion and Public Life.[13] That study found that millennials are significantly less affiliated than baby boomers were at a corresponding age. They also found that a high percentage of Americans under the age of forty are open to associating with religious and spiritual organizations different than the affiliations of their childhood.[14] In one key question in the survey, "How important is religion in your life?" 69 percent of respondents over the age of sixty-five said "very important." That response compares to 59 percent of respondents aged fifty to sixty-four and only 45 percent of respondents aged eighteen to thirty.

The survey data above paints a dire portrait for the future of American religious institutions. It puts into perspective the declining number of Jews who join synagogues or JCCs or who contribute to Jewish Federation campaigns—all classic indicators of Jewish identity and communal solidarity.

At the same time, there are trends in American life that present opportunities for a spiritual revival, albeit with a set of rules far different than is part of the playbook of most American religious institutions. In the last section of this chapter, I will lay out four strategies that present unique opportunities for synagogues and Jewish organizations promoting Jewish identity. But first a few words about the symptoms of what can only be described as the American spiritual malaise of the twenty-first century.

An American Spiritual Malaise

Although it is far too early to make generalizations about this new century, the jury is clearly in on its first decade. If the twentieth century
was the "American Century," characterized by America's dominance in
the world by virtue of its military might, economic power, and cultural
influence, then the terrorist attacks of September 11, 2001, provided a
disturbing signal that that century was over. No longer do Americans feel
secure in the knowledge that those around the world view us with respect.
Closer to home, even before the start of the twenty-first century, there
were growing concerns about the erosion of the American civic fabric.
Robert Putnam's groundbreaking book *Bowling Alone*[15] raised far more
serious concerns than the decline of bowling leagues. He cited how key
features of American democracy were eroding—membership in civic
groups, neighborhood associations, participation in American politics,
and so on. Other students of American culture followed Putnam's analysis
by citing the dangerous side effects of the age of technology. Although the
conventional wisdom is that the Internet has helped to get people more
connected, one recent study found that one-third of those who use text
messaging prefer that medium to a phone call or an in-person encounter to communicate with another individual.[16] Anyone with a teenager
knows this phenomenon well; the implications about the declining skills
of young people to engage in normal social interactions are scary indeed.

Perhaps of even greater immediate consequence to the health of our
society is the impact of technology on our political culture. MoveOn.org
emerged as one of the most highly successful organizations that mobilized
the younger generation into politics via the Internet. They burst onto the
scene in 1999 to support President Bill Clinton against the efforts of Repub-
licans in Congress to impeach him. They then began online organizing to
oppose the war in Iraq. In 2003 their online primary catapulted Howard
Dean to the front of the pack for the 2004 Democratic nomination for
president and built a base of more than a million young people that they
subsequently organized for a variety of progressive causes. But MoveOn.
org's own former executive director, Eli Pariser, now makes the case that
the Internet has had some very negative consequences for American politics.

It has resulted, he argues, in people being exposed only to opinions with which they agree. The growing sophistication of search engines essentially customizes every person's computer, feeding them information that they will like. The strength of any democracy depends on a healthy debate in the public square about contemporary issues so as to advance the common good. A generation ago, Americans got their news from a handful of major media sources that felt a responsibility to fairly represent a broad range of public opinion. Today, that market has fragmented into hundreds of highly partisan niche sources. Pariser sees a direct connection between the growing hegemony of technology in American society and the partisanship and political gridlock that now characterizes the American political process.[17]

> I believe that the crisis in American society at the dawn of the twenty-first century cries out for a spiritual response.

Finally, the twenty-first century brought with it a growing concern about America's economic decline. The stock market crash of 2008 was the tip of the iceberg as economists noted the twenty-five-year shift of manufacturing out of the United States and the rise of America's trade deficit and long-term indebtedness to other countries. For several generations it was assumed that children would outearn their parents. With unemployment hovering in the 7 to 9 percent range in the second decade of the twenty-first century and little chance that that number will shift dramatically in the near future, the prospect for America's younger generation seems less bright than ever before.

All four of these factors—the crisis in religious inheritance and the rise of the "nones," America's declining economic hegemony and prestige in the world, the breakdown of America's civic fabric, and growing partisanship and political paralysis—contribute to a culture with a deep spiritual malaise.

Four Propositions

There is a Rabbinic saying: *makdim refuah l'maka*, "even before the onset of the malady, the antidote already exists." It is another way of saying that embedded in every social problem lies the seed for its remedy.

In that vein, I believe that the crisis in American society at the dawn of the twenty-first century cries out for a spiritual response. Here I will frame that response in the language of Judaism with specific reference to how it might play out in the Jewish community. But I believe that the four strategies I set forth would have considerable appeal to Americans beyond the Jewish community. I will, however, leave it to others to translate these strategies for the other ethnic and religious subcultures of America.

If the strategies that sustained the American Jewish community for much of the twentieth century now fail to attract generation X (aged thirty to forty-five) and, even more so, Jewish millennials (aged eighteen to twenty-nine), what new strategies might be more effective? If the analysis above focused on the changes taking place in the *marketplace* (society), then we must also focus on the change in the *market* itself—next-generation Jews who we hope will carry on the legacy of Jewish heritage and Jewish life. To that end I offer four propositions that I believe hold the key to a renaissance of Jewish life. For each proposition, I will identify several examples of Jewish organizations or programs that are already experiencing success tapping into that trend. Hopefully, the analysis and examples will convince other Jewish institutions to follow suit.

Wisdom/*Chochmah*

Proposition 1: In an age of globalization, Jewish institutions need to offer multiple avenues to explore *chochmah*, the wisdom of our sacred texts put into the context of the world's religions and in the language of contemporary culture.

Globalization is often discussed in economic terms as global markets become increasingly independent due to advances in transportation and telecommunications. Yet far more significant than the fact that you might be wearing a shirt from China, pants from Indonesia, and shoes from Brazil is the fact that we live in a world where culture and ideas know no borders. Chief Rabbi Jonathan Sack's important book *The Dignity of Difference* explores the implications of globalization on the way people think about their respective religious traditions. Provocatively he asks the question: Can we hear the voice of God in a language and a culture not our own?[18]

19

Jewish institutions need to dramatically rethink the way they will engage in the enterprise of transmitting the Jewish heritage. When so much information is available through computer terminals or smart phones and language can be taught with online language learning software, Jewish educators must increasingly get into the business of imparting wisdom and not just knowledge. Furthermore, the wisdom that gets imparted cannot be of a parochial nature. Judaism is part of a world wisdom tradition, and next-generation Jews are hungry to understand the similarities and differences between Judaism and other faiths and cultures in the world. Jewish "lite" will no longer appeal to the next generation of American Jews. Though it is true that the vast majority of Jews are Judaically illiterate (and even less competent in Hebrew language), younger Jews yearn for authenticity. It is no surprise that on college campuses and in their travels around the world there is a strong attraction to the Chabad Houses, an ultra-Orthodox approach to Judaism that has emissaries and houses all over the globe. Most American Jews that gravitate to Chabad Houses will not adopt the rigorous ritual observance that characterizes the Chabad rabbis themselves. Yet the young people like the feel of "doing the real thing," even if they don't show up every week.

> In an age of globalization, Jewish institutions need to offer multiple avenues to explore *chochmah*, the wisdom of our sacred texts put into the context of the world's religions and in the language of contemporary culture.

There are other indicators as well. In 1980 a few young British Jews launched a program called Limmud. It was a multiday Jewish learning retreat over the Christmas holiday that attracted about eighty participants. Now Limmud rents an entire college campus and accommodates more than three thousand participants for a five-day program, attracting Jews from all over Europe and featuring some of the best Jewish teachers in the world. Nor has Limmud remained an exclusively United Kingdom operation. There are now sixty different communities sponsoring Limmud conferences throughout the year on five continents, and the phenomenon is still growing.

Starting in the 1970s Jewish studies programs were established on college campuses throughout America. Thousands of Jewish college students who got little out of their afternoon Hebrew school experiences were now studying about Judaism at an advanced level. But what is interesting about gen X and the millennials is that their interest in Judaism is no longer restricted to courses for college credit. Many Jews find their way to Israel to study at Pardes, an open and pluralistic yeshiva in Jerusalem, or at Bina, a secular yeshiva in Tel Aviv. In New York, several young rabbis started Yeshivat Hadar in 2006, a noncredit learning academy where young people, college and postcollege, commit to full-time study of Jewish texts for a summer or for a full year.

In a previous generation this seriousness about Jewish learning would have been restricted to Orthodox Jews. But the programs described above are attracting largely non-Orthodox Jews, and it is a phenomenon to be celebrated. The interest is also not restricted to Judaism. Increasingly, Jews want to be able to access the wisdom traditions of many different cultures around the world.

It is not uncommon to find more and more Jews engaging in "do-it-yourself" Judaism because there is so much material on the web for anyone who is so inclined. Jews who once would have been satisfied with using the Maxwell House Haggadah for their Passover seder will now put together their own booklets, and it will integrate the passages of the traditional text with excerpts from Mahatma Gandhi, Martin Luther King Jr., and Nelson Mandela. Many of the young people I meet who are most serious about Judaism are intensely interested in how their heritage compares to Christianity, Islam, Buddhism, and other religions of the world. They explore those faiths not because they want to convert, but because they refuse to live and learn in an intellectual and cultural ghetto.

From 1997 to 2000, the organization that I founded and led, PANIM: The Institute for Jewish Leadership and Values, sponsored a program called the *E Pluribus Unum* (EPU) Project. Our flagship program, *Panim el Panim*, brought Jewish high school students to Washington to be exposed to politics, social justice, and community service, all through the lens of Jewish texts and values. Over several years we had fine-tuned an educational methodology that used the wisdom of the

Jewish tradition to inspire greater social and political activism. I became intrigued by the possibility that the same methodology could be applied to other faith traditions as well. With funding from the Ford Foundation, the Lilly Endowment, and the Righteous Persons Foundation, we launched the EPU Project, a three-week program each summer for sixty entering college freshmen exploring religion, social justice, and the common good.

With equal representation from Jews, Catholics, and Protestants, and including a small Muslim cohort in year three, the program had participants study the social teachings of their respective faith traditions and then explore both similarities and differences with the other traditions represented at the program. We learned together, did community service together, prayed together, and played together, all in the close quarters of a college campus. I had a faculty that represented all faiths, races, and ethnicities. I recall one prominent head of a national Jewish organization who served on my advisory board express shock that I would create such a program. He told me that he supported PANIM because he saw it as a great Jewish identity enhancer. What did I think would come of a program that put Jews ages seventeen to eighteen in close quarters with *gentiles*!

> For post-tribal, next-generation Jews, Jewish wisdom also needs to open a window to the wisdom of the world's great religions.

Well I know what came of it, and I had a pretty good hunch even before we enrolled our first participant. Evaluations showed that our EPU Project had a much greater impact on our participants than did our *Panim el Panim* program. The ability of these young people to explore faith, politics, ethnic identity, and social responsibility in a religiously pluralistic setting was nothing short of transformative. Though it was seemingly counterintuitive to my skeptical board member, participants emerged more committed to their own faith, because they had to live and explain their faith to others who did not share their path. Faith communities are in the business of transmitting the values and practices of their respective heritage to the next generation. They mostly do so by creating programs that are totally insular, essentially educational and intellectual ghettos. It won't work anymore.

For post-tribal, next-generation Jews, Jewish wisdom also needs to open a window to the wisdom of the world's great religions. Some of our teachings are unique. Other teachings have fascinating parallels in cultures and religions that are rarely if ever mentioned in Jewish educational settings. Jewish institutions that understand this will need to totally rethink their programming. If they do, they will find themselves able to engage younger Jews in new ways.

Social Justice/*Tzedek*

> **Proposition 2: At a time when our political culture seems so dysfunctional and the social and environmental threats to the planet grow exponentially every year, the Jewish community needs to provide ever more ways to advance *tzedek* in the world.**

One of the bright spots in American Jewish life over the past few decades is the explosion of organizations that have been created that offer Jews the opportunity to advance social justice through the framework of Judaism. The phenomenon started in the 1980s as a reaction to the growing parochialism of the organized Jewish community. It was a phenomenon not dissimilar to the way that the excesses of the American counterculture in the 1960s gave rise to the religious Right.

Several factors combined to drive the organized Jewish community into a more defensive, if not reactionary posture. First, the Yom Kippur War of 1973 revealed that the American progressive Left, a political sector that reflected the sympathies of most American Jews, was an unreliable ally when it came to Israel and the Middle East. Second, the Reagan presidency seriously challenged the premise that it was the government's responsibility to ensure a social safety net for the most vulnerable sectors of the population. Third, rising rates of intermarriage and assimilation increased concerns about the future strength and viability of the American Jewish community. Taken together, the organized Jewish community's priorities shifted decidedly toward "continuity," a buzzword for communal survival.[19]

Although it can be argued that this was a justified priority for the organized Jewish community, it nonetheless spurred a grassroots response from Jews whose priorities were becoming post-tribal. The affluence and organizational know-how of American Jews resulted in the birth of an amazing array of new Jewish organizations whose priorities were decidedly more universal. The 1980s saw the creation of the New Israel Fund (supporting progressive causes in Israel), Mazon (hunger relief), the Jewish Fund for Justice and the Shefa Fund (domestic social justice, later to merge together with the Progressive Jewish Alliance in California to form Bend the Arc), and the American Jewish World Service (aid and support to the developing world), to name just a few. The 1990s saw the creation of Avodah (postcollege Jewish service houses in urban neighborhoods), Hazon (food and environmental justice), Tzedek Hillel (social justice initiatives via college campus Hillels), and the Jewish Coalition for Service (an umbrella for more than twenty Jewish groups that promoted community service, later to evolve into Repair the World). In 2009 the Nathan Cummings Foundation further helped to build the field by creating the Jewish Social Justice Roundtable, made up of the executives of all the national organizations pursuing a justice agenda. By 2012, twenty-six organizations were part of the Roundtable.

These are just some of the larger, national initiatives in the realm of Jewish social justice. In dozens of communities around the country *tikkun olam*, "repairing the world," programs were popping up everywhere. Synagogues sponsored Mitzvah Days that attracted families to spend a day in service to those in need. It became commonplace to have young teens undertake a *tikkun olam* project as part of their preparation for Bar and Bat Mitzvah. By the year 2000 there were more than a dozen Jewish organizations focused on some form of environmental work.

When I founded the PANIM Institute for Jewish Leadership and Values in 1988, it was a novel idea. Our mission was to inspire, educate, and train the next generation of American Jews for lives of commitment to leadership, activism, and service for the Jewish people and the world at large. PANIM did not force young Jews to choose between commitment to Judaism, the Jewish people, and the rest of the world. Its premise was that each of those commitments was core to what it meant to be a good

Jew. In so doing, PANIM reflected a new ethic that characterized much of the emerging Jewish social justice movement. Jews who might otherwise walk away from Jewish commitments and affiliations found a growing number of organizations that aligned with their values. Jews who increasingly saw themselves as global citizens were able to fulfill those passions through Jewish-sponsored programs. For many, it was the only way that they would be prepared to remain identified with the Jewish community.[20]

Part of what is exciting about this phenomenon is that it represents a much healthier integration of Jewish identity than was so long the case in the American Jewish experience. For the better part of the twentieth century, you could divide the Jewish organizational universe into religious, educational, and secular baskets. Synagogues covered the religious agenda. Hebrew schools, day schools, camps, and Hillels were engaged in the work of transmitting Jewish identity to the next generation, and a large array of organizations dealt with everything from social services to caring for the elderly to community relations, which included relations with Jewish communities around the world and Israel. In the third basket were the Jewish communal organizations that, despite being part of the Jewish communal umbrella and funded with dollars from the Federation community campaigns, did not see themselves as being in the Jewish content business. That was the work of synagogues and schools.

> At a time when our political culture seems so dysfunctional and the social and environmental threats to the planet grow exponentially every year, the Jewish community needs to provide ever more ways to advance *tzedek* in the world.

When I left my first pulpit in Media, Pennsylvania, in 1984 to become the executive director of the Jewish Community Relations Council (JCRC) of Greater Washington, D.C., I experienced a bit of culture shock. The community relations field was in its heyday. The agenda included defending Jews against anti-Semitism, saving Soviet Jewry, mobilizing for the State of Israel, and when there was time and energy, some local interfaith and social justice work. I was deeply committed to the entire agenda of the agency. Yet when I attempted to introduce some Judaic perspectives into the social policy issues that we were debating week in and week out, I was chastised for being "too rabbinic." Let synagogues do the Jewish content thing, I was told. We were in the business of ethnic politics and advancing group self-interest. Indeed, the Jewish community had become amazingly effective at doing just that.

Some fifteen years after I got that scolding, I was invited to offer a keynote talk to the annual convention of the Jewish Council for Public Affairs, the national umbrella for all the Jewish community relations agencies around the country and a dozen or so national defense agencies like the Anti-Defamation League, the American Jewish Committee, Hadassah, and the like. My talk was on integrating Torah (Jewish learning and values) and *tzedek* (social justice). It was an indication of how far the community had come in a relatively short time. Indeed, looking around today at the fast-growing sector of Jewish social justice organizations, I celebrate how many produce outstanding educational materials that do exactly what I had tried, unsuccessfully, to do during my tenure at the JCRC in Washington.

> Because next-generation Jews more closely identify as covenantal Jews than as tribal Jews, the only way to reach them is to make sure that the Judaism they experience as youth reflects Judaism's millennial commitment to *tzedek*, justice.

Because next-generation Jews more closely identify as covenantal Jews than as tribal Jews, the only way to reach them is to make sure that the Judaism they experience as youth reflects Judaism's millennial commitment to *tzedek*, justice. Many Jews my age recall their Bar and Bat Mitzvah with a certain scorn and cynicism. The "values" they recall from the event were about the ostentation and the party. I would hope that when this generation of tweens has children of their own, they will be able to recount how, as part of their Bar/Bat Mitzvah, they served food in a soup kitchen, collected sports equipment for children in a developing country, sent packages to wounded Israeli soldiers, and volunteered to work with developmentally disabled children.

Hopefully that is how they will recall how they became "*mitzvah* men and women," the meaning of the term Bar/Bat Mitzvah.

Synagogues that make social justice central to their programming, like B'nai Jeshurun in New York and IKAR in Los Angeles, are thriving while dozens of other synagogues are losing membership. According to innovation labs such as Jumpstart and the ROI Community, and in social entrepreneurship incubators like UpStart Bay Area, New York's Bikkurim, the Joshua Venture Group, and PresenTense, a significant number of the projects being created by younger Jews in the United States, Europe, Latin America, and Israel have a social justice or environmental focus. Mainstream Jewish organizations that understand this trend and are prepared to modify their modus operandi will flourish. Those that don't will see themselves hard-pressed to maintain their current membership levels and support.

Community/Kehillah

Proposition 3: At a time when technology has made meaningful social intercourse much harder to come by, the Jewish community must offer places where people can find support in times of need, communal celebration in times of joy, and friendships to make life fulfilling.

We have already cited the extent to which America has suffered a breakdown of its civic fabric over the course of the past twenty-five years. There is no doubt that the very factors that contribute to this trend have exacerbated the membership/affiliation declines in the Jewish community. The two largest national synagogue umbrella organizations, the Union for Reform Judaism and the United Synagogue of Conservative Judaism, have suffered significant drops in their respective membership rolls during that period.[21] Even more dramatic is the fact that donors to the Jewish Federation system in America—the central fundraising and allocation arm of the organized Jewish community—has dropped from 900,000 donors to 450,000 donors since 1985.[22] One recent study found that even as American Jewish philanthropy to Israel increased from $1.05 billion in 1975 to $2.06 billion in 2007, the share of that philanthropy that passed through the centralized Federation system dropped from 79 percent to 16 percent.[23] All of this points to the fact that American Jews are voting with their feet and with their wallets in ways that signal the weakening of the central, national institutions that have been at the center of American Jewish life for more than a century.

This is not to suggest that Jews are no longer seeking each other out. It simply means that Jews are turning their backs on larger, mainstream organizations that are experienced as top-down institutions in an era when Jews want to do it themselves. Even as synagogues and Federations have experienced sizable declines, there has been significant growth in other sectors of American Jewish life. One such sector is independent *minyanim*, which are prayer groups that meet at least once per month, are not affiliated with national synagogue bodies, and have no paid clergy. The New York–based Mechon Hadar has taken the lead in organizing a national conference for independent *minyanim* since 2006, which has grown from eleven participating groups that year to forty-five in 2010. As Hadar has tracked and defined the phenomenon, they count more than one hundred such *minyanim* in the United States today, as compared with six in the year 2000. This does not count the many *minyanim* that take place within synagogues throughout the country, attracting members of the synagogues who prefer a do-it-yourself prayer experience over the service led by the rabbi and cantor.[24]

> At a time when technology has made meaningful social intercourse much harder to come by, the Jewish community must offer places where people can find support in times of need, communal celebration in times of joy and celebration, and friendships to make life fulfilling.

It is clear that, as compared to independent *minyanim*, there are even more Jews involved in groups that gather with a Jewish focus other than prayer.[25] These would include Jewish book clubs, groups that gather periodically for Shabbat or holiday celebrations, and Jewish study groups that explore every Jewish topic imaginable. I am aware of many such groups where the participants have dropped their synagogue membership because the self-run groups meet their needs just as well for a fraction of the cost. Ironically, the Internet, which has contributed to the decline of membership-based institutions, also makes it easier for informal networks of like-minded people to come together and access the resources necessary for running such a group. The fact that those resources are available for free makes it hard for synagogues or JCCs, whose dues run into the thousands of dollars, to compete. It doesn't take much for a volunteer to use the Internet to prepare to lead a group in a prayer, a book discussion, or a conversation about Jewish mysticism.[26]

In my 2000 book *Finding a Spiritual Home*, I profiled four synagogues, one from each denomination of American Judaism, that represent a new and more effective approach to engaging the next generation of Jews. I suggested that the factors the four synagogues had in common represent a new paradigm for the American synagogue called the synagogue-community, and I contrasted that new paradigm with the one that is still predominant in the American Jewish community—the synagogue-center. One of the key differences between the synagogue-center and the synagogue-community is that in the former, the clergy and staff are primarily responsible for the program of the institution. Members have a consumer relationship with their synagogues. They pay a fair market price for an array of programs and services that they want.[27]

In contrast, synagogue-communities realize that there is enormous creative talent and energy among the membership if only it were invited. Members still pay dues to the synagogue, but significant parts of the synagogue program are generated and led by laypeople. People of talent are drawn to such institutions because they thrive when they are provided with avenues to give back or provide leadership for a worthy endeavor. The synagogue-community requires rabbis to adopt a very different leadership style than they have been trained for. Rabbis must move from talk/control mode to listen/empower mode. In synagogue-communities the emphasis shifts from an obsession with membership (the number of members matters most) to ownership (Jews who see themselves on a journey toward more engaged Jewish living). Rabbis, who so often complain about congregants with little commitment to Jewish life, find that this more empowered leadership style actually moves their congregations to precisely the kind of engaged Jewish life that the synagogue enterprise should be about.

While the universe of American synagogues has a long way to go to adopt this new paradigm, the principles underlying the approach have been central to the major synagogue change initiatives over the past twenty-five years. Those initiatives, which have affected dozens of synagogues and several hundred rabbis, have included Synagogue 2000 (now Synagogue 3000, or S3K), the Legacy Heritage Synagogue Innovation Project, and STAR (Synagogues: Transformation and Renewal). The seminaries that train rabbis and the national synagogue bodies were initially resistant to these change initiatives, but with declining rates of affiliation, all seem eager to rethink their approach. The Reform movement was recently put on the defensive when a loose confederation of large Reform congregations and their rabbis voiced their dissatisfaction with the direction of the denomination. The Conservative movement, experiencing dramatic declines in membership, undertook a major strategic plan in 2010 under newly appointed United Synagogue executive director Rabbi Steven Wernick. Among the recommendations of the Conservative movement's study was to put a greater emphasis on the communal dimension of synagogues (they use the Hebrew word *kehillot*) as well as on spirituality.

Synagogues that understand the generational shifts that are already in play and adapt their models accordingly will have the best chance to capture the energy and loyalties of younger Jews. But I think that there are also opportunities for initiatives that are not yet so well tested.

One area of dramatic growth is the Jewish food movement. An extension of the interest among Americans for healthier and more locally grown food, the Jewish phenomenon is also deeply spiritual in its approach, grounding its work in the Rabbinic teachings about proper stewardship of God's creation. The New York–based organization Hazon has both shaped this trend and capitalized on the interest. They started a national Jewish Food Conference in 2006 that had 150 attendees. In 2010 that conference, held in the San Francisco Bay Area, attracted 600 participants. Hazon has also seen dramatic growth in their network of Community Supported Agriculture (CSAs) based in synagogues and JCCs throughout the United States. I believe that the next few decades will see the emergence of more and more environmentally focused co-ops based on locally grown food and sustainable living, which will attract people looking for small networks of like-minded neighbors committed to the same values and lifestyles. It is a trend that Jewish institutions would do well to embrace, because it could provide a new form for Jewish engagement.

Even less well developed right now but also a trend that Jewish institutions should explore is co-housing. The nascent co-housing movement develops properties in which families can share common living spaces and, depending on the specific community, common tasks like preparation of meals, child care, and the like. With a stagnant American economy, serious rethinking about the benefits of mortgaged-based home ownership, and the search for community that is the by-product of an over-techified, individualistic society, co-housing has significant potential. Jewish leaders who want to anticipate trends instead of playing catch-up may want to explore ways to seed Jewish co-housing communities.

Lives of Sacred Purpose/*Kedushah*

Proposition 4: In an age when we better understand the shortcomings of capitalism and the culture of consumerism, the Jewish community must offer a glimpse of *kedushah*, experiences that provide holiness, transcendent meaning, and a sense of purpose.

One of the most wrongheaded assumptions of Jewish leaders over the past generation is that Jewish communal life is suffering because it costs too much money and it takes too much time. Don't get me wrong. Many Jews will use the costs associated with Jewish institutions (e.g., synagogue dues, Jewish day schools, expectations for charitable gifts by Jewish Federations and an array of Jewish organizations) as an excuse to disaffiliate or avoid affiliations altogether. It is also true that there is a small segment of the community that is truly unable to bear the high cost of Jewish living.

Yet the Jewish community is still among the most affluent groups in American society. Jews will pay enormous sums of money for the highest caliber theater/symphony subscriptions, second homes, spa/wellness getaways, personal coaches, trainers and therapists for themselves, and private school education for their children. One study of more than a dozen (non-Jewish) spiritual retreat centers in America noted that many of the attendees were Jews.[28] The fact of the matter is, Jews will spend significant sums of money and find the time to access experiences that provide value for their lives.

Surely, Jewish institutions must provide the funds so that Jews who cannot afford dues or tuitions can fully participate in Jewish life. But, for the most part, the Jewish community has not had the self-confidence to bring to the marketplace programs of great quality that pass on the costs of providing those goods and services. Jewish schools are notoriously under-resourced, as are Jewish elder care facilities, JCCs, and synagogues.

> In an age when we better understand the shortcomings of capitalism and the culture of consumerism, the Jewish community must offer a glimpse of *kedushah*, experiences that provide holiness, transcendent meaning, and a sense of purpose.

Each of these institutions relies on a small cadre of wealthy Jews to subsidize their respective programs and facilities via charitable contributions. The cadre of such philanthropic Jews is aging out and is not being replaced by younger Jews who possess the wealth or the commitment to Jewish life of the previous generation. It is a time bomb with serious consequences for the Jewish future.

The irony is that in the American marketplace, some of the services provided by the above-mentioned institutions are run as private businesses and are enormously profitable. There is probably no issue that raises more concerns about the future of American Jewish life than the high rate of intermarriage. Millions of philanthropic dollars have been spent by Jewish organizations over the past few decades to increase the in-marriage rate among young Jews and/or to attract interfaith couples into Jewish communal programming. Yet the private company JDate may have had a more positive impact on increasing Jewish in-marriage than all of the Jewish organizational efforts combined.

Founded in 1997, JDate now has 750,000 users a year across the globe. Almost a third of them, almost a quarter of a million Jews, pay thirty dollars per month for the premium service, over three times what one would pay for a non-Jewish dating site. In the United States alone, in any given year there are about 1.8 million single adult Jews and over 20 percent of them are active on JDate. There isn't any Jewish communal effort that comes close to this kind of market penetration. How did this happen? The founders of JDate set out to build a business. They identified a market—single Jews who wanted to meet other Jews—and then invested the money to make a Jewish dating service cool. JDate ads can be found in Times Square and on the London Tube. Not only does this effort not require any philanthropic dollars, but the company also currently makes thirty million dollars a year![29] Two other entrepreneurs with impressive track records of business success in Washington D.C. have recently created a company called ShalomLearning, believing that they can deliver quality after-school Jewish education to children more effectively than the current after-school synagogue model, and they believe that they can make money doing it.[30]

Clearly not every Jewish communal challenge can be addressed through private business ventures. Yet the Jewish community needs to be far more nimble and creative to respond to the challenges it faces. Both elder care and pre-schools are areas that seem ripe to explore private solutions rather than continuing the current subsidized communal models. Where are the Jewish institutions that will take up the challenge of the capitalist marketplace to create programs of such quality that they will pay for themselves? Instead, the Jewish community creates a mentality of scarcity and subsidy, assuming that Jews will never pay a fair market price for their programs.

The most heralded program of the past decade in the Jewish world is a classic example. Earlier I cited the impressive achievements of Birthright Israel in sending hundreds of thousands of young Jews to Israel. Though some have criticized Birthright with not doing enough to engage alumni of the program after their return, overall studies indicate that there is a huge positive impact on the participants' connection to Israel and their Jewish identity. But then there is the law of unintended consequences. Even as Birthright programs generate significant increases in Jewish identity among its participants, might the largesse of the Jewish community in making the programs free come back to haunt us?

The long-term message of Birthright may be as serious a time bomb for the Jewish community as the aging of Jewish philanthropists. The next generation of Jews is learning by experience that someone else will pay them to "do Jewish." Among the early casualties of Birthright was the array of programs that took Jewish teens to Israel. Families quickly figured out that it was foolish to pay $3,000 to $5,000 to send their teen to Israel on a summer program when they could get it for free in college. In addition, participation on an organized teen trip to Israel made that teen ineligible for the free Birthright trip, because the organization wanted to privilege the under-affiliated. Thus, despite its positive, short-term impact on participants, Birthright both undermines other Israel trip programs that have viable, fee-for-service business models and creates a generation of Jews who are conditioned to put their hands out to Jewish institutions for subsidy and scholarships despite being more than capable of paying their fair share.

> Where are the Jewish institutions that will take up the challenge of the capitalist marketplace to create programs of such quality that they will pay for themselves? Instead, the Jewish community creates a mentality of scarcity and subsidy, assuming that Jews will never pay a fair market price for their programs.

Some will argue that free trips are a good investment given the long-term, positive impact on the Jewish identity of participants. Yet there are dozens of great programs in the Jewish community that have been launched at highly subsidized rates due to the generosity of funders, only to disappear a few years later when the funders lose interest and move on to their next project. There is no question that the Jewish community benefits enormously from the fact that we are an affluent community and that not an insignificant number of those affluent Jews choose to give money to Jewish organizations and programs. Yet as the influence of Jewish family foundations grows and that of the Federation system wanes, the community suffers from a lack of centralized planning. Too many wonderful initiatives get launched without sustainable models, and the community is poorer for it.

Similar challenges face synagogues. Jews are among the most avid spiritual seekers in American society. Yet, for the most part, gen X and millennial Jews are turning their backs on synagogues as places to feed their spiritual hunger. About 70 percent of Jews affiliate with synagogues at some point in their lives. Typically, a family will join when their oldest child is ready to begin after-school religious education, and they will drop their membership after the Bar or Bat Mitzvah of their youngest child. During the time of their membership, few of the parents or children feel themselves touched or transformed by the experience of being part of a religious community. In interviews I did with dozens of young adults who were asked about their synagogue experiences, few recalled being engaged in discussions about God, life's purpose, or the possibility that Jewish worship, ritual, and study might give them a sense of the sacred. When many of these post-tribal Jews become adults and begin to ask questions about life's ultimate meaning, they have already concluded that such a spiritual search cannot be fulfilled by membership in synagogues, and they seek out spiritual alternatives beyond the Jewish community.[31]

A handful of rabbis and synagogues are beginning to address this spiritual hunger among Jewish seekers. The Institute for Jewish Spirituality (IJS) has programs that train rabbis in the practice of meditation and silent retreats. Since its founding in 2000, IJS has trained more than two hundred rabbis and close to one hundred cantors and Jewish educators. Jewish spiritual retreat centers like Isabella Freedman in Connecticut and Chochmat HaLev in the Bay Area attract Jews who might shun other forms of more conventional Jewish learning.

The fact that the past twenty-five years has seen the growth of new seminaries to train rabbis even as synagogue membership is shrinking is evidence of the fact that the well-established rabbinical seminaries may not be producing rabbis who understand the changing trends of the younger generation of Jews. These newer seminaries include the Reconstructionist Rabbinical College (Philadelphia), the Ziegler School of Rabbinic Studies (Los Angeles), the Academy for Jewish Religion (one in New York and one in Los Angeles), Yeshivat Chovevei Torah (New York), the Rabbinical School at Hebrew College (Boston), and the Aleph Rabbinic Program (Philadelphia).

A comparison of the curricula of these schools with the more estab-lished seminaries shows a shift away from graduate-style academic rigor in favor of training that might better meet the spiritual needs of a changing marketplace and a changed market. The graduates of these alternative seminaries are also more inclined to think of ways to pursue the rabbinate beyond the realm of conventional congregations.

Yet there is both risk and reward inherent in this fact. Some rabbis of talent, with the right mentorship, a creative idea, and a little bit of good fortune, will create innovative models that will succeed in engaging next-generation Jews. Many more will fail. The majority of the graduates of American rabbinical seminaries will find employment in the synagogues and Jewish communal institutions that were established by the genera-tions that preceded their ordination. They will enter those positions filled with idealism and passion for Jewish life. Yet, for the most part, they will be frustrated.

The constituency of those institutions is graying at an alarming rate, and it will telegraph to these freshly minted rabbis a bleak future. Even if they have the self-confidence not to take this fact as a signal of their per-sonal failure, few will have the ability to see the forest for the trees. The institutions they serve are part of the larger established Jewish community that has not understood well enough the changes taking place in the Ameri-can marketplace and in the American Jewish market (e.g., the tastes and predilections of the millennials). Until or unless the community "gets it," it will squander the talents of the next generation of Jewish spiritual leaders, and no community can thrive unless it positions its leadership for success.

American society has caught the spiritual bug. Wherever they turn Americans can now find their spiritual interests indulged—yoga centers, organic diets, meditation training, personal gurus, ashrams, holistic heal-ing centers, and dozens of organizations that sponsor multiday retreats with the latest big names in the field of spirituality. American Jews no longer need synagogues or rabbis to feed their spiritual hunger, and syna-gogue affiliation numbers are proof of that fact. Yet within Judaism is spiritual wisdom and spiritual practice that can compete more than favor-ably with what is available in the general American marketplace. And there is a growing cadre of rabbis and Jewish teachers who can deliver this wisdom and practice. Yet this phenomenon is still happening only on the margins of the American Jewish community.

Have all Americans become seekers? Hardly. Similarly, not every American Jew wants to chant and meditate. Yet what I know to be true is that if you show Jews how Judaism can offer a glimpse of a life of sacred purpose, they will come in droves. The programs of most synagogues are not yet geared to do this in an effective way, and most rabbis, even when they have the interest, do not have the skill sets to re-engineer their institutions in ways that will challenge the status quo.

I once heard Rabbi Harold Schulweis (the longtime rabbi of Valley Beth Shalom in Encino, California, and one of the most respected rabbis of his time) offer an observation that has stayed with me for more than thirty years. In many ways, it has shaped my own approach to the rabbinate. He said, "Most rabbis have answers to the questions that Jews no longer ask." I did not take this to be a criticism of rabbinical schools. Most Jewish seminaries in the United States are engaged in constant reassessment of their curricula, and they have the unenviable task of conveying a vast body of knowledge in five or six years. Rather, I took Schulweis to mean that the issues that differentiate good rabbis from great rabbis have little to do with the knowledge they have of Jewish tradition. It has to do with their ability to read the market (the Jews they want to reach) and the marketplace (the social context in which the Jews live). Rabbis who can do that will quickly understand that synagogues have to be radically transformed. They then need to have the ability to put out an alternate vision and the political savvy to implement that vision, bringing along the many lay stakeholders of the congregation.

> Within Judaism is spiritual wisdom and spiritual practice that can compete more than favorably with what is available in the general American marketplace. And there is a growing cadre of rabbis and Jewish teachers who can deliver this wisdom and practice. Yet this phenomenon is still happening only on the margins of the American Jewish community.

The community needs to invest resources in postgraduate training for rabbis to give them the training and support not only to be effective spiritual leaders but also to become agents of institutional transformation. Compared with other fields in American society (e.g., teachers, doctors, lawyers), the American rabbinate is sorely lacking in the kind of practical professional training that is needed to give rabbis the tools to offer compelling models of Jewish engagement for Jews. It makes no sense for American synagogues to remain empty while American Jews spend millions of dollars to travel to generic spiritual retreat centers to feed their souls.

If the American Jewish community wants to capture the next generation of American Jews, it needs to get into the *kedushah* business—helping Jews live lives of sacred purpose.

The Future

The Talmud says that since the end of the period of the biblical prophets, the business of predicting the future falls to fools. We are thus engaged here in a risky endeavor. Yet we are not entering into unchartered waters. Each of the trends outlined above and framed by a proposition that suggests a clear direction for the future already enjoys the benefits of some pioneering innovators and nascent institutions that are showing the way. Leaders of vision, often with limited resources and the skepticism of a community that is slow to change, are nevertheless charting the course for a vibrant Jewish future. The challenge, of course, is whether the major institutions of Jewish life and those that fund them will pick up on these trends fast enough to stem the tide of Jews who are voting with their feet in ways that threaten Jewish life and culture.

In the pages that follow you will meet some of these leaders. Each of them is working in a different sector of the Jewish community, and each of them is deeply engaged with efforts to advance the kind of changes that I have outlined above. Their perspectives help provide a fuller picture of the shape of the American Jewish future, because no one person can possibly be aware of all the challenges and opportunities that exist in a community as multifaceted as ours. Their responses to this lead essay also offer a healthy debate on the analysis that I have offered.

The good news is that each of the trends that I have outlined in this lead essay represents pockets of Jewish renaissance. They tell us that Jews are in fact seekers of wisdom (*dorshei chochmah*), seekers of social justice (*dorshei tzedek*), seekers of community (*dorshei kehillah*), and seekers of lives of sacred purpose (*dorshei kedushah*). A handful of rabbis and Jewish communal leaders are demonstrating that they understand the dynamic social trends that have already changed American society and the changing needs and interests of the next generation. Instead of focusing on what is wrong with Jewish life, they are reinventing it.

It is just such spiritual leaders who will help usher in a new and vibrant era of American Jewish life. They will redefine the terms of Jewish identity and the structures of the institutions that guide the Jewish community. Their success will determine how well an ancient Jewish heritage can navigate the dizzying social changes that are destined to characterize the twenty-first century.

Part 2

Perspectives from the American Jewish Community

Jewish Culture

What Really Counts?

Elise Bernhardt

The sign of every great civilization is the art, architecture, literature, music, and theater it creates. That cultural legacy tells us much about the people who made up that civilization, conveying to future generations what their ancestors valued, and it also serves as a considerable source of pride. As Jews living in a time of great wealth and power, it is fair to ask ourselves, What is it that Jews are now producing that will be worth reflecting on in two hundred years?

Can Good Culture Be Popular?

More than once I have heard a concern from lay leaders that contemporary artistic programs are not sufficiently appealing to Jewish young adults. My own experience is quite different. I once attended a concert of young composers at the Brooklyn Academy of Music as part of a festival that received a two-page advance article in the *New York Times*. One of

Elise Bernhardt has been president and CEO of the Foundation for Jewish Culture (formerly the National Foundation for Jewish Culture) since 2006. Before that, Bernhardt was the artistic advisor of New York City Center's Fall for Dance Festival and executive director of The Kitchen, the performance space in Manhattan, from 1998 to 2004. She founded the organization Dancing in the Streets, which produces performances in public spaces, and directed it from 1983 to 1998. She received the Chevalier des Arts et Lettres from the French Ministry of Culture, the BAX 10 Award, and the Doris C. Freedman Award for enriching the public environment.

the composers, Judd Greenstein, is a recipient of the Foundation for Jewish Culture's Six Points Fellowship. Greenstein, whose influences seem to include Pulitzer Prize–winning composer Steve Reich, perhaps Leonard Bernstein, and possibly Crosby, Stills, and Nash, had nine stellar musicians performing, several singing in Hebrew about the life of King Solomon of Temple days. An audience of hipsters and families alike listened raptly. This was anything but pop culture, as its appeal might seem somewhat limited. It is the kind of work that gets widespread critical attention and often travels around the world. Greenstein made a real, successful connection to a broad swath of people, including many young Jews, just the audience the Jewish community is so concerned about. From the perspective of both Jewish culture and Jewish continuity, this event was a home run.

Yet Jewish culture remains a hard sell to the institutional Jewish world. The sad fact is that many people assume that Jewish culture is one of two very limited genres. The first category is mainstream, assimilated art that retains a "Jewish sensibility," like the movies of Woody Allen or Mel Brooks that include a couple of inside jokes for folks who know what *trayf* means. The second category is earnestly Jewish, often religious art, featuring transparent Jewish themes that will ensure a built-in audience of the Jewish faithful. Unfortunately, the quality of this art is often subpar.

The good news is that there is a new Jewish culture emerging today that is real, exciting, and innovative. Beyond old-fashioned bagels-and-*shiksas* shtick, this new Jewish culture has depth and is nuanced enough to connect young, bright, and often skeptical Jews to their heritage. It is this type of Jewish culture that our community must support.

There are numerous pockets of Jewish cultural renaissance that fly under the radar screen of Jews who care about the future of the Jewish community. In 2011 the Folksbiene, the oldest and only remaining Yiddish theater in America, remounted its extraordinary production of *Shlemiel the First*, a collaboration between Robert Brustein, the founder of the Yale Repertory Theatre in New Haven; the award-winning postmodern choreographer David Gordon; Hankus Netsky, the director of the Klezmer Conservatory Band; and Zalmen Mlotek, one of the most prominent Yiddish actors and singers alive today. Talk about great worlds coming together! With the ironic irreverence of Gordon meeting the brilliant inanity of Isaac Bashevis Singer's "Wise Men of Chelm," Jewish culture achieved a new level of profundity *and* artistic excellence. And yet the show has never played outside of the New York metro area, for lack of financial support to mount a national tour.

Notably there are a few Jewish cultural institutions that have been able to build bridges between the artistic intelligentsia, Jewish philanthropists, and Jewish cultural arts programming. The Jewish Museum in New York, whose extraordinary exhibitions over the years are too numerous to name, has found ways to focus on the innovative through such shows as *Reinventing Ritual* and *Off the Wall* (curated respectively by Daniel Belasco and Andrew Ingall, past assistant curators at the Jewish Museum), both of which featured young artists exploring the Jewish tradition through a variety of media, including digital and architectural. The Contemporary Jewish Museum in San Francisco, in conjunction with Reboot (a network of thought-leaders and tastemakers who work to "reboot" Jewish culture, rituals, and traditions), has presented such groundbreaking events as *Dawn*, an all-night exploration of Shavuot through the work of artists, and exhibitions such as *In the Beginning: Artists Respond to Genesis* (Fred Wasserman, curator), which included brilliant installations by visual artists Mierle Laderman Ukeles, Alan Berliner, Ben Rubin, and others.

> The good news is that there is a new Jewish culture emerging today that is real, exciting, and innovative.

Ukeles, mother of the feminist manifesto in the art world, is also an Orthodox Jew, and her work was recently featured along with several other Orthodox feminist artists, including Hadassah Goldvicht, a Six Points fellow who takes rituals of Orthodox Jewish life and reframes them through video installations, and Andi Arnovitz, a Jerusalem-based artist who works in textiles. These women bring incredible knowledge of Torah, Rabbinic commentaries, and other classical Jewish sources along with their own observant, and intellectually and emotionally rigorous perspective to their beautifully material work. It would be easy to imagine the interest such an exhibition would generate if it went on tour to Jewish museums and women's studies departments in colleges all over the country and if there were a fund to support similarly worthy touring exhibitions within the American Jewish world.

The Richness of Israel

To consumers of Jewish culture, Israel represents a gold mine of creativity. The art, film, music, and dance coming out of the country today are as impressive as its success in the high-tech industries. Philanthropist Lynn Schusterman has almost singlehandedly inspired a revival of the city of Jerusalem through her generous support of the Jerusalem Season of Culture (JSOC), a new annual summer festival during which the city hosts a series of artistic experiences spanning the worlds of dance, music, poetry, philosophy, visual art, new media, and more. JSOC's successes, and those of the many smaller cultural institutions creating new work in Jerusalem, demonstrate how culture can affirmatively change and revitalize a city and its population. The fact that a major Jewish philanthropist is putting her money behind such a comprehensive and ambitious cultural experiment is to be applauded and emulated. Indeed, other Jewish philanthropists are joining in the JSOC as well as other culture-focused endeavors, such as the American Academy in Jerusalem.

In 2011, the Foundation for Jewish Culture created the American Academy in Jerusalem (AAJ), a ten-week fellowship for senior-level artists and cultural leaders modeled on the successes of the American Academies in Rome and Berlin. The program provides each fellow with travel to Jerusalem, accommodations, a living stipend, personal workspace, and additional resources to develop individual projects emphasizing social engagement with diverse populations in all parts of the city. During their residency, fellows work closely with local cultural organizations, NGOs, and the municipalities, where they teach master classes, serve as mentors, and offer professional development to peers. Israel is an incubator of extraordinary talent, and cultural organizations in Israel are hungry to interact with world-class artists. The AAJ fills this need by bringing serious American Jewish artists to Israel. Among the organizations that have worked with the AAJ fellows are the Bezalel Academy of Arts and Design, Yaffo 23, HaZira Performance Art Arena, Hebrew University of Jerusalem, Israel Museum, Jerusalem Academy of Music and Dance, Jerusalem Cinematheque, Jerusalem Inter-Cultural Center, Jerusalem Print Workshop, School of Visual Theater, Machol Shalem–Jerusalem Dance Festival, and the Vertigo Dance Company.

Happily, there are too many examples of the renaissance of culture in Israel to mention, yet a few can be singled out as exemplars. The Schusterman Visiting Artist Program, supported by the Charles and Lynn Schusterman Family Foundation, brings Israeli artists from various disciplines to North America for residencies of two to four months at some of the nation's most esteemed universities, museums, and other cultural organizations. Artis, the brainchild of Rivka Saker, supports and promotes contemporary artists from Israel, and brings important American curators and museum directors to Israel to meet their peers. That these curators and directors of secular institutions are eager to bring the work of Israeli artists to the attention of their constituencies, which are not necessarily Jewish, demonstrates that Israeli art is quite often taken seriously in a way that "Jewish art" is not, not even by Jews.

A significant amount of credit for the success of Israeli arts goes to the Israeli government, which, despite many pressures, consistently funds cultural projects in the Jewish state. Of course, Israeli arts also require additional aid from philanthropists, but the government has a deep commitment to culture and to freedom of expression. While many find fault with Israel's democracy, one has to admire the fact that it has not made support for culture contingent on agreement with government policy. Documentaries by Israelis that are critical of Israeli policy are often supported by government-funded programs in Israel. The choreographer Donald Byrd, a recent AAJ fellow, observed that "in Israel, the word of the writer and poet (and artist) is taken really seriously."[1]

In the United States, Jewish culture remains starved for adequate financial resources. While philanthropic support of major cultural institutions in America comes disproportionately from Jews, there is startlingly little support for Jewish cultural endeavors from Jewish philanthropists. According to *Following the Money: A Look at Jewish Foundation Giving*, a report from February 2012, Jewish non-Israel giving accounts for only 16 percent of total dollars given by Jewish foundations, and of that 16 percent, only 7 percent goes to arts and culture.[2] Jewish arts and culture outside of Israel thus accounts for only about 1 percent of all Jewish foundation giving! About 5 percent of Jewish philanthropic dollars goes to Israeli arts and culture. In other words, Jewish philanthropists value secular and, to a lesser degree, Israeli culture. Jewish art and culture in the Diaspora remains a tough sell to Jewish philanthropists. Until that situation changes, it is hard to imagine Jewish culture reaching its full potential.

Making the Holy Secular and the Secular Holy

According to Harvard psychologist and writer Dr. Howard Gardner, who has written about the theory of multiple intelligences, the arts provide a variety of portals to learning. By bringing their creative energy and perspective to a Jewish issue or concept, artists can reframe an idea and offer metaphors to allow a person to consider that idea in a new way.

Jewish art can be considered an extended midrash on the Jewish tradition. While the classical body of midrash is a piece of literature, its authors allowed their imaginations to run wild as they filled in the spaces between the sparse words of Torah. In so doing, they offered a different lens through which Jews of subsequent generations could understand the biblical narrative. Jewish artists are also creating an extended commentary on our Jewish heritage. Many of their forms are nonverbal, such as music, dance, and art, yet in these ways they open up the "book" for the "people of the book."

Not every Jew is capable of reading classical Jewish texts and making meaning out of that text. For some, an art form may be far more accessible than the text. In other cases, the artist's work might instill or inspire a curiosity that will lead a person back to the book. But even if it doesn't, the exposure to the idea in a nonverbal form may be the switch that turns on the light for someone who has been disconnected from the Jewish tradition. The emotional energy of a piece of music may provide the hard to define but deeply memorable experience that a piece of liturgy or a Bible story might fail to provide at face value.

A wonderful example of this phenomenon is the emergence in Israel of secular academies that are devoted to the study of classical Jewish sources. Ruth Calderon, who founded one of the best known of these academies—Alma in Tel Aviv, an educational institution for adults in the field of Hebrew culture—has helped us understand the elasticity of our cultural heritage. Calderon recognized that the majority of Israelis are secular, but she was troubled that they rarely looked at or took seriously the rich heritage of classical Jewish texts. She helped pioneer a way for secular Israelis to treat the texts as worthy of exegesis in a manner that combines freedom and the commitment to see oneself as a link in the chain of culture.

Calderon suggests that this new community of Torah students is engaged in a revolution. They do not look for *Yiddishkeit* or nostalgia in their study, nor do they attempt to modify the text to make it compatible with their own values. Ambivalence and opposition to the text are an integral part of the study experience. The underlying assumption that makes this entire revolution possible is that the material—the text—is resilient and durable, well able to deal with any intellectual challenge and benefit from the encounter. Secular academies like Alma do not function based on the premise that the texts are sacred in the religious sense. However, the students do ascribe to them the vigor of the great classics, in the same way that artists attribute power to their paints or poets attribute power to their words. The text is regarded as raw material for individual creation, for the understanding of oneself and the world. In this respect, the text is unique or holy, even in secular terms, and its wisdom is then filtered through the eyes and hands and ears of incredibly talented artists. It informs their work, which reaches audiences around the world. Neither didactic nor always obvious, it is the next level of commentary, and its impact is very real.

> The emotional energy of a piece of music may provide the hard to define but deeply memorable experience that a piece of liturgy or a Bible story might fail to provide at face value.

The Foundation for Jewish Culture has tried to seed similar alternative approaches to the riches of the Jewish tradition in the United States. Like

Alma in Tel Aviv, its Six Points Fellowship for Emerging Jewish Artists offers substantial Jewish learning as well as professional development workshops. Since 2007, thirty Six Points artists in New York and Los Angeles have produced more than 115 separate readings, workshops, and performances, which have reached over thirty-five thousand people. The projects and artists have been featured in more than six hundred articles and blog posts, including major mainstream and Jewish outlets, radio, and national TV, and have attracted more than 350,000 individual visits to the artists' websites and blogs. New York Cohort I fellows (2007–9) and their projects continue to engage audiences as far away as Mali in West Africa. The visual artist Ofri Cnaani, a Six Points fellow and a student of Calderon's, created *The Sota Project*, a multimedia installation based on a Talmudic story of two sisters, one of whom is accused of adultery. Originally shown to acclaim at the mainstream Galapagos Art Space in Brooklyn, New York, it moved to Los Angeles then to Montreal. For many attendees, it may be their first encounter with Talmudic thought.

Another powerful transmitter of culture is film. The Lynn and Jules Kroll Fund for Jewish Documentary Film has given nearly $2 million to approximately one hundred films exploring a wide range of subjects, including interracial adoption, the criminal justice system, the Holocaust, the kibbutz, Susan Sontag, and Shalom Aleichem. These films have received Academy Award nominations, Emmy Awards, and honors from major Jewish and secular film festivals worldwide, and have reached millions of viewers via public television broadcasts and educational screenings in schools, giving audiences a new understanding of Jewish life, history, and heritage.

A critically important demographic for nurturing and expanding Jewish culture are young adults. The Kroll Fund grantees have screened for young people on college campuses (including at Hillels) and in JCCs, Moishe Houses, and synagogues via the Inside the Docs program, which uses thematically connected film series to engage adults aged eighteen to thirty in conversation about contemporary Jewish life.

Inside the Docs comes at an appropriate time, as the past forty years has seen an explosion in Jewish studies programs in universities across the country. In 2008, the Foundation for Jewish Culture launched its Jewish

Studies Expansion Program (JSEP) for campuses that have many Jewish students but few Jewish studies opportunities. By funding two-year fellowships for charismatic, learned young scholars on these campuses, JSEP is helping to provide in-depth Jewish learning for students as well as employment in the field of Jewish studies. The program has provided these professors with a toolbox of films, books, authors, and musicians so that they have multiple ways to engage with students on their campuses. These programs provide a glimpse of what a rich Jewish culture can look like, and it helps make Jewish ideas exciting to the next generation of college students.

JSEP fellows have taught new courses at twelve universities, reaching more than three thousand students through classes and an additional one thousand through activities, including screenings, concerts, and other cultural events. JSEP also has a lasting impact on those students. Even a year after taking a JSEP course, 78 percent of Jewish respondents reported a stronger connection to their Jewish heritage and identity "to a great or moderate extent," while 33 percent of Jewish respondents said the course inspired them to get more involved with Jewish life on campus and beyond. One respondent reported that her JSEP course "made me realize the importance of passing Judaism on to my children, which is something I never really thought about." Yet another student said the course "energized my own commitment to Zionism" and motivated her to visit Israel. Every fellow produced at least one event that was attended by more than one hundred students and community members. Jewish studies directors, students, and the fellows themselves described how they became "the face of Jewish studies on campus."[3]

> The text is regarded as raw material for individual creation, for the understanding of oneself and of the world. In this respect, the text is unique or holy, even in secular terms, and its wisdom is then filtered through the eyes and hands and ears of incredibly talented artists.

The Future

Supporting scholars and artists in Israel *and* the United States is the wisest possible investment in the Jewish future. We should honor them for their incredible efforts. Send them around the country and the world. Make them keynote speakers at our conferences. Help them disseminate their work on tour. Provide traveling exhibition support. Fund teaching materials on Jewish culture for young people and support their efforts to form affinity groups to encourage more Jewish cultural creativity. Hebrew schools would be more well-rounded and enticing places with an artist in residence. One of the past Six Points artists, a secular Israeli, offers his teaching services at a Hebrew school in Brooklyn in exchange for rehearsal space, and he is planning a full-scale artists residency program there for himself and other choreographers. More synagogues should reimagine themselves as houses of study through artistic practice. Think how many more people might come to a synagogue on a weekend if a Jewish artist offered some kind of performance or class or discussed his or her latest work of art.

We have only to look at our own sacred text to see the importance of the artist. In the biblical chapter *Ki Tissa*, Bezalel, an individual endowed with craft, knowledge, and *ruach Elohim* ("divine inspiration" or, more literally, "the spirit of God"), is selected to build the Tabernacle, where God's presence is made manifest to the people. This monumental task is not left to just anyone. Although the people participate, they are led and overseen by a singular human being of extraordinary talent. The placement of the Bezalel story just before the commandment of Shabbat and the second giving of the Ten Commandments demonstrates his and the story's centrality to our people. Imagine if today we were to recognize the artist as key to the future of our people in the same way! In my perfect world, a fund for culture in the Jewish world, international and multidisciplinary in scope, would provide serious support for intelligent, artistically meritorious projects that stretch our understanding but are also grounded in the wisdom of our ancient civilization. One of the keys to Jewish survival has been the Jewish people's uncanny ability to adjust to new social and historical milieus, moving forward even as we honor our heritage by giving it new forms.

There are extremely talented and intelligent individuals delving into their heritage who want to be recognized both in their artistic field and in the Jewish world. If we put the bright, talented, creative individuals at the center of Jewish life instead of on the fringes and invest in them appropriately by encouraging, promoting, and disseminating their efforts, we will reward talented artists and scholars who embrace their often complex Jewish identities. Even better, we will make sure that the Jewish culture we create and pass on is exciting and inspiring for generations to come.

Synagogues

Reimagined

Rabbi Sharon Brous

Once there was a beloved king, teaches Levi Yitzchak of Berdichev, whose court musicians played beautiful music before him. The king loved the music, and the musicians felt honored to be able to use their talent to bring him joy. Every day for many years the musicians played enthusiastically, and the king and the musicians developed a deep love for one another. But eventually, after years of dedicated service, all of the musicians died. Their children were called into the king's court to take their parents' place. Out of loyalty to their parents, they began to appear every morning to perform. But unlike their parents, the children did not love the music. While they could play basic tunes, they did not understand the hidden power of their instruments, and in their hearts they believed that they had better things to do than spend time trying to please some king. Each day that they played, their resentment grew. And each day the king became more and more frustrated—as much by their dismissive attitude as by their cacophony.

Rabbi Sharon Brous is the founding rabbi of IKAR (www.ikar-la.org), a spiritual community dedicated to reanimating Jewish life through soulful religious practice that is rooted in a deep commitment to social justice. She has been noted as one of the leading rabbis in the country in *Newsweek/Daily Beast* and has been listed among the *Forward*'s fifty most influential American Jews numerous times. She serves on the faculty of the Wexner Heritage Program, the Shalom Hartman Institute, and Reboot and sits on the board of Rabbis for Human Rights.

After some time, for reasons nobody really understood, a few of the children developed a renewed interest in serving the king. They realized that playing beautiful music was the way to connect with him and bring him joy. But because they had abandoned serious practice for so long, their instruments were rusty and out of tune, and their skill was embarrassingly inadequate.

So these children set out to remember what their parents had known so well. They arrived early each morning and found a remote corner of the palace to practice together. They began to experiment with sound, rediscover harmony, and rededicate themselves to service spawned by love. In the evening, after the other musicians went home, they'd practice more, trying desperately to make their instruments sing.

The king witnessed their efforts and was deeply moved. Their music was different from their parents', but like them, it was driven by dedication and love. And for this reason, their efforts were received as a blessing.

Many American Jews—third- and fourth-generation immigrants—carry within them the distant echo of their parents' and grandparents' Judaism. They know that there are stories to tell but can't remember the major plot lines, let alone the sacred details. They know that there was a Jewish song that guided and propelled, that healed and held for many generations, but they have no idea how to access the memory of that song. The first time I taught Levi Yitzchak's story to a room full of Jews—all young, all unaffiliated—one woman stood up and said, with tears, "This is my story!" And many others concurred. Our grandparents and great-grandparents came to Ellis Island clutching sacred books, memories, recipes, and traditions. Their children tossed them overboard to become American, go to drive-ins, and play baseball. But now many of us, *uber*-American, find ourselves wondering if there may have been anything in those forgotten books that could help us navigate life's most challenging questions. For so many young American Jews, the experience of the musicians' children is all too familiar.

In 1948, as the devastation of the Jews of Europe became known, Simon Rawidowicz wrote an essay called *Am Ha-Holekh Va-Met*, "Israel—The Ever-Dying People."

> The world has many images of Israel, but Israel has only one image of itself: that of an expiring people, forever on the verge of ceasing to be.... He who studies Jewish history will readily discover that there was hardly a generation in the Diaspora period which did not consider itself the final link in Israel's chain. Each always saw before it the abyss ready to swallow it up.... Often it seems as if the overwhelming majority of our people go about driven by the panic of being the last.[1]

Rawidowicz claimed that pessimism and uncertainty were not unique to a generation that had witnessed the destruction of European Jewry, but were intrinsic to the Jewish psyche, present in every generation. And just as it was true then, it is also true now. The past couple of decades have produced major studies identifying the shrinking of the Jewish community in America (outside Orthodoxy), with sociologists painting an ominous picture: Will the Jewish community continue to dwindle until it is unrecognizable? Will it be reduced to an insular, extremist religious community, devoid of the breadth of Jewish intellectual, spiritual, and cultural expression? One wonders, is this just the latest iteration of eternal Jewish anxiety, or is there something distinct about this round of panic attacks, something that signals a true shift in Jewish consciousness and community?

Alienation

But unlike their parents, the children did not love the music. While they could play basic tunes, they did not understand the hidden power of their instruments, and in their hearts they believed that they had better things to do than spend time trying to please some king.

The thesis of Sidney Schwarz's lead essay is entirely consistent with my experience working with young, disengaged, and disaffected American Jews over the past decade. There is no question that we are witnessing a generational shift, one that manifests itself in a deep and growing disconnect from the institutional loyalty and communal affiliation of previous generations. No longer will young people invest in large organizations and institutions that do not move them as spiritual beings, stimulate their intellects, captivate them socially, or inspire them to be better citizens of the world. The significant difference between this generation of American Jews and the musicians' children is that the musicians still felt compelled to show up every morning, albeit resentfully. Today's young Jews would rather opt out. In other words, guilt no longer generates synagogue attendance or support for Jewish Federation campaigns.

To be sure, the Jewish community is suffering from a perception problem: many young Jews won't even look to conventional institutions for answers to the most penetrating questions—from the practical (where am I going to meet my partner?) to the transcendent (what is the meaning of my life?). But the problem is more than perceptual. If the Rabbis believed that the world stands on three pillars—*Torah* (Jewish core teaching), *avodah* (sacred service), and *g'milut chasadim* (acts of love and kindness)—then the prevailing belief is that twentieth-century Jewish communal and institutional engagement was similarly predicated on three pillars: anti-Semitism, Israel in crisis, and intermarriage. And, as Sidney Schwarz argues, the twentieth-century communal agenda simply does not speak to a generation of young Jews who see the world—Jewish and beyond—through a very different set of priorities, commitments, and attachments.

> No longer will young people invest in large organizations and institutions that do not move them as spiritual beings, stimulate their intellects, captivate them socially, or inspire them to be better citizens of the world.

Alienation from the prevailing values and agenda of the Jewish community is not the only driving social force redefining the Jewish landscape. Just at the moment that so many young people are experiencing a deep and very real sense of disconnect from conventional Jewish organizations and synagogues, they are also experiencing unprecedented access to American social and cultural experiences. Even when I was growing up in the 1980s in suburban New Jersey, there were two country clubs in our town—neither of which accepted Jews as members. Temple youth group was our response to the popular Protestant after-school dance class. But today it is far too easy to find community, intellectual engagement, and spiritual fulfillment outside the insular Jewish communal structure. Today we have Sundance and South by Southwest. Jews no longer need a refuge from a cold and unwelcoming American cultural scene. What they need is a reason to come back into a Jewish one.

This is only one factor in what makes the social and spiritual reality of young Jews today—whether gen X or millennials—substantially different from any previous generation. I have heard more than one sociologist identify this generation (today's twenties through early forties) as the most narcissistic in history. Technological advances and social realities have affected every aspect of their lives, from the intellectual to the spiritual to the political. In 2005 and 2006, Reboot funded two studies: *"Grande Soy Vanilla Latte with Cinnamon, No Foam …": Jewish Identity and Community in a Time of Unlimited Choices*[2] and *OMG! How Generation Y Is Redefining Faith in the iPod Era*.[3] The studies concluded that "if the Baby Boom was characterized as a 'generation of seekers,' their offspring, generation Y, is a 'generation of individuals.'[4] For many, pursuing the American Dream simply means, 'doing whatever I want.'"

The early twenty-first century is a time of radical individualism and instant gratification. With an iPod, a person buys whatever music she wants immediately and deletes it the minute she tires of it. Many have argued that the democratization of news—with instant access to every possible political perspective—has had the unintended consequence of narrowing people's exposure to ideas and perspectives that differ from their own. When you can special-order your music and your news commentary, you bypass a whole world of accidental learning and growth. With parking apps and GPS devices, we never get lost anymore. Technology and access, for all that they have made possible, have also created a culture of narrowness and superficiality in which virtual community has taken the place of real community, in which the newest technology makes the old obsolete in an instant and people put more thought into one-line posts to Facebook friends than cultivating meaningful relationships with actual friends.

How does a culture of narcissism, over-entitlement, and personalization manifest itself in terms of Jewish communal engagement? How can an iPod generation find rigorous exploration of Talmud and Jewish

WIN A $100 GIFT CERTIFICATE!

Fill in this card and mail it to us—
or fill it in **online** at

**jewishlights.com/
feedback.html**

—to be eligible for a
$100 gift certificate for
Jewish Lights books.

JEWISH LIGHTS PUBLISHING
SUNSET FARM OFFICES RTE 4
PO BOX 237
WOODSTOCK VT 05091-0237

Place
Stamp
Here

Fill in this card and return it to us to be eligible for our quarterly drawing for a $100 gift certificate for Jewish Lights books.

We hope that you will enjoy this book and find it useful in enriching your life.

Book title: _____

Your comments: _____

How you learned of this book: _____

If purchased: Bookseller _____ City _____ State _____

Please send me a free JEWISH LIGHTS Publishing catalog, I am interested in: (check all that apply)

1. ☐ Spirituality
2. ☐ Mysticism/Kabbalah
3. ☐ Philosophy/Theology
4. ☐ History/Politics

5. ☐ Women's Interest
6. ☐ Environmental Interest
7. ☐ Healing/Recovery
8. ☐ Children's Books

9. ☐ Caregiving/Grieving
10. ☐ Ideas for Book Groups
11. ☐ Religious Education Resources
12. ☐ Interfaith Resources

Name (PRINT) _____

Street _____

City _____ State _____ Zip _____

E-MAIL (FOR SPECIAL OFFERS ONLY) _____

Please send a JEWISH LIGHTS Publishing catalog to my friend:

Name (PRINT) _____

Street _____

City _____ State _____ Zip _____

JEWISH LIGHTS PUBLISHING
Tel: (802) 457-4000 • Fax: (802) 457-4004
Available at better booksellers. Visit us online at **www.jewishlights.com**

literature compelling and life-sustaining? How can those taught to walk away/delete/unfriend on a whim be taught to cultivate a serious relationship with Israel, even when it doesn't always feel good? How can they be stimulated to discover a spiritual practice that actually requires *practice*? Is there a way to cultivate a sense of obligation, enchantment, and spiritual hunger in a generation that is essentially able to log off or sign out in all other aspects of life?

In light of these trends, a growing sense of dissatisfaction and disconnection from conventional Jewish institutions among young Jews should come as no surprise. The past couple of decades have seen a widening gap between the programs and services being funded and offered in the Jewish communal world and the people who need meaningful connection the most.

Regeneration

After some time, for reasons nobody really understood, a few of the children developed a renewed interest in serving the king.

At the same time that the organized Jewish community has been losing market share in the under-forty demographic, the past decade has also demonstrated a growing trend toward revitalization in the form of inspired, purpose-driven communities and communal efforts. There is a whole new crop of Jewish leaders—many from the disappearing demographic—putting their best thinking into addressing the question: How can the relevance, power, and possibility of Judaism be translated to the next generation? As much as the prevalent trend is toward alienation and disaffection, there is a simultaneous (albeit much smaller) trend toward wholehearted and meaningful Jewish engagement, sometimes manifesting itself within the institutional world, sometimes emerging in autonomous efforts in bars, cafes, living rooms, and JCCs around the country.

Schwarz prescribes four essential, defining principles that are necessary for institutions and organizations to survive and thrive in the coming decades. I propose a slightly different framework, with some significant areas of overlap. My sense is that there are three, core definitional characteristics that must form the foundation of vibrant Jewish organizations and institutions, especially synagogues, in the years ahead: authenticity, creativity, and moral courage. All of these are grounded in Jewish text and tradition, and all are a response to the discontinuity and spiritual disorientation that define the Jewish landscape today.

Authenticity is the buzzword that studies reveal is the essential ingredient young people are both driven to and most cynical about in the Jewish community. Given the culture of instant gratification, if someone is going to invest time and money, it had better be for something real and something that offers the potential for transcendence and transformation. When I was a young, disaffected Jew living in New York City, I was desperately searching for a place to learn, and I found nearly every synagogue I visited to be cold and unwelcoming. But I was equally repelled by the services in which I knew and understood—even as an essentially illiterate Jew—everything that was going on. Where is the mystery? The challenge? For years, the Jewish community has made the mistake of equating *accessible* with *simplistic*. In reality, people are willing to invest in their learning—but the reward has to be not only deep and meaningful but also challenging.

> There are three, core definitional characteristics that must form the foundation of vibrant Jewish organizations and institutions, especially synagogues, in the years ahead: authenticity, creativity, and moral courage. All of these are grounded in Jewish text and tradition, and all are a response to the discontinuity and spiritual disorientation that define the Jewish landscape today.

I once consulted for an aging synagogue that was losing families to the local Reform temple, which required only three hours a week of religious school, compared to their six. They were considering scaling back as well, to stay competitive. My advice: Why not double the hours of your program each week instead? Make it the most rigorous program in the city, with intensive study of Mishnah, Talmud, *chasidut*—texts they'd never see in another after-school program. Develop real expectations around Hebrew fluency, and speak with them frankly about what it means to be a Jew and a human being in the world. Let the word on the street be that when their kids graduate from your program, they'll be serious Jews, knowledgeable and engaged. You'll have a waiting list within a couple of years. Not surprisingly, they didn't take my advice. But I strongly believe that our communal instinct—toward ease and convenience—is a recipe for generational disengagement.

The reality is that the young Jews we assume will never dedicate the time or energy needed to take themselves seriously as Jews—who will go on a program only if it's free (because we can't expect them to pay money for their own Jewish experience), who will only go to Shabbat services if they promise to be short, sexy, and conveniently located—these are the same young people who will dedicate many hours each week and significant amounts of money to their yoga practices. They will preregister for Burning Man and prepare months in advance for the spiritual desert experience. Why? Because this generation has a finely tuned instinct for authenticity. If a Jewish experience feels cheap and watered down, they won't sit through it, and they certainly won't come back. But if it feels real—if it feels mysterious, enchanting, and powerful, if it feels like the revelation of truths that have been hidden in the past and might help them uncover hints about how to live meaningfully today, then they will invest. In the 1970s, Rabbi Abraham Joshua Heschel criticized the synagogue for perpetuating the lie of prayer by proxy. Some hired hand—a rabbi, a cantor, a choir master—stands on stage and simulates prayer, and the people, by virtue of being witnesses, are excused from their own soul-work. This model no longer holds—if nothing is being asked of me, why should I waste my time? And even more to the point, if the rabbi and cantor are not being moved—deeply moved—by the experience of prayer, if they never cry and never dance and never feel that they are pleading before the gates of heaven, why should I trust that they'll guide *me* to that place?

When considering what authenticity looks like in Jewish engagement, I often think of Hannah, from the book of Samuel. Hannah's heart was broken by her struggle with infertility, and in her suffering she realized that she could no longer abide by a religious life that felt empty, distant, and meaningless. In her devastation, she cried out to God. She wept, she shook, she accused. And she redefined what Jewish prayer ought to look

61

like. There is no room in a Jewish prayer experience for falsehood or faking, for empty ritual that is devoid of spiritual truth or disconnected from moral action.

Jewish engagement efforts that will be sustainable and long-lasting can't be shticky attempts to attract young people, but must offer access to a very old Jewish conversation that remains provocative and enlivening in every generation.

The necessary partner to authenticity is creativity. Imagination. A willingness to breathe something very new into the very old. Torah teaches us that the greatest expression of human freedom is the ability to deny inevitability, to defy expectations, and to believe that with creativity and imagination we can create a new reality for ourselves. An ethic of inevitability responds to demographic trends toward disaffection and disaffiliation by saying, "These people are narcissists. None of this is our fault—they'll come back when their kids need a Hebrew school." But an ethic of imagination, creativity, and possibility looks at what's broken and says, "What can we learn from what we are seeing? What can we do to shift the trends?" *New York Times* columnist and Pulitzer Prize–winning author Thomas Friedman argues that there really are only two kinds of countries in the world today—not developed and developing. Not first world and third world. Today there are only nations that harness imagination and those that do not. The same is true about synagogues, Federations, and day schools. Are we willing to be imaginative, to take risks, to fail, in order to keep our communities vibrant and vital—truly alive?

> Jewish engagement efforts that will be sustainable and long-lasting can't be shticky attempts to attract young people, but must offer access to a very old Jewish conversation that remains provocative and enlivening in every generation.

When IKAR began its search for a place to hold its religious services, I insisted that we find a space in which the chairs were not rooted to the ground. No theater seats and certainly no pews. I knew that physical fluidity was absolutely essential to spiritual fluidity. People had to be able to get up and dance without first saying "excuse me" to the fourteen people between them and the aisle. And we needed to be able to experiment. To set chairs up in circles and straight lines and arcs and diamonds and even sometimes to uproot in the middle of a service when the vibe isn't working and try something completely new. I learned this as a rabbinic fellow at B'nai Jeshurun (BJ) in New York. One Thursday afternoon, in my weekly meeting with the rabbis, I suggested that we rearrange the seats in a certain formation that I suspected might be more conducive to communal prayer, sketching my idea on a tiny notepad. The moment passed and we went on to discuss something else, and I thought little of it until I showed up for *Kabbalat Shabbat* the next night. To my astonishment, eight hundred chairs in that sanctuary had all been moved to match my scribbled model from the day before. It was breathtaking—and one of the most important lessons I learned going into the rabbinate. The service was awful. The spiritual vibe was off, people felt uncomfortable and out of sorts, and the next week they went back to the standard setup. But I loved that they tried—and I am still convinced that BJ's extraordinary success in capturing the hearts and minds of thousands of disaffected Jews is because their modus operandi has always been to think creatively, experiment, flow, fail, and then try again. This is a mandate that we have taken very seriously in building IKAR over the past eight years.

Finally, our organizations have to be defined not only by a sincere rootedness in the tradition and a simultaneous commitment to building a culture of experimentation but also by the recognition that creative and authentic religious practice must *necessarily* lead to a broadening of moral concern and moral action. Our tradition is unambivalent about the need for concrete acts of compassion and justice to flow from our religious practice. It is clear to me that for a spiritual and religious life to be authentic, it must strive to catalyze a kind of spiritual activism.

At IKAR, we talk about Judaism as an inheritance of willful opposition, Torah as an eternal challenge to the status quo. Our community organizes around a Shabbat experience that is both rich in spiritual and ritual practice and dedicated to awakening the Jewish heart to work toward social and political change. We work to cultivate a kind of holy audacity that calls us to do better, to fight harder, to manifest our core values on the street. I see this as the great Jewish legacy, woven through biblical and Rabbinic texts over the past four thousand years and a standard-bearer for a Jewish life of courage and conviction.

This is the moral courage of Abraham, who refuses to acquiesce to God's plan to destroy Sodom and Gemorrah. Instead, Abraham takes God to task, arguing with deep certitude that it is unjust and unbefitting of God to punish the innocent with the guilty. This is a classic act of *chutzpah k'lappei sh'maya*—chutzpah thrust toward the heavens—the ultimate in spiritual audacity, which seems to delight rather than enrage God when it comes from a place of humility and love. Later in the Torah, God is apoplectic when the Israelites build a Golden Calf, just days after witnessing the miracle of the Sea. It is then that God prepares to destroy the entire nation, but Moses pleads for mercy. According to the midrash, he refuses to leave God's presence until God relents and reverses the decree. Both Abraham and Moses demonstrate extraordinary chutzpah in their refusal to allow God's worst instincts to prevail. And there are many others who similarly demonstrate a severe and unyielding posture when it comes to overturning social structures and fighting injustice.

> We work to cultivate a kind of holy audacity that calls us to do better, to fight harder, to manifest our core values on the street.

There is Rebecca, who refuses to accept birth order as destiny and helps Jacob trick his father into receiving the blessing of the firstborn. Tamar refuses to accept her permanent imprisonment under unjust laws binding a woman to the family of her dead husband. The prophet Natan berates King David (the king, after all!) for having an adulterous relationship with Batsheva and then killing her husband, Uriah. The Jew as bearer of moral courage is ubiquitous in our text and literature. Some of the central moments and characters of Israelite and Jewish history are characterized by a holy refusal to accede to social norms or their presumed fates. It seems clear that as much as Judaism is about obedience to God and *mitzvot*, it is also about a legacy of willful defiance against unjust social, political, and religious structures and even at times against God.

Jews are known in America to be bold and courageous, to challenge unethical laws and norms, and to stand at the forefront of movements for social change, from civil rights to labor and immigration. But all too often, this holy assertiveness does not translate into our Jewish lives—precisely the place where it ought to be nurtured. The Jewish posture in synagogue is sitting quietly, not disturbing the order—"Please rise. Please be seated. Please turn to page 82 for *Aleinu*." Don't dare speak out of turn, cry out in pain, or, God forbid, say anything too "political"—especially about Israel.

Cultivating a community that is driven by moral courage requires the full integration of the spiritual and the political, the social and the ritual. We *daven* with all our hearts and souls because we believe that Shabbat is a spiritual revolution—it temporarily relieves us of the world as it is and allows us to think and dream again about the world as it could be. This is not only a spiritual value, but it is also a call for social and political change, and it must be at the heart of a deep and meaningful Jewish practice and at the core of a vibrant Jewish synagogue or organization.

Opportunity

Their music was different from their parents', but like them, it was driven by dedication and love. And for this reason, their efforts were received as a blessing.

So how can Judaism remain relevant and vital in an instant gratification world? My sense is that there are three prescriptions: (1) speak an eternal message, one that helps us understand what it means to be a Jew and a human being in the world, and do so in a voice that is both strong and vulnerable; (2) imagine what is necessary but not yet seen and then work creatively to manifest something new, taking a risk; and finally, (3) expand your heart beyond what is comfortable. Recognize that, as the Slonimer Rebbe teaches:

> Much is required of us. Though we do not fully under-
> stand it, we intuit that we live in a very great time of his-
> tory. We need to recognize the importance of our mission,
> our obligation, and our task in this generation—we need
> to utilize what has been given to us—so that we not despise
> the King's gift, God forbid.... This generation calls us to

great things. Rabbi Moshe of Kobrin commented on the verse: "The day is vast. It's not a time for gathering cattle. The great and awesome day is approaching." This is not a time to gather up "cattle" and worldly possessions.[5]

In small pockets around the country, for reasons we don't fully understand, musicians have been coming together because they have found a renewed interest in serving the king. They come early and stay late to practice and tune and try to find a way to do something beautiful, something heartfelt that is rooted in their parents' and their grandparents' music. Sometimes it sounds completely new. They often have to practice in some obscure corner of the palace because our community is not always encouraging of innovation. If they start to find success in their art, while some established leaders will welcome and encourage them, others will scorn and dismiss their efforts, worried that these holy rollers will steal market share (membership) or attention from long-standing, conventional efforts. Others fear that adaptations and improvisations will compromise the sanctity of the music. But these musicians persist, and hopefully will for many years to come, because it is from those obscure corners that we are learning about what the future might have in store for us. Not the panic-driven-ever-dying-people version of the future, but the hope-and-possibility version of the future.

The failure of institutional Jewish life to capture the imagination of young Jews today is irrefutable but not immutable. We have the ability to bridge the disconnect between the needs and interests of young Jews and the organized Jewish world. I believe that the greatest response to disaffection of a generation of Jews is to reclaim the power of our tradition, to find a way to think creatively about the future, and to remind ourselves of a profound and unrelenting truth: We who have been blessed with a legacy of moral courage must find our courage anew. We must work together—through acts of love and kindness, justice, and courage—to reignite a sense of purpose and mission in our community.

Jewish Family Foundations

"Come Together, Right Now"

Sandy Cardin

I n 1969, the Beatles released what is now considered their finest record, *Abbey Road*. While many remember that album more for its iconic cover of the shaggy-haired band crossing the street than for its music, several of its tracks contain timeless lyrics that still resonate more than forty years later. The opening track, "Come Together," is one such song. Originally penned by John Lennon to help rally support for Timothy Leary during his abbreviated run for governor of California against Ronald Reagan, the words of the chorus could and should serve as another kind of urgent call, this time to the American Jewish philanthropic community: "Come together, right now."

Sanford R. ("Sandy") Cardin is president of the Charles and Lynn Schusterman Philanthropic Network (CLSPN), a global effort to ignite the passion and unleash the power in young people to create change for themselves, in the Jewish community, and across the broader world. Cardin is a frequent presenter and panelist in global forums on topics related to catalytic grant making, innovative program building, Jewish identity, young adult engagement, Israel, and more. He acknowledges Roben Kantor Smolar, director of communications for the Charles and Lynn Schusterman Philanthropic Network, who contributed to this article.

The American Jewish community is in a state of flux and transition. Demographic challenges, behavioral shifts, religious differences, attitudinal disparities, and re-prioritizations—especially insofar as Israel is concerned—are just a few of the incredibly complex issues confronting and dividing American Jewry. Many of the large, consensus-driven organizations and congregations that served our people so well for years—the so-called "established" Jewish community—are sagging under the weight of these changes, and many of the start-up enterprises striving to gain a foothold in Jewish life are struggling as well.

The response to this reality by the American Jewish philanthropic community—composed primarily of Federations, private foundations, and individual funders—has been largely ineffective and, in some ways, counterproductive. Rather than finding ways to meaningfully work together to address common concerns and leverage the limited resources available to our community, we have generally pursued the larger mission we share—securing a vibrant future for Jewish people everywhere—independently and with remarkably little communication among ourselves.

Of course, the fact that many of us have become distracted from our larger mission is hardly surprising. As my friend and mentor Charles Schusterman (*z"l*) used to say, "It's hard to think about draining the swamp when you're knee-deep in alligators."

All of the news, however, is not bad or bleak. American Jews have never enjoyed so much social, political, or financial success. In virtually every walk of life, including philanthropy, Jews can be found at the top of the list; nearly half of the signatories to the Giving Pledge—an effort to encourage the wealthiest people in America to give the majority of their wealth to charitable causes—are Jewish. In fact, American Jewry has never been stronger and more capable of charting its own course, a truly remarkable and humbling thought. The key question is, of course, will we?

The Good News and the Bad News

To the extent that the future of American Jewry rests on the financial resources made available to Jewish programs and organizations, the conclusion we can draw from what little data actually exists about American Jewish philanthropy is inconclusive at best and conflicting at worst.

On the positive side of the ledger, the Federation system continues to raise and distribute hundreds of millions of dollars each year through its annual campaigns and endowment funds, and many other Jewish funders contribute impressively to Jewish life. According to a recent report from the Institute for Jewish and Community Research (IJCR), approximately $335 million of the funds distributed by fifty-six Jewish foundations went to Jewish causes in 2009 and 2010.[1] The IJCR study also shows that the number of foundations in the United States increased more than 50 percent, to 76,545 between 1999 and 2009, of which an estimated 10,000 made grants to Jewish causes.

At the same time, however, there are many reasons for alarm. Information from the 2000–2001 National Jewish Population Survey (NJPS) showed that among more engaged Jews, just under 33 percent gave to the Federation system. In the decade since that survey was published, the number of donors to the Federation system has diminished by almost 50 percent (from 925,000 to 480,000).[2] Perhaps of even greater concern is the fact that 92 percent of the funds raised by the Federation system in its annual campaign comes from just 7 percent of its contributors, and on an inflation-adjusted basis, overall Federation giving is lower today than it was ten years ago.

Outside of the Federation world, the picture is no prettier. According to the NJPS, a mere 26 percent of Jews gave one hundred dollars or more to Jewish causes, and the $335 million figure cited in the IJCR report represents just 24 percent of total giving from Jewish foundations. Indeed, only a very small percentage of American Jewry donates to Jewish causes, and the sums they contribute represent a very small portion of their total giving. Some estimate the percentage going to the Jewish community to be around 15 percent, and the figure is even lower for most of the Jews who have signed the Giving Pledge. That the resources exist is beyond question; whether those resources will be directed to supporting and strengthening American Jewish life is not so clear.

But rather than seeing the glass as half empty, I prefer to see it as half full and would like to address three promising, albeit nascent, trends of convergence within the American Jewish philanthropic community. Properly encouraged, nurtured, and promoted, the following three trends have the potential to make greater collaboration and communication in the American Jewish community the rule, not the exception:

1. A growing recognition among the most influential funders of Jewish life about the importance of engaging young Jewish adults in ways that speak to their unique needs and interests
2. A greater appreciation among those same funders about the importance of facilitating greater collaboration among all kinds of programs that seek to inspire young Jewish adults
3. A growing similarity between the way in which public and private grant makers are raising and distributing their funds

These three points of convergence are important for two reasons. First, they provide evidence that the American Jewish philanthropic community may finally be starting to work together to help young Jews strengthen their Jewish identities. Second, they may represent the dawn of a new era of greater cooperation and collaboration in addressing the many other areas of concern with which American Jewry is struggling.

Of course, these emerging trends could prove illusory. There are many within American Jewish life who still cling to the hope that the tidal wave of changes over the past decade is a passing fad and that the pendulum will eventually swing back to business as usual. They pay lip service to the changes that Sidney Schwarz identifies so well in his lead essay, even as they refuse to reprioritize their time or resources so as to optimize their chances of success in engaging and inspiring young Jews in their respective communities.

Still, if all three of these phenomena continue apace, they will do more than just go a long way toward resolving the specific concerns Schwarz raises about young Jewish adults; they will also have a profound and very positive effect on American Jewry for years to come.

Coming of Age for Young Jewish Adults

It is generally accepted that with an ever-growing number of opportunities open to them in American society, young Jewish adults need a reason to become or remain involved in Jewish life, one that resonates and speaks to them personally and authentically. Study after study have found that the young Jewish adults of the early twenty-first century have complex, multifaceted identities, only one of which is "Jewish."[3] Now that young Jews have the freedom and ability to participate in every aspect of American life, Judaism itself is competing for time and shelf space in the marketplace of ideas.

This understanding of young Jewish adults has taken a long time to embed itself within the halls and boardrooms of the established Jewish community. Until a decade or so ago, most Jewish organizations failed to realize that the rules of the game had changed. For a host of reasons, including inertia, resistance to change, and fear of the unknown, many within the Jewish community chose not to address intergenerational differences and operated on the erroneous assumption that future generations would ultimately turn out to look like their predecessors.

In hindsight, this laissez-faire approach was a true tactical error. It resulted in accelerating the ongoing exodus of young Jewish adults from organized Jewish life soon after their *B'nei Mitzvah*. We are left today with a younger generation with weak Jewish identities and few memories of meaningful Jewish experiences. While some return to Jewish life when they have children, far too many remain uninvolved.

Although it is difficult to pinpoint any one moment or event that caused attitudes to shift within the established Jewish community about young Jews, the founding of the Taglit-Birthright Israel program in 1999 is probably as good a place as any to start.[4] Its success in attracting and exciting young Jewish adults soon led other Jewish foundations and individual funders to take a more serious look at how the Jewish community was serving that age cohort, and what they found was not very impressive. The available options were limited and reflected an outdated model of engagement. Many of the institutions that constitute the established Jewish community were either unwilling or unable to build more accessible and attractive portals into Jewish life. Even more depressing and distressing was the desire by many in the

> The American Jewish philanthropic community may finally be starting to work together to help young Jews strengthen their Jewish identities.

Jewish establishment to "blame the customer"—to put the responsibility for their own inabilities and failures at the feet of the very young people they were trying to reach.

Those who forged ahead and began working closely with young Jewish adults quickly discovered that many of them, much like their peers from other faith communities, found the traditional institutionalized paradigm of twentieth-century religious practice uninteresting and uninspiring. What they wanted and demanded in return for their time and attention were opportunities to connect to their Jewish heritage and homeland in ways that allowed them to shape their ethnic-cultural identity on their own terms and in their own image.

In short order, the individual funders and foundations desirous of tapping into the passion, power, and talent of the "next generation" of global Jewry realized they needed to adopt a new set of approaches and initiatives.[5] They began to take chances on supporting those with the greatest potential to create and operate such programs: innovative, resourceful, energetic young Jewish social entrepreneurs, who understood their peers far better than most of those working in the established Jewish community.

In the early part of the twenty-first century, undeterred by the lack of interesting and relevant opportunities offered to them within the established Jewish world, these social entrepreneurs began "making Shabbat for themselves." Supported and inspired by incubator programs such as Joshua Venture[6] and Bikkurim,[7] young people began creating their own Jewish experiences, periodicals, programs, and networks. Collectively, they created what has become known as a Jewish "innovation ecosystem."[8]

As these start-ups were getting off the ground, much of the established Jewish world continued to function as if these enterprises were fads. Bolstered by the dramatic increase in the availability of social networking technology, the leaders of the innovation ecosystem continued to experiment with new ways of exploring their Jewish identities and participating in Jewish life, largely without the help or involvement of the established Jewish community.

And they succeeded. Independent organizations such as American Jewish World Service, Avodah, IKAR, Hazon, Mazon, and JDub, to name but a few, started to reach young Jewish adults in a way that the established Jewish community could never have imagined. A handful of private foundations—ours included—started developing proprietary projects that found favor among young Jewish adults. As this new approach manifested itself in successful new programs, organizations, and initiatives, the established Jewish community took notice, and its attitude toward young Jewish adults began to change. By the middle of the decade, a few of the largest and most visible Jewish organizations in the world began to shift their approaches to this age group, and several others started increasing the staff time and attention they were giving to it. Where young adults were once considered just one of several age cohorts in Jewish life worthy of support, many now perceive them to be the most important group, at least at this moment.

One example of this reorientation can be found within the Jewish Agency for Israel (JAFI), an institution that adopted a new strategic plan in 2011. For years known as an organization for which *aliyah* (immigration to Israel) was the number one priority, JAFI has decided to focus on strengthening the connections of young Jewish adults to Israel and to the Jewish people.

Two other entities with an increased emphasis on young Jewish adults are the American Jewish Joint Distribution Committee (JDC) and the Jewish Federations of North America (JFNA). Prior to 2008, JDC had no strategy to engage young Jews. Four years later, the amount of money spent by the JDC on this age cohort has increased more than fourfold, and the investment is paying real dividends: more than five hundred young adults now participate in JDC service projects every year. Steve Schwager, then JDC's CEO, pointed with pride to the fact that the organization "has embraced the operating spirit of start-ups and social entrepreneurs, borrowing from the trends around us, creating the space for intra-preneurs."[9]

For JFNA, the shift in attitude and approach to young Jewish adults started in July 2009 upon the hiring of Jerry Silverman as its president and CEO. As the former president of the Foundation for Jewish Camp, Silverman was well familiar with the wisdom and importance of reaching out to young people as a way to help secure the Jewish future, and under his leadership, JFNA is doing more for young Jewish adults than trying to recruit them as donors. As one example, JFNA has enticed more than fifteen hundred participants to its young-adult-oriented TribeFest conference in each of the past two years.

Even though it took many of the established Jewish institutions a long time to fully recognize and appreciate the importance of young Jewish adults and to begin adopting new approaches to reaching them, the fact that many within the Jewish community are currently using a shared language to speak about ways to engage that population is a very positive development.

Integrating the New with the Establishment

With an emerging consensus about the importance of focusing on the next generation, conditions are ripe for the further advancement of our second convergence: greater interaction among and integration of the efforts to inspire young Jewish adults by the established Jewish community with those being offered by the emerging Jewish innovation ecosystem. The benefit of this trend is obvious. To do otherwise would be a waste of precious communal time and resources. Why should we build new organizations if existing ones can be successfully retooled?

And yet, as anyone who has ever purchased an old house can tell you, it often takes longer and costs more to renovate an existing property than it does to build anew. Even when renovating makes sense, you are often left reliant on systems and structures that simply cannot accommodate the most recent advances in style, design, and technology. Sometimes, things become obsolete, and no amount of repairing or hand-wringing can make them worth saving.

Having to choose between these two alternatives is a dilemma those of us in the private foundation world often face, especially when thinking about how best to invest our resources in the American Jewish community. We are constantly weighing how much time, effort, and money we should expend working with the "established" institutions versus how much effort we should put into helping start-up organizations find their initial footing. The answer is not always clear, and funders are forced to consider complex factors in making their decisions. We need social entrepreneurs to continue pushing our community forward and to keep educating us about how best to connect with young Jews. And we need the enlightened leadership of the established Jewish community to serve as mentors and to help bring innovative projects to scale.

The good news on the philanthropic front is that many Jewish funders are making it clear that they realize both the establishment and the innovators are needed. According to the research from the IJCR, Jewish foundations continue to "help fund the vast network of Jewish communal institutions, while also acting as catalysts for innovative programming and upstart organizations meeting the diverse needs of the Jewish community."[10]

Indeed, we need to approach and fund Jewish life holistically, as part of one system with common goals, sharing responsibility—and credit—for the outcomes. Two good examples of how to do this well can be found in the stories of the PresenTense Group,[11] founded by Ariel Beery and Aharon Horwitz, and Moishe House,[12] founded by David Cygielman. Each of these respective organizations faces the typical growing pains of young nonprofits, including funding their infrastructures and building toward self-sufficiency. To their credit, each has also understood the value of partnerships with large, established organizations in the Jewish community. The results of these collaborations are larger and deeper levels of service to young Jewish adults than would have been the case if the fledgling organizations were to have insisted on going it alone.

> We need social entrepreneurs to continue pushing our community forward and to keep educating us about how best to connect with young Jews. And we need the enlightened leadership of the established Jewish community to serve as mentors and to help bring innovative projects to scale.

Among the lessons being learned as a result of these emerging partnerships is that accomplishing meaningful change and forging strong, durable relationships will require a serious commitment of resources, both human and financial. After all, virtually every Jewish organization operating today, established or emerging, needs help strengthening its infrastructure, attracting new donors, and upgrading its programs.

Here it is important to note that even the early successes of the Jewish community in fostering young innovative organizations have created another challenge: helping them move beyond the start-up phase to a place where they can expand and build sustainable organizations. Their need for additional financial support (sometimes known as "mezzanine" or "second stage" funding) often comes at precisely the moment in which the excitement generated by the original project or organization is fading. Dana Raucher, the executive director of the Samuel Bronfman Foundation, recently called on the Jewish community to better define and understand growth in order to make sustainable innovation possible.

Achieving the goal of an unprecedented degree of cooperation between and among the Jewish Federation system (including the donor-advised assets they control) and all other funders of Jewish life, private foundations and individuals alike, will not come easily or inexpensively. Shifting tides and structures in the philanthropic landscape just may be creating the necessary circumstances for it to happen.

The Realignment of Jewish Philanthropy

It was not so long ago that American Jewish philanthropy was virtually monolithic. In this way, it is not dissimilar to the broader American philanthropic landscape. For close to one hundred years, Jewish giving was largely defined and controlled by the Federation system. Jewish philanthropy was a collective endeavor. Members of the community gave funds to a central body responsible for assessing needs and allocating the resources at its disposal. Large givers, the kind of people and families that today are likely to engage in philanthropy through private foundations or donor-advised funds, may have been given priority in terms of board seats and committee assignments, but they were nonetheless part of a consensus-driven institutional structure that did its best to meet a wide spectrum of communal needs.

Over the course of the last quarter of a century, however, shifts in the general and Jewish philanthropic worlds have weakened "umbrella" organizations such as the Federations and the United Way. The rise of "directed giving," "venture philanthropy," and other more individualized forms of funding signaled the ever-increasing activism and influence of private foundations and individual donors, a paradigm shift still in process today. The emergence of the independent Jewish foundation sector "has revolutionized the American Jewish polity from one built around centralized and communally governed philanthropy into one built around multiple, independent power centers with few, if any, formal bonds of accountability toward one another."[13]

And so, while the ascendancy of private foundations has contributed in many ways to the breadth and depth of Jewish philanthropy—especially in promoting leadership development, nurturing the innovation ecosystem, and otherwise supporting some of the more creative efforts in American Jewish life—it has also created a few challenges. Among the most obvious are (a) the disproportionate influence large and activist foundations can have over an entire Jewish community; (b) the "balkanization" of giving in which each foundation, or small groups of foundations, pursue projects and programs of their own design and control, often without seeking input from the general Jewish community and sometimes in direct competition with the community; and (c) the creation of unnecessary strife and conflict between private foundations and communally governed organizations, especially when foundations challenge and criticize the communal groups for not sufficiently helping to take their proprietary projects "to scale" and/or otherwise providing the foundations with the kind of "exit" early-stage investors in the business world consider a sign of financial and programmatic success.

Many Federations, of course, have their own ideas as to how their communal funds should be used and the other philanthropic responsibilities they must fulfill. Private foundations and individual funders have the luxury of picking and choosing from among the areas of interest they wish to pursue, not to mention the ability to focus their financial resources in ways that Federation leadership can only dream about. Without open lines of communication and a willingness to blend the strategic advantages of the Federation system with that of the private foundation world, opportunities for synergy are lost. In the worst cases, it leads to outright competition.

Thankfully, our final convergence, which can be found in both the Jewish and the general philanthropic communities and whose effect is only just beginning to be felt, has the potential to lead to far greater cooperation and collaboration among Federations, private foundations, and individual donors. Until recently, public charities like the United Way and the Jewish Federation system operated primarily by seeking support from the community at large and distributing their funds across a wide range of organizations and causes. Endowed private foundations, on the other hand, avoided fundraising of any sort and gave their resources away in a narrower, more focused manner. Neither group ventured very often onto the turf of the other.

Today, these distinctions are fading. Public charities are much more deeply engaged in targeted grant making than ever before, and private foundations are boldly stepping into the fundraising world. Indeed, in early 2012, one of the largest privately endowed foundations in the world—the Getty Trust—announced it was adding a development director to its team. We are also seeing the growing democratization of philanthropy, a trend that takes advantage of online tools that allow anyone to make a charitable contribution according to particular interests.

Where some see these shifting sands as a sign of impending disaster, others believe the "flattening" of the philanthropic world is a long overdue step in the right direction. Those who rue these changes point to the problems the shifts are causing, including greater competition for scarce resources as well as for development professionals capable of raising money. They are also concerned that those with special interests will dominate the communal philanthropic agenda in unhealthy ways.

But while these are real concerns that must be addressed, the benefits of convergence within the philanthropic community far outweigh the costs. It has contributed to the development of a shared literature, a shared language, and a shared perspective about giving—the necessary precursors to the maturation of the field of philanthropy. Conversations within the giving community are more focused, and philanthropic organizations that have long despised each other are communicating more often and more effectively than ever before. Even the long-pilloried donor-advised funds at Fidelity, Schwab, and Vanguard, once derided as too commercial in nature, are now being welcomed into the philanthropic community as valuable players in the field.

Within the Jewish philanthropic world, a similar pattern of behavior is unfolding. Private foundations and large funders in the United States and Israel, often with the help and guidance of the Jewish Funders Network, are actively raising money and pursuing the creation of philanthropic partnerships that they believe will increase their financial and programmatic leverage. Among those doing it particularly well is the Israel-based Rashi Foundation, which is building public-private partnerships to promote education and social welfare for children and youth in the geographic and social periphery. Indeed, many of their actions mirror what organizations like the Jewish Agency for Israel, the Jewish Federations of North America, and the Joint Distribution Committee have done for years.

Among the first of these kinds of private philanthropic partnerships to be formed were PEJE (Partnership for Excellence in Jewish Education), STAR (Synagogues: Transformation and Renewal), Foundation for Jewish Camp, Reboot (an organization for culturally creative young Jews exploring Jewish identity and community), and of course, Birthright. More recent examples include Areivim (developing a network of Hebrew-language charter schools), PELIE (Partnership for Effective Learning and Innovative Education), Repair the World (inspiring American Jews and their communities to serve those in need), NEXT (connecting Birthright alumni to their peers and home communities), and the iCenter (promoting high-quality Israel education in the Diaspora). In each of these cases, the donors have decided to work together out of the belief that only successful collaborations can make the kind of difference necessary to achieve large-scale change. It is also a way to share the risks involved in starting new ventures.

At the same time, community foundations and others who control donor-advised funds are becoming much more active in the philanthropic world. No longer content to serve primarily as passive "pass-through" entities, they are developing and pursuing a much more activist and interventionist approach to resource allocations. They are beginning to operate more like foundations in the way that they assess communal needs, develop targeted interventions, gather data, and evaluate the effectiveness of their funding approaches.

In short, funders are becoming more focused and strategic in pursuing their core missions of enhancing the quality of life for all Jews within the communities that they seek to serve. If this particular trend continues, the relationships between Federations and foundations will no longer be defined by what one side can do for the other, but rather by what they can achieve together as partners. This shift in Jewish philanthropy is creating an environment that has the potential to strengthen our community by providing greater opportunities for cooperation, collaboration, and innovation.

The Road Ahead

Even as these three trends of convergence point toward greater cooperation and collaboration within the American Jewish philanthropic community, achieving our goal of ensuring that the future of Jewish life in the United States is vibrant, dynamic, and inclusive will require much more than what we have accomplished to date. Although we have taken a few small steps toward abandoning our silos and collaborating across institutional lines to more effectively reach younger generations of American Jews, the Jewish world remains fragmented and divided in a way that puts the broader Jewish communal endeavor at risk, even as some individual organizations and local communities are stronger than ever.

> The Jewish world remains fragmented and divided in a way that puts the broader Jewish communal endeavor at risk, even as some individual organizations and local communities are stronger than ever.

Our only recourse in the face of these challenges is to reclaim and rebuild a sense of a unified community, one in which service providers, foundations, Federations, and individual funders subordinate their own self-interest for that of the greater community. We must find ways to work together to open more doorways into the Jewish world and to encourage greater participation in Jewish life. We have to present a stronger case to those with wealth about why they should be investing in the Jewish community and then hold ourselves accountable for measuring and achieving the outcomes we promise those investors. And we must leverage our resources—human and financial—in unprecedented ways.

To be a community, we must act like a community. We have to do more than speak about collective responsibility—*Kol Yisrael arevim zeh lazeh,* "All Jews are responsible for one another" (*Shavuot* 39a)—we have to embrace and model it. Only then will we have a realistic chance to realize the full potential of our community in the years to come.

The famous quotation from Rabbi Tarfon applies as much to this work as it does to studying text or repairing the world: "Ours is not to complete the task, but neither are we free to desist from trying" (*Pirke Avot* 2:21). Indeed, it is time to answer John Lennon's prescient clarion call: it is time to come together, right now.

Israel and Jewish Life

A Twenty-First-Century Educational Vision

Dr. Barry Chazan and Anne Lanski

The establishment of a modern Jewish state over six decades ago has changed the canvas of the Jewish experience in ways not yet fully comprehended. The change has been profound and powerful—and, ironically, perplexing and problematic. This seminal event in the narrative of the Jewish people has been a Janus-faced coin: we cannot live without it, yet it has created new issues, challenges, and dilemmas.

We are two educators, and we see the world from the vantage point of education. In this essay, we shall present a view on Israel and contemporary American Jewish life that proposes a different direction from the status quo. We want to challenge some of the contemporary conceptions about Israel and propose a new way to approach the subject.

Dr. Barry Chazan is professor emeritus of the Hebrew University, founding educational director of Birthright Israel, and professor of education and director of the Masters of Arts in Jewish Professional Studies Program at Spertus College in Chicago. He is married to Anne Lanski, with whom he coauthored this chapter.

Anne Lanski is the executive director of the iCenter, a national organization established by the Charles and Lynn Schusterman Family Foundation and the Jim Joseph Foundation to build and support the field of precollegiate Israel education. Lanski was founder of Shorashim, a nationally acclaimed Israel experience program, and she is widely regarded as the pioneering figure in the formulation and implementation of the *mifgash* as a seminal context for experiencing Israel.

Some Contemporary Commonplaces

"Israel Is a Problem"

We often hear Israel described as a "problem." Some see Israel as a political problem for American Jews caused by Israel's territorial policies since 1967. Others regard Israel as a religious problem caused by intolerance toward the nonreligious or toward liberal Jewish religious movements. Still others are troubled that Israel has become a "secular" state of Israelis rather than a "religious" state of Jews. Finally, there are those who feel that Israel is a financial drain on American Jewry and that Jewish life would be better served if those resources were invested in local needs.

We believe that Israel represents a remarkably significant achievement of the Jewish people in the twentieth century. It has returned a people to its ancestral homeland and established a modern Jewish society. Like other societies, Israel encompasses achievements and successes along with complexities and problems. It is both a state like all other states and, at the same time, a state like no other state. We need to resist turning the problems of Israel into the "problem" of Israel.

"Israel Is No Longer a Struggling Democracy Trying to Make the Desert Bloom"

It is often argued that the romantic narrative of yesteryear (canonized in Otto Preminger's film version of *Exodus*) has been replaced by the narrative of Israel as a secular, Western, militarist Goliath. This commonplace is flawed by its very romanticism. It is rooted in a Hollywood movie whose heroes are Paul Newman and Eva Marie Saint.

A truer narrative is likely to be found in the sweaty arrival of Yitzhak Kummer at the Tel Aviv port in S. Y. Agnon's 1945 novel *Only Yesterday* (*Tmol Shilshom*), which tells the tale of an Eastern European idealistic immigrant trying to adjust to his new life in Palestine.[1] Similarly, Meir Shalev's novel, *The Blue Mountain* (*Roman Russi*), explores the foibles and ironies of those who came to Palestine from the Ukraine prior to the creation of the state in 1948.[2] These two books describe real people coming to a real country and undergoing a kaleidoscope of experiences—glorious, humorous, romantic, and tragic.

What about the often clichéd phrase that "Israel once made the desert bloom"? Indeed, Israel did make the desert bloom, and it continues to conquer many new "deserts"—in science, hi-tech, music, and art. As for democracy, Israel has been a democracy since its founding in 1948, even if it is a challenged democracy and even if the choices made by the electorate are not always pleasant to the ears of Jews outside of Israel (or to all Jews in Israel). But they are the voice of the people.

"Contemporary American Youth Have Distanced Themselves from Israel"

This claim has been made about youth and Israel since the early years of statehood. The contention that "the good old days were better" or "today's youth don't care about Israel" is a perennially debated subject. In 2010 Peter Beinart created a stir with an article in the *New York Review of Books* titled "The Failure of the American Jewish Establishment,"[3] followed by the book *The Crisis of Zionism*,[4] in which he argued that an entire generation of young Jews was being alienated from the State of Israel because of Israel's settlement policies over the Green Line and the lack of attention paid to that "sin" of Israel by the established Jewish community.

There is an extensive literature in the social sciences of adolescence and emerging adulthood that suggests that the distancing thesis is more often a perception of adults than a true reflection of the attitudes of the younger generation itself. In fact, the empirical evidence is not at all conclusive. Cohen and Kelman in *Beyond Distancing* suggest that today's youth are distancing themselves from Israel more than has been the case with previous generations of American Jews.[5] At the very same time, that research was challenged by Saxe, Sasson, et al. based on a systematic and extensive review of data collected over the years.[6] Indeed, a very recent study by Steven Cohen himself suggested that contemporary Jewish youth aged twenty-five to thirty-four are more attached to Israel than previous generations, a phenomenon that Cohen calls "the Birthright Bump."[7] One striking fact is clear: in the past decade, more young Jews between the ages of thirteen and twenty-six have visited Israel than during any comparable time since the destruction of the Second Temple.

Clearly, Taglit-Birthright Israel has proved to be a game changer. Since 1999 approximately three hundred thousand young Jewish adults have participated in these trips to Israel. Approximately 80 percent of those participants have come from North America. The evaluation data on Birthright Israel's impact on both attitudes and behaviors is overwhelmingly positive.[8] It indicates that the program creates significantly stronger attitudinal ties to Israel and Jewish peoplehood among Birthright alumni than among Jewish young adults who did not go on such trips. Birthright alumni also exhibit other behaviors in dramatically higher percentages than their peer group such as reading about Israeli daily life, maintaining contact with Israeli peers, and taking courses in Jewish studies. The most recent studies indicate statistically significant higher levels of in-marriage among Birthright alumni than among other Jews of the same ages.

> To the extent that younger Jews have some ambivalence about the State of Israel, there is plenty of blame to go around. The media, Jewish communal activities, and Jewish education have not been particularly effective at making the Israel story come alive for young Jews.

Still, there are many American Jewish youth who have not and will not be touched by the Birthright program. To the extent that younger Jews have some ambivalence about the State of Israel, there is plenty of blame to go around. The media, Jewish communal activities, and Jewish education have not been particularly effective at making the Israel story come alive for young Jews.

"Jewish Education Is at Fault Because It Doesn't Teach the Young to Know about and Defend Israel"

This commonplace is half true. Jewish education does not do a particularly good job of teaching Israel (there are some who say this is true not just about teaching Israel!). This claim actually points to a deeper problem related to a faulty understanding of the word "teaching." Predominant notions of "teaching" in both Jewish and general education are rooted in a long philosophic tradition that suggests that if you *know* something, then you will *feel* and *act* in certain ways. An unlikely confluence of classical Jewish education and contemporary neuroscience suggests that the formula may be backward. More accurate is that if you *feel* and *do* something, then you will come to *know* it. Let's remember that the Bible first says, "And you shall *love* the Lord your God" (Deuteronomy 6:5), and only then it says, "You should *teach* these words" (Deuteronomy 6:7). Authentic knowing and thinking may well begin in matters of the heart, in dispositions and affinities that then lead one to reflect, seek, pursue, and examine. We have learned well from general education how to sacrifice the heart at the altar of SAT scores.

In truth, the problem of Israel education is not the lack of curricula, books, or Internet apps; it is that we have not engaged enough American Jewish youth in true "education." Israel is not in textbooks. It's not only facts and figures about longitude and latitude. Rather, it is connection to real people, real places, real relations, and real emotions.

A New Set of Commonplaces

The above-mentioned commonplaces have emerged over time, and they are as likely to be the result of circumstance and events as much as of maliciousness or intent. It is probably not helpful to find someone to blame—the Arabs, contemporary Israel, or the Jewish establishment. Stuff happens. Education, however, doesn't just "happen"; it is a conscious activity. Education is an act of choice and will—it is an intentional activity. Israel education should not be left to fate or to CNN. Jewish educators and communal professionals need to be more proactive in providing a sophisticated yet compelling portrait of Israel to contemporary Jews.

There are clearly good intentions vis-à-vis Israel in American Jewish life, but this has been accompanied for decades by ambivalence, lack of clarity, and unclear vision. What is called for in Jewish education is an *aleph-bet* of Israel education—a new set of consciously chosen commonplaces, values, and beliefs that will serve as the linchpins of Israel education in the decades to come. This *aleph-bet* of Israel education needs to include the following practices and principles.

Israel and Identity Development

Israel plays a powerful role in the shaping of Jewish identity. Convincing research suggests that experiencing Israel has important implications for such social psychological phenomena as linkage, lineage, social bonding, mirroring, peer impact, self-verification, social networking, and transformative experiencing. Visiting Israel provides an array of transformative experiences—for some spiritual, for some historical, for some familial. An Israel connection links Jews to their roots and to a collective history. For many, Israel opens the door to a significant social network of peers and relatives. Israel in a person's life is a gallery of diverse and alternative ways of being Jewish. All of these elements are components of personal identity.

It is important to add that identity development is not an abbreviated process but rather a continual developmental dynamic that unfolds over a lifetime. The famous psychologist Erik Erikson talked about "the eight ages" (eras) in the development of a person.[9] Similarly, Israel as a part of Jewish identity should not begin in late adolescence or college (indeed, some might claim this already is too late). A serious approach to the development of a Jewish identity that includes Israel implies a developmental approach and pedagogy that begins in the earliest years and continues through "the eight ages."

Israel and "I"

We take an "I-centered approach" to Israel education. An I-centered approach means that education works best when the person feels him- or herself as the subject. In John Dewey's words, "Education is not preparation for life, education is life itself."[10] This approach maximizes the potential meaning of Israel for youth in their everyday life. Israel will only become an inner force in the lives of American Jews when it is linked to their genuine search for personal meaning, spirituality, and self-fulfillment as Jews. The person-centered approach assumes that people seek meaning, and it also implies that our Jewish youth may be able to find it in Judaism if it is presented in the context of that search for meaning. This is not egocentrism but rather part of the contemporary (and perhaps timeless) desire for personal-meaning making. This approach sees a direct connection between Israel, Judaism, and meaning. For those worried about a next generation that will care about Israel, this approach assumes that inner-directed, Israel-engaged young people are the best guarantors of a continued American Jewish community that supports Israel.

The Land of Israel, the State of Israel, the People of Israel

The word "Israel" has multiple meanings.[11] This is not accidental. The word suggests (a) the ancient land of biblical times that served as the cradle for Jewish civilization; (b) the covenantal land, a sign of the pact between the Holy One and the people of Israel; (c) the remembered land, a semi-mythical entity and symbol for Jews living all over the world; (d) the envisioned land, the ideal of a new homeland where Jews would live, create, and survive; (e) the lived land, a contemporary state of more than 7 million people; and (f) *Am Yisrael*, the worldwide community of Jewish people with shared legacies, beliefs, present, and future.

A comprehensive approach to Israel education will encompass all of these dimensions. This approach avoids dichotomies that have plagued contemporary Jewish thinking and practice between "Israel" and "Jewish"; "heavenly" and "earthly" Jerusalem; and "contemporary Israel," "Jewish peoplehood," and "Judaism." It will help Jews better understand the complexity of the State of Israel and its relationship to the history of Judaism and the Jewish people. For much of Jewish history, Jewish identity included both Judaism and the Land of Israel. Ironically, the reestablishment of the State of Israel has sometimes undermined that inherent unity. It is essential that we reintegrate the diverse elements of our Jewish heritage.

Multiple Narratives

Narratives are ways of looking at the world. They represent a particular weave that gives facts a meaning or a perspective. There are diverse narratives of Israel within the Jewish world and even more varied narratives of Israel in the non-Jewish world. There are several educational responsibilities concerning narratives. Jewish education has a primary obligation to present core Jewish narratives that are legacies of our people. We have to help our students learn the Israel narrative from the perspective of Jewish history and Jewish life, rooting it in both knowledge and understanding. At the same time, we owe it to our audiences to acknowledge that other narratives exist. We should not pretend that the narrative we present is the only one out there (indeed, the Jewish hermeneutic tradition reflects a methodology that consistently honors multiple narratives and allows them to be presented alongside each other). Our task is to empower our students to become confident narrators in their own right. Having heard and appreciated diverse narratives, we hope and trust that they will begin to give voice to a narrative that incorporates a Jewish perspective that then becomes their own.

The issue of multiple narratives is most strikingly reflected by the alternative Israeli/Jewish and Arab/Palestinian narratives to the region. This is not merely a political issue; it is also an educational concern. We often hear from young adults that they felt helpless (or sometimes even betrayed) when they first encountered the Arab narrative in their college years at a campus demonstration or in a university course. They lament the fact that their Jewish education did not better educate them about this subject.

We have a responsibility to: (1) provide a sound basis in the cornerstones of the Jewish narrative; (2) introduce components of other views at developmentally appropriate moments and to examine their premises, documents, and arguments; and (3) provide our youth with the conceptual "tool kit" and reflective skills to think about and respond to other perspectives. We trust both the intelligence and sophistication of our youth and the legitimacy of the Jewish perspective to make its case and be convincing. In this way, we have the opportunity to prepare a generation

> We often hear from young adults that they felt helpless (or sometimes even betrayed) when they first encountered the Arab narrative in their college years at a campus demonstration or in a university course. They lament the fact that their Jewish education did not better educate them about this subject.

of young adults who intelligently and passionately feel comfortable in articulating and representing a grounded Jewish perspective.[12]

Ivri daber Ivrit

Jewish education has failed to effectively teach Hebrew to American Jews. The Zionist movement consciously encompassed land, culture, and language. These three components reflect a social psychology of Jewish identity. The role of language in identity, sense of self, and group lineage is an important theme in the contemporary sociology of language.[13] Unfortunately, in the United States, Hebrew has been relegated to learning of prayers or to preparation of students for their Bar or Bat Mitzvah. Leonard Fein has quipped, "Hebrew school is remembered by most Jews as the place where they failed to learn Hebrew."[14] Successful language acquisition is deeply related to rich personal identity. This is not an easy task, but there are models of communities and educational practices that show that it can be done.

Jews in contemporary South Africa, Australia, Mexico, Argentina, and other Latin American countries are Hebrew-literate, and Hebrew constitutes a core component of their Jewishness (it is mainly in the United States that Birthright Israel is known by that name; in other countries it is known by its Hebrew name, Taglit). For decades the Massad and Ramah camps in America successfully created intensive Hebrew immersion experiences. There are also several dozen institutions across the United States that have shown that it is possible for preschools, middle schools, and high schools to create proficiency in Hebrew language and culture. There are new techniques and methodologies in Hebrew instruction that promise achievement and competence similar to other second-language education. The American Jewish community would do well to reexamine its approach to Hebrew and consider its potential for how Jews relate to Israel and to their Jewish identity.

Life Is with the People

The life of contemporary Israel—its youth, music, foods, rhythm, pop art, and tempo—speaks to contemporary Jewish youth. It says to them that being Jewish need not be suits and ties, beards and head coverings, or aged and holy. It can be young and alive, tanned and athletic. It can be like "us" and of our century.

The reality is that it is often easier to get young Jews to appreciate this fact on a trip to Israel than in a school classroom in America. Indeed, the opportunity to personally experience a total Jewish society in the State of Israel is one of the major educational breakthroughs of recent times. Nothing can take the place of spending time in Israel, where one experiences a society that functions on a Jewish calendar—when traffic slows down on Friday afternoon, stores begin to close, and people walk home, buying flowers on the way. It is difficult for a classroom experience to transmit an appreciation for Jewish history like visiting a site—along with Israeli peers—where the tour educator reads from a Bible in one hand and points to the site mentioned with the other hand. And finally, it is difficult to replicate the impact on young Jews of a place where even the dogs and cats can respond to commands in Hebrew!

Perhaps more than anything else, the *mifgash* (personal encounter) has become a staple of the trip to Israel for young Jews from abroad. *Mifgashim* are symmetrical interactions of Israeli and overseas peers in which the experience of Israel becomes highly personal. Israel is no longer only holy sites, museums, walls, and graves. As powerful as those places might be, it is meeting Israelis that makes the country real. Meeting Israelis born in the former USSR, Ethiopia, Tel Aviv, or Jerusalem brings alive the story of the many faces of Jewish life while at the same time underscoring the shared lives and experiences of young people from all over the world. It shows Israel's diversity while at the same time personalizing Israel.

The Israeli poet Yehuda Amichai captured the magic of encountering the ancient and modern Israel with this vignette in his poem "The Tourist": "Do you see that arch over there from the Roman period? It doesn't matter, but near it a little to the left, and then down a bit, there's a man who has just bought fruits and vegetables for his family."[15]

At the same time, we must be wary of fabricating a perfect Israel. It is a real country with diverse people, practical issues, and genuine dilemmas. Because of the complexity of Israel, we know that different aspects of Israel strike Jewish visitors differently. There are things that are foreign and strange. Other things are very familiar. There are things that are complicated, and there are other things that are very attractive. For some people, the Western Wall is a sacred spiritual site; for some important sectors of contemporary Jewish life, it is a painful symbol of chauvinism and inequality. For some people, the security fence is an unavoidable structure that successfully protects Israeli citizens from terrorism. For others, it is an unfortunate symbol of separation that inflicts undue hardship on Palestinians.

As we have seen, the research on the Israel experience quite definitively points to its role as a significant force in strengthening Jewish identity.[16] The research on this subject is probably the most conclusive we have about any aspect of Jewish education, and the Birthright Israel studies enrich what we already knew. The research tells us that: (1) an Israel trip rooted in an experiential approach has the power to significantly affect Jewish identity; (2) the genuine encounter with Israeli peers significantly affects a sense of Jewish peoplehood for both sides; (3) presenting Israel in a way that acknowledges Jewish pluralism and the complexity of Israeli society shows respect for the intelligence of travelers and increases the chance for serious engagement with Israel over time; (4) experiencing Israel helps link the Jewish present with the biblical past; (5) Israel powerfully reflects the Jewish will to survive; (6) Israel symbolizes Jewish pride and achievement—along with the complexities of striving for survival while remaining committed to universal values; and (7) with all its complexities, once Israel is genuinely experienced in an educational context, it becomes a positive and admirable exemplar of being Jewish in our times.

> American Jewry is among those communities with the highest percentage of Jews who have not visited Israel. If we are going to meaningfully connect people to Israel, it will best be done by enabling them to experience it.

In light of this data, it is surprising and disappointing that world Jewry has not made a trip to Israel a Jewish norm. Of course Birthright has begun to change this reality. Still, American Jewry is among those communities with the highest percentage of Jews who have not visited

Israel. If we are going to meaningfully connect people to Israel, it will best be done by enabling them to experience it.

Teaching from Within

The Israel education we have described here focuses on identity formation, personal narratives, experiential education, and authenticity. Obviously, it requires unique educators. They must be knowledgeable, be communicative, and have experienced Israel. But most important, they must be able to teach from within. They must be able to teach from their own selfhood. They must "become" Israel, and it must be part of their DNA.[17] This is another way of saying what the educational philosopher Parker Palmer has long taught: true education takes place when we connect with the deepest part of people's psyches, which includes not only their mind but also their heart and their spirit.[18] If we are going to do a better job of connecting young Jews to Israel, we are going to have to train Israel educators who are true role models, who represent Israel on all levels of their being—thinking, feeling, and behaving. We don't need fanatic or close-minded ideologues, because we should not be in the business of offering only one perspective on Israel. Loving Israel does not preclude questioning or disagreeing with one or more aspects of Israeli society. But it does imply teaching love by loving.

Ultimately, Jewish education is about opening the treasure chest called Jewish civilization and modeling a lifestyle called the Jewish experience. We hope that such a process will lead young people to shape a personal narrative that reflects the values and behaviors of the Jewish heritage, which will, in turn, offer the person a life of significant meaning. The contemporary State of Israel is a central part of Jewish history, and it needs to be integral to the way Jews experience and express their Jewish identity. It should be part of the personal narrative of every Jew. Although Israel will mean different things for different people, we know that for tens of thousands of Jews, the encounter with Israel is a chance to fall in love with a land, a language, a history, and a people. We think that people should be allowed to fall in love.

Denominationalism

History and Hopes

Dr. David Ellenson

Jewish religious denominationalism arose in Germany at the beginning of the nineteenth century as a way for the Jewish community to cope with the revolutionary political, cultural, religious, and social changes brought on by the onset of the modern world. While Moses Mendelssohn and his circle of *maskilim* (followers of the Jewish Enlightenment) represented the first individual responses to these dramatic changes through their affirmation of and participation in the culture of the larger German world in whose midst they dwelt, it was the Reform movement in the first decades of the 1800s that articulated the first communal denominational response to these transformations in Jewish life. Reform was, at first, a lay-led movement that aimed to recast traditional modes of Jewish worship in accord with nineteenth-century German standards of aesthetics.

The rise of *Wissenschaft des Judentums* (academic study of Judaism) introduced the idea that Judaism was not only *in* but *of* history, that is, that Judaism developed through time and had to be understood in its cultural context. This provided an ideological basis that would allow for the

Dr. David Ellenson is president of Hebrew Union College–Jewish Institute of Religion. Dr. Ellenson was ordained as a rabbi at HUC-JIR and received his PhD from Columbia University. His book *After Emancipation: Jewish Religious Responses to Modernity* won the National Jewish Book Award. His most recent book, *Pledges of Jewish Allegiance: Conversion, Law, and Policymaking in Nineteenth- and Twentieth-Century Orthodox Responsa*, was coauthored with Daniel Gordis.

growth of non-Orthodox liberal movements in Germany. The Reform strand centered around Abraham Geiger and the Hochschule für die Wissenschaft des Judentums in Berlin. The positive-historical school, which would be a predecessor to Conservative Judaism, was more committed in principle to *halachah* (Jewish law) than its Reform counterpart was, and it was centered around the Breslau-based Positive-Historical Jewish Theological Seminary of Zecharia Frankel.

Cultural conditions in Germany were such that the ritual observance patterns among rabbis as well as lay adherents of these respective trends—ideological differences notwithstanding—were similar. Thus, these two wings of German liberal Judaism functioned within a common institutional framework where graduates of both institutions joined the same rabbinical organization and served the same communal synagogues. At the same time, a distinct modern Orthodox movement arose in opposition to these liberal movements. Neo-Orthodoxy, as it came to be called, was devoted, in the words of its chief ideologue, Rabbi Samson Raphael Hirsch, to a philosophy of *Torah im derech eretz.* What this meant was an affirmation of Western culture and mores combined with a commitment to the traditional ahistorical Jewish notion of divine revelation of Torah at Sinai and classical observance of Jewish halachic practice. Hirsch's colleague, Rabbi Esriel Hildesheimer, proceeded to establish a seminary in Berlin to serve this new movement. Denominational divisions in Germany were thus twofold—Orthodox and liberal. It would take America, with its cultural-social divisions between the Jews of German descent and the Jews of Eastern European descent, to foster the development of more than one non-Orthodox denomination.

American Developments

When Isaac Mayer Wise came to the United States and established the Union of American Hebrew Congregations in 1873 and the Hebrew Union College in 1875, he avoided the label "Reform" in the titles of his institutions because he did not believe that he was a creating a denominationally distinct form of American Judaism. Instead, his intention was to create an "American Judaism" for a German-speaking American Jewish community that was overwhelmingly Germanic and culturally homogeneous prior to 1881. Wise aspired to speak for all of American Judaism and even claimed that the Hebrew Union College would educate both "Orthodox" and "Reform" rabbis.

However, Wise's dream of a united American Jewish religious community vanished in the 1880s with the arrival of hundreds of thousands of Eastern European Jews to these shores. The cultural and religious cleavages between the Eastern European immigrants and their earlier-arriving German coreligionists were quite pronounced, and it soon became apparent that a union between these disparate groups was impossible. Liberal Judaism may have been possible in Germany, where cultural homogeneity promoted a similarity in observance that allowed two trends to coexist in the non-Orthodox camp without erupting into distinct denominations. But the differences between Eastern European and German Jews would not permit this coexistence in the United States, and soon two major non-Orthodox denominations—Reform and Conservative—emerged at the end of the nineteenth century.

One infamous episode points to how the fissures caused by ethnic and religious divisions began to widen at this time. In 1883, the Hebrew Union College ordained its first class of rabbis, and Jewish leaders throughout the United States were invited to the graduation ceremony. At a banquet held to celebrate the ordination, traditional Jewish dietary restrictions forbidding the mixing of milk and meat at the same meal were flouted, and all types of forbidden seafood were served. While most historians assert that what has come to be labeled as the infamous "*Trefa* Banquet" was the result of a caterer's error, there is no doubt that this banquet delivered a powerful message to Eastern European immigrants and other Jewish religious traditionalists. Judaism, at least as the Reform movement envisioned it, was no longer wedded to traditional Jewish law and practice. At this moment, American Jewish religious denominationalism was fully born.

The Reform movement gave explicit ideological expression to this denominational stance in the Pittsburgh Platform of 1885. Authored by the German-born Kaufmann Kohler, who would eventually succeed Wise as president of Hebrew Union College, this platform asserted that Judaism was a universal faith ever striving to be in accord with the postulates of reason. Kohler looked askance at Jewish ritual behaviors and was a fierce opponent of Jewish nationalism. The posture Kohler and the Reform movement now championed found practical liturgical expression within the walls of Reform temples. The removal of head coverings for men during worship now came to be a near-universal Reform custom, and in 1895, the *Union Prayer Book*—composed almost entirely in English and highly universalistic in its orientation—was adopted as the official liturgy of the Reform movement. Such steps on the part of the Reform movement were anathema to Jews of Eastern European descent, who were then pouring onto American shores.

The Jewish Theological Seminary (JTS), which was first established in 1886 in opposition to Reform, flourished under the leadership of the Romanian-born scholar Solomon Schechter. Schechter articulated the twin ideological foundations upon which Conservative Judaism was to be established—a non-fundamentalist fidelity to Jewish law that recognized the historical character of Jewish tradition and law as well as an uncompromising devotion to "Catholic Israel," the community of the people Israel. These ideological positions, combined with a warm embrace of cultural Zionism as well as an affirmation of modern American aesthetic standards and sensibilities, appealed to the Eastern European Jews and their children as they began their process of acculturation into American life.

The commitment of Conservative Judaism to Jewish law clearly differentiated it from the Reform movement. Yet the rise and growth of denominationally distinct forms of non-Orthodox Judaism in America almost a century ago resulted primarily from the sociological divide that marked the American Jewish community at that time. The religious attitudes and cultural patterns that divided first-generation American Jews of Eastern European and German descent from one another were too large to bridge. Reform Judaism thus

> The rise and growth of denominationally distinct forms of non-Orthodox Judaism in America almost a century ago resulted primarily from the sociological divide that marked the American Jewish community at that time.

came to be the denominationally distinct expression of the "folk Judaism" of German Jews in this country, while the Conservative movement came to express the "folk Judaism" of Eastern European Jews and their descendants as they successfully integrated into American society.

Nevertheless, it is crucial to note that Jews of Eastern European background were as anxious to acculturate into America as the German Jews had been before them. As they did so, the cultural distance that separated them from their German Jewish coreligionists began to diminish, and Reform itself came to change as children of Eastern European Jews began to join Reform temples. As the Reform Columbus Platform of 1937 demonstrates, more positive attitudes toward religious ritual and Zionism began to make inroads in Reform Judaism through the leadership of figures such as Rabbis Samuel Cohon, Stephen Wise, and Abba Hillel Silver.

The 1934 publication of *Judaism as a Civilization* by Rabbi Mordecai Kaplan and the ideal of Jewish peoplehood that stood at the center of his Reconstructionist philosophy had a profound influence upon many in the Reform movement. Kaplan similarly exerted a powerful influence in the Conservative movement through his teaching at JTS, even as he initially opposed the creation of a distinct Reconstructionist movement during the first half of the twentieth century. The influence and numbers of Conservative Jews grew throughout most of the twentieth century, and Conservative Judaism became the dominant movement within American Judaism for most of this period. But at the same time, the divide among culturally homogeneous, non-Orthodox Jews on matters of observance and belief became narrower and narrower as the century progressed. This change would ultimately come to have a significant impact on minimizing distinctive denominational allegiances among American Jews.

This tale would not be complete without some attention being paid to Orthodox Judaism during this period. During the 1920s and 1930s, Orthodox Judaism began to establish itself more securely in America. The Orthodox at this time represented the least successfully acculturated elements among the Jewish immigrant population who came to these shores. However, under the leadership of Rabbi Bernard Revel, a nascent modern American Orthodoxy began to strike real roots. The establishment of Yeshiva College in New York in 1928 and the incorporation of the Rabbi

Isaac Elchanan Theological Seminary into Yeshiva University provided an institutional framework that would later prove to be critical for the growth of Orthodox Judaism in the United States.

The birth of Yeshiva University in 1928 was complemented by the arrival of elite Orthodox scholars such as Rabbis Moses Soloveitchik and his son, Joseph Baer Soloveitchik, to these shores. These men were able to spread the influence of Orthodox Judaism among rabbis and laypersons alike. Perhaps the most significant of these Orthodox immigrant leaders was Rabbi Aaron Kotler, who established a traditional Orthodox yeshiva in Lakewood, New Jersey, in 1941 and who inspired his students to establish a network of Torah Umesorah Orthodox day schools throughout the United States long before parochial schools became part of the landscape of American education. The appearance of large numbers of Orthodox Hungarian Jews who entered America after World War II also contributed to the resurgence of Orthodox Judaism in this country during later decades. It also laid the groundwork for the emergence of two types of Orthodox Judaism—a modern centrist variety and a more sectarian, ultra-Orthodox one.

Contemporary Trends and Directions

By the 1960s, even as denominational allegiances remained strong, the sociological makeup of the community began to change. The American Jewish community was no longer an immigrant community seeking to adjust to the United States. Old ethnic patterns that formerly preserved and divided the Jewish religious community were no longer present, and the rivalry that had existed between American Jews of German and Eastern European descent was little more than a historical memory.

During this same period, America witnessed the emergence of "the new ethnicity." In the Jewish community this gave rise to new forms of Jewish expression. The *havurah* movement offered Jews a way to be part of a religious practice outside of the walls of a synagogue. Jewish feminism empowered women's voices in ways that were rarely heard in the hallowed halls of rabbinical seminaries. *The Jewish Catalog* became a mini–best seller and planted the seeds for a "do-it-yourself" Judaism that no longer made Jewish practice dependent on rabbis. The near-miraculous Israeli victory during the Six-Day War in 1967 also unleashed an enormous amount of pride among American Jews and led to a renewed sense of "tribal" Jewish commitment as well as newfound religious commitment among hundreds of thousands of American Jews.

In short, the attitudes and beliefs that had so sharply divided Reform from Conservative Jews in the first half of the twentieth century now began to blur, and crossover between denominations was no longer unusual. The 1990 National Jewish Population Survey indicated that more than seven hundred thousand of the million-plus persons who claimed to be Reform Jews stated that they had Conservative Jewish backgrounds.

Sidney Schwarz correctly notes in his discussion of "covenantal Jews" in his lead essay that this growing uniformity among American Jews took place against an ever more intense universalistic backdrop in which American Jews—particularly those who came to adulthood during the past twenty years—feel completely at home in America. For these Jews, tales of anti-Semitism and the memory of the Holocaust embody a distant past that has virtually no impact on promoting their allegiance as Jews. Indeed, as the election of Barack Obama as president indicates, older forms of prejudice and discrimination—while they have surely not disappeared—do not possess the power and influence they once did.

American Jews have now been fully accepted into American life, and Jews of all stripes and ethnic backgrounds as well as sexual orientations are now full participants in the cultural, social, political, and economic spheres of the United States. Ivy League colleges that formerly had strict quotas limiting Jewish admission now have Jewish presidents, and businesses like DuPont that once banned Jewish executives now frequently have Jewish CEOs.

As Jews have become fully accepted by gentiles as social equals and as traditional Jewish attitudes that opposed exogamy have weakened, intermarriage rates have soared, and traditional Jewish communal attitudes opposing intermarriage have undergone revolutionary changes. Younger American Jews do not feel the sting of social anti-Semitism that their forebears did, and this makes their attitudes toward Israel and Jewish identity different than those of their parents and grandparents. Those Jews who seek out affiliation with the Jewish community do so with an indifference to denominations that was unknown earlier in the century. Indeed, the appeal of the individual rabbi and the ability of specific congregations to serve the personal religious and spiritual needs of congregants are far more important factors than denominational identification in attracting most non-Orthodox Jews to membership in particular synagogues.

In addition, there are new forms of Jewish identification being created by younger Jews that take place completely outside the realm of Jewish denominations. Reboot was founded in 2002 to appeal to "Jewishly un-connected cultural creatives" and supports their development of new projects for both Jews and non-Jews. Storahtelling, founded in 1999, works with clergy, educators, and artists to make Torah more accessible to Jews through dramatic presentations. Even as print Jewish magazines have trouble staying financially solvent, *Tablet* emerged as an online Jewish magazine with a wide and young Jewish following. Of the hundreds of new Jewish initiatives that have emerged in just the past decade, few of these phenomena are dependent on Jewish denominations and almost all are trans-denominational.

Nor is the cultural and religious excitement that marks present-day American Judaism limited to the few examples cited in the previous paragraph. There are larger trends that underscore the vibrancy of Jewish life in America, including the rapid and significant growth of Jewish day school education among a significant minority of non-Orthodox Jews in the United States, the explosion of Jewish studies programs at universities, Birthright and the rise of trips to Israel, the dramatic growth of Jewish camping, the growth of Jewish renewal study centers, the rise of Jewish social action projects, and the appearance of Limmud conferences, where thousands of Jews come together each year to learn and socialize. Indeed, these developments can rightfully be described as contributing to a renaissance in Jewish religious and cultural life among a core minority of American Jews.

> It would be easy to give a dozen or more examples of new Jewish initiatives that have emerged in just the past decade. Few of these phenomena are dependent on Jewish denominations and almost all are trans-denominational.

Some look at these developments as signs of a golden age for Judaism in America, and the impact of such creativity and vitality has been felt both within and beyond denominational boundaries.

Judaism beyond Denominationalism

All these developments have promoted the growth of alternative modes of Jewish religious and cultural expression and have propelled many committed Jews to seek out Jewish community and religion apart from denominations in a manner that was unknown to earlier generations of American Jews. My own impression here comports with those of Schwarz, when he speaks optimistically and hopefully of the emergence of significant pockets of "covenantal Jews" whose activity in the community is quite independent of the structures of Jewish denominations.

For all the reasons cited above, more and more American Jews are indifferent to denominational labels in their highly eclectic and idiosyncratic search for meaning and community. To employ Leo Baeck's felicitous phrase, more and more Jews are likely to move away from "an adjectival Judaism," in other words, a Judaism where the adjective—whether it be Reform, Conservative, Reconstructionist, Renewal, or Orthodox—is more important than the noun, "Judaism." They will not hesitate to shop among movements and individual rabbis and religious teachers as they engage in their own personal religious and communal quests. The distinctions in theology and ideology that are so crucial to the elite leaders of the different movements are increasingly irrelevant to these Jews. Many of the debates that occupy the leaders of these movements are regarded by most Jews as needlessly divisive and extraneous to the larger task of creating a Judaism that is vital and vibrant in the face of the challenges that modern-day America presents to Jewish life and commitment.

Of course, denominations are in no immediate danger of extinction. Any elementary course on sociology can tell us that well-established and powerful institutions do not simply disappear. Furthermore, the movements themselves and their institutions are not blind to these trends, and they strive mightily to reinvent and adapt themselves to these forces of change. The current preference of Jewish foundations for cross-denominational collaboration has led to unprecedented institutional cooperation between

The Jewish Theological Seminary (JTS, Conservative) and Hebrew Union College–Jewish Institute of Religion (HUC-JIR, Reform) in innovative programs sponsored by the United Jewish Appeal (UJA) of New York, the Charles and Lynn Schusterman Family Foundation, and the Jim Joseph Foundation. As a result, some of the most significant trans-denominational programs for the renewal and reconfiguration of synagogue life are taking place within denominationally sponsored structures. Synagogue 3000, which has done cutting-edge work with synagogue transformation, was cofounded by professors from the American Jewish University (Conservative) and HUC-JIR (Reform). The Institute of Jewish Spirituality is doing important training of clergy in meditation and mindfulness, and they work in close cooperation with American rabbinic seminaries. JTS, the Reconstructionist Rabbinical College, and HUC-JIR are also collaborating on work in the area of health and healing. The bottom line: the denominational centers of American Judaism are striving to adapt to the new post-denominational reality.

> Many of the debates that occupy the leaders of these movements are regarded by most Jews as needlessly divisive and extraneous to the larger task of creating a Judaism that is vital and vibrant in the face of the challenges that modern-day America presents to Jewish life and commitment.

However, all of this begs the question of whether such adaptation is as rapid and flexible as it ought to be to meet the needs of the hour. After all, the larger and more pervasive reality at play in American Judaism today as reported in all surveys of the American Jewish community indicates that "unaffiliated" is the largest growing category among contemporary American Jews, even as many of these Jews seek spiritual meaning and renewal. The recently conducted (2012) New York UJA demographic study indicates that denominational affiliation among Reform and Conservative Jews has decreased over the past decade, and record numbers of Jews now define themselves as "just Jewish" or nondenominational. Crossover among denominations is more common than ever for thousands and thousands of Jews, as it is for millions of non-Jewish Christian

Americans as well. Indeed, a recently conducted U.S. religious landscape survey indicates that no more than 25 percent of American Christians remain in the Protestant or Catholic denomination into which they were born.[1] Jewish indifference to denominations and crossover among denominations therefore reflects larger trends in American society.

Many commentators suggest that the heyday of Jewish religious denominationalism in the United States is not only over, but they also predict that the non-Orthodox movements in Judaism (Conservative, Reconstructionist, and Reform) will one day merge and that sectarian Orthodox Judaism will triumph over more modern manifestations of Orthodox Judaism found in institutions like Yeshivat Chovevei Torah. From this perspective, the prospects for maintaining traditional Jewish denominational patterns do not appear particularly bright, and there is surely a great deal of evidence to suggest that this assessment may well be right. Yet even as the trials facing Jewish religious denominations today are admittedly great, the challenges in forging meaningful expressions of Judaism for millions of Jews without the support of national denominations may well be even greater. After all, denominations still possess great resources, and the programs that emerge from their institutions would be hard to duplicate by the innumerable Jewish start-ups that currently dot the communal landscape.

> Yet even as the trials facing Jewish religious denominations today are admittedly great, the challenges in forging meaningful expressions of Judaism for millions of Jews without the support of national denominations may well be even greater.

Still, given the current access to the tools of mass communication and social media, a power shift has taken place in society. Institutions and movements no longer own their messages, nor do they have a complete monopoly over knowledge. Jews—and, for that matter, even synagogues—need no longer rely solely on their rabbis or their denominational movements for knowledge. The web and a wide variety of teachers available in every community provide viable options for Jewish learning. Additionally, through the wonders of technology, groups can easily form without organizations. Online Jewish communities like My Jewish Portal and Our Jewish Community are more common than ever and promise to grow over the next decade. Ours is a world of niche markets and customer customization. People coalesce around interests and values, not institutions. People seek personalization rather than institutional affiliation. No wonder numbers in denominations have declined. Synagogues and movements need to respond to these changed realities. They need to reach out to people beyond the synagogue in informal settings where people gather, like coffee shops and shopping malls. They also need to find ways of fostering participation and engagement in the community without insisting on the payment of membership dues.

Schwarz gives a compelling rationale for why we must make such adaptations. While I am highly sympathetic to Schwarz's call, I would still ask, does the emerging symmetry between universal and Jewish values bode well for the ongoing vitality of Jewish life in this country? American Jews have overwhelmingly internalized the dominant values of their host society. We in the liberal Jewish community and movements are decidedly universalistic in our orientations. Even our particularistic affirmations are made in the service of a universal cause. Whether such affirmations will prove strong enough to sustain a cultural and religious identity in the future is open to debate. Jews have been blessed with freedom in this country. Whether such blessing will strengthen Jewish commitments, values, and identity or whether America will be the solvent in which Jewish continuity dissolves remains to be seen. The resiliency of Judaism as it confronts the future will surely be tested.

As we move into the twenty-first century, the tasks that confront traditional religious movements in the modern American context—whatever the ideological distinctions and organizational commitments that mark and sometimes divide them—are essentially identical. The challenge that confronts all of them is how to make Judaism relevant, compelling, joyous, meaningful, welcoming, comforting, and challenging to American Jews who, as "sovereign selves," have infinite options open before them. Both within and beyond denominations we must ask boldly whether Judaism can succeed in doing this for large numbers of Jews.

American Judaism today stands at a crossroads where trends of weakened Jewish commitment and attachment compete with pockets of intense Jewish revival and knowledge—and all this takes place across denominational boundaries and institutional lines. The task of all Jews will be to strengthen these pockets of revival and knowledge. This task will compel us to recognize that such revival and knowledge must take place both within and beyond the denominational universe. The future of Judaism in the United States depends on the ability of all Jews, regardless of denominational identification, to maintain and revitalize Jewish religious tradition in light of the conditions that confront our community today.

"Getting" the Next Generation

Young Adults and the Jewish Future

Wayne L. Firestone

Many people think trend spotting is about predicting the future, but in fact, it's less ambitious than that. It's about accurately seeing the present. For the past decade I have had the unique opportunity to view the Jewish world through a distinct lens—the university experience—125 campuses in twelve countries at last count. My position allows me to meet and interact with the "next generation"—the nearly one hundred thousand Jewish students who enter college every year. One of the greatest pleasures of my job is to observe what is taking place on university campuses around the world. Without understanding the present, we can't possibly predict the future. And when we tune in to our young adults, we have the privilege of experiencing what's coming down the (Jewish) pike.

Wayne L. Firestone is the president and CEO of Hillel: The Foundation for Jewish Campus Life. He is a lawyer, writer, and Jewish community professional who has lived and studied in Israel for almost a decade. He is the founding executive director of the Israel on Campus Coalition and serves on the advisory boards of Repair the World, Mazon, and the National Urban Debate League.

While there may be good cause to be concerned for the Jewish collective future, it is important that we focus on the right things. To that end, I want to help nullify four myths about Jewish students and reframe those concerns based on both the daily observations of Hillel staff and the research garnered from Hillel's network of more than five hundred campus affiliates around the world.

Myth 1: The younger generation doesn't care about Jewish life.

Myth 2: The way to reach young Jews is through technology and gimmick marketing.

Myth 3: The Jewish community has a young-leadership talent pool crisis.

Myth 4: The younger generation's obsession with individuality and personal choice will undermine Jewish communal solidarity and will weaken the ability of the Jewish community to engage with other ethnic and religious communities in a coherent fashion.

The unmasking of these myths is not only the result of personal observation; it is also informed by quantitative data about the millennial generation that suggests we are witnessing a significant shift in how students view their Jewish identity and Jewish leadership.[1] Just one generation ago, Jewish students still exhibited particularistic (e.g., tribal and ethnic) loyalties. Hillel served these students by creating a welcoming home for particular Jewish experiences. Fast-forward to 2012. Everything has turned upside down. Young Jewish students today are largely universalists. Most are not looking for a place to "do Jewish." They are happy and comfortable participating in activities with their friends—whether they are Jewish or not.

As a result, Hillel has progressively embraced a new role over the past two decades, one that is different from how

> Jewish organizations that will survive and thrive are those that succeed in connecting with the next generation of Jews. I believe that the winners will be those who really understand this generation's leaders and the unique ways in which they celebrate their Jewish identity.

Hillel functioned in its first seventy years. Instead of primarily being a place where committed Jews can go to find a refuge from mainstream culture and society, Hillel has taken on the responsibility to reach out and serve less-committed Jews while encouraging them to celebrate their Jewish heritage. Our student engagement approach deploys educators and peer interns to go out into the campus community and meet students on their own terms.

In the coming decades, the Jewish organizations that will survive and thrive are those that succeed in connecting with the next generation of Jews. I believe that the winners will be those who really understand this generation's leaders and the unique ways in which they celebrate their Jewish identity. The good news is that successful strategies for reaching and engaging millennials are neither new nor particularly complex. It requires real engagement, relationship building, community organizing, and network weaving—approaches that have in recent years become a major focus of the philanthropic, not-for-profit, entrepreneurial, and political sectors.

What will success look like? No one has a crystal ball, but we must start by finding a new mix between particularism and universalism. If we get it right during the college years, we might then have a shot at keeping young Jews engaged in the Jewish community after their graduation. Let's unmask the myths so that we can reveal what the new combination of strategies might look like.

Myth 1: The Younger Generation Doesn't Care about Jewish Life

Reality: **Jewish students today care deeply about Jewish life but in different ways than Jews did decades ago. They have a fundamentally different view of identity than prior generations do. They are not yearning to "fit in"; rather, they are actively seeking to carve out safe spaces to be different. They want to find their authentic voices, and Jewish identity is often one piece of that.**

Case Study: Eli, a student at Scripps College in California, is a great example of this phenomenon. I first met her on a Hillel-sponsored advocacy mission to Israel. Eli wanted to promote awareness and activism about genocide in Darfur. She invited uninvolved students to bake challah together and then sell them to benefit the cause. Along with the challah, she provided information on how the students could take on the issue or get involved in local hunger efforts. Word soon spread that the activity was fun for guys as well as girls. The *challot* were delicious and invited creativity and customization (from dill to chocolate chip). The effort spread to more than one hundred campuses and communities under the name "Challah for Hunger." Upon graduation Eli joined a social entrepreneur network and fellowship in Israel—PresenTense, created by two other Israel campus activists who made *aliyah* from New York. She later was selected to be part of the Joshua Venture Fellowship.

This vignette illustrates how we increasingly see the next generation reaching out as a catalyst—organizing and creating communities of meaning. It also exposes the limitations of older assumptions about how Jews engage. Those who invested in the Israel advocacy trip could easily have interpreted Eli's interest in Darfur as a distraction or, worse, a failure. Conversely, those students interested in the Darfur issue might have found Eli's project as too Jewish and challah baking as too old school. Yet many uninvolved students found Eli's project enormously compelling. What was it about her initiative that worked?

In order to understand Eli and her peers, we need to look at some of the latest data on millennials. Millennial Jews are proud of their distinctiveness and of their Jewish identity—even when they have very little knowledge or connection to Jewish institutional life. According to the March 2012 national survey of Jewish university students conducted by Penn Schoen Berland, 85 percent of Jewish undergraduates say that they like people to know that they are Jewish. Seven in ten say that being Jewish makes them feel "special." Nearly one in three Jewish college students say that given a choice between fitting in and feeling different, they prefer to feel different.

This newfound joy in being distinctive, in standing apart from the mainstream, is a fundamentally different environment from the one that existed when Hillel was born. Young Jewish adults are also falling in love with Israel and with the global Jewish people. As they personally encounter Israelis, Russian-speaking Jews, and Jews from Africa and Yemen, they begin to experience the greater narrative of Jewish life around the world. Millennials are less ideological and partisan than prior generations are, causing them to clash with baby boomer employers, professors, and frankly, many of the leaders of the organized Jewish community.

Moreover, despite their addiction to gadgets and the Internet, millennials are remarkably communal in their orientation and behavior, which makes them very different from gen X and baby boomers, who prize individualism. Indeed, much of their use of technology is aimed at generating and supporting a variety of communities in which they find value.

> Millennials are less ideological and partisan than prior generations are, causing them to clash with baby boomer employers, professors, and frankly, many of the leaders of the organized Jewish community.

In short, it is a misdiagnosis to view the decline in membership and affiliation with existing Jewish organizations, both nationally and locally, as evidence of a disinterest in Jewish identification. Certainly, over the past decade, the record participation rates in Taglit-Birthright and the increased activity in a wide variety of Hillel activities indicate that this next generation is open to particularistic choices, ranging from service learning trips to Shabbat.[2]

One key to understanding the next generation of Jews is to realize that choice is an important precondition for their Jewish engagement. Jews are the people who ask questions, and the university is arguably the ideal venue in which to honor the spirit of free and rigorous inquiry. The Jewish community will have to embrace the spirit of this generation. Many millennials will accuse the Jewish community of feeding them programmed answers that do not ring true for them. Rabbis, Jewish educators, and Jewish communal professionals will need training to hear the questions and honor the choices of millennials rather than feed them a set of limited options. Millennials want to tap the wisdom of Jewish professionals, but it can't be taught or preached top-down. It needs to emerge from authentic relationships that are designed to support the quest for knowledge and the personal life journeys of these young adults.

111

Let's begin to redefine the parameters of the universalism/particularism tensions, even if we are not able to fully resolve them. At one time, the predominant mood on American campuses was one of universalism. But today young Jews go to college in search of their uniqueness. The range of opportunities that they can choose from—athletics, Greek life, student government, volunteer service, and so on—do not have any Jewish strings attached. Because Jewish values, learning, and traditions are increasingly unknown to these Jewish millennials, our challenge is to make the richness of the Jewish experience accessible to them on their terms.

Myth 2: The Way to Reach Young Jews Is through Technology and Gimmick Marketing

Reality: Jewish students are yearning for meaningful conversations about the "big questions" that confront Jews and all human beings.

Case Study: A few years ago, a group of Jewish student interns and their Hillel rabbi at Northwestern University sought to engage the campus in the kinds of conversations they weren't having in class. Just in time for the High Holy Days, they made a banner that read, "What will you do better this year?" and hung it in the middle of campus. Students started having conversations. Faculty became involved. More banners went up, the group built a website, the provost provided a grant, and soon a regular series of reflective conversations was taking place, led by Hillel and including students of all backgrounds.

At the same time and unbeknownst to this group, students and staff at the University of North Carolina Chapel Hill created a "Three Cups of Tea" initiative to promote campus-wide dialogue following an event with Elie Wiesel and Greg Mortenson, the author of *Three Cups of Tea*. The success of those initiatives inspired students, staff, and alumni from these and thirteen other campuses to join together to launch "Ask Big Questions." Go to www.askbigquestions.org to experience how these students share all of their content and conversations through social media. Craigslist founder Craig Newmark labeled the program as "one of the sixteen bold ideas with the potential to change the world" in 2012.[3]

Over the past several years we have both observed and partnered with students to develop peer-driven social networks that have organically attracted Jews and non-Jews into meaningful Jewish conversations/experiences. Admittedly, some have asked, "What is Jewish about this?" The short answer is that Jewish students are more attracted to casual settings where they can discuss Jewish responses to universal questions than they are to pursuing Jewish knowledge for its own sake. In addition, a recent evaluation of Hillel's peer-to-peer engagement efforts suggested a correlation between "Jewish talk" (discussions of Jewish identity topics including Israel, faith, holidays, and so on) and Jewish growth.[4] This data reinforces comments Hillel frequently hears from students in our own evaluative work, like that of Ariel from UCLA:

> Jewish students are more attracted to casual settings where they can discuss Jewish responses to universal questions than they are to pursuing Jewish knowledge for its own sake.

> As an intern I am constantly thinking about how to better engage others, how to make Judaism appeal to others, and how to make others appreciate [Jewish life on campus]. As a result I am finding the ways that Judaism appeals to me … and how I can connect with my Jewish self.

As we merge our traditional commitments to *chesed* (loving-kindness), *tzedek* (justice), and *tikkun olam* (repairing the world) with an increasingly flat and borderless world, the bonds of Jewish peoplehood seem in conflict with universalism. We should not fear this conflict. The fact that Jews are so well accepted and integrated into American society combined with Jews taking on an increased sense of responsibility for humanity at large is a good thing. It has fostered an extraordinary resurgence in Jewish pride and a deep interest among young Jews to discover, explore, and embrace their Jewish roots. The millennial generation exhibits an inherent desire to help those less fortunate, and many are increasingly proud of seeing this as a Jewish value.

The pride that young Jews take in Judaism's fundamental value of helping others presents us with an opportunity. The universalist ethic comes in a secular package that eliminates many elements that have emotional resonance for Jewish students—roots, purpose, passion, collective memory, and Jewish belonging. We find that ethical ethnicity has greater appeal than soul-less secularism. Jewish institutions need to leverage this approach so that they can inspire thousands of Jews who might otherwise be beyond reach.

Over the past few years, Hillel has proactively facilitated deep, substantive, compelling, and meaningful Jewish learning among Jewish students across the globe. Perhaps our greatest discovery during this time has been that marginally affiliated Jewish students are willing to seek out such meaningful Jewish learning experiences. Hillel did not employ flashy marketing techniques, and we did not water down our program to simply offer social hours. Of course, the approach is not as simple as posting a class and enrolling dozens of students. Success depends on connecting students with talented and skilled educators capable of interpreting and translating the richness of our texts, tradition, and values in relevant and compelling ways.

Myth 3: The Jewish Community Has a Young-Leadership Talent Pool Crisis

Reality: **The superstar students we encounter demonstrate some of the key ingredients needed to be successful leaders: communal loyalty, comfort with particularism, a love for Israel, and a desire to make an impact.**

Case Study: Among the participants at the 2011 Davos Leadership Conference in Switzerland were Facebook COO Sheryl Sandberg and Uri L'Tzedek cofounder Rabbi Shmuly Yanklowitz. While Sandberg has become a role model and champion for secular issues that range from advancing women in the workplace to alleviating poverty in Africa, Rabbi Yanklowitz, a former Texas Hillel activist, helped develop restaurant certification for ethical treatment of workers and animals. Today, both play on a global platform, influencing and learning from the best practices and networks of successful social and business entrepreneurs. Though they work in completely different fields, both draw wisdom, inspiration, and pride from their Jewish identities and their activism.

How can we help cultivate more leaders like Sandberg and Rabbi Yanklowitz? Almost fifty years ago, young Jews hijacked the agenda at the 1969 General Assembly (GA) of the Council of Jewish Federations, demanding more money from the Federation system for Jewish education. Those who were seen by establishment leaders as young radicals are now prominent rabbis, Jewish scholars, and Jewish professionals. Twenty-five years ago, when I was in college, I participated on a panel at the GA about student leadership. Most of my peers at the time would never step foot into this national Jewish leadership gathering, and they were certainly not interested in precipitating a revolution. Thankfully, today hundreds of young Jews participate at national Jewish meetings, from the GA, to the American Israel Public Affairs Committee (AIPAC) Policy Conference, to the annual J Street Conference, and many more. Jewish students have come out in droves for rallies on the genocide in Darfur, traveled to New Orleans to help with Katrina relief efforts, and traveled to Israel to learn more about the modern Jewish experience. If anything, the Jewish community has been criticized for focusing too much on building Jewish leadership among youth while overlooking other important constituencies within the Jewish community.

The phenomenon of young leaders in their twenties and thirties was the focus of a much discussed study by Dr. Jack Wertheimer.[5] The study revealed that Jewish leaders are emerging from three distinct sectors: establishment organizations, nonestablishment start-up organizations like Yanklowitz's Uri L'Tzedek, and hybrid organizations that are supported by the established Jewish community and that attract a younger and niche constituency. I am not sure that this analysis sufficiently captures the breadth of venues where we can find the next generation of Jewish leaders. There are future business, philanthropy, and social sector leaders like Sheryl Sandberg who are being shaped in non-Jewish fraternities and sororities, volunteering for Peace Corps or City Year, and interning at the World Bank. How can the Jewish community benefit from this talent pool of leaders who are Jewish but who did not come up through the ranks of our own organizations?

115

In the second half of the twentieth century, the Jewish community had enviable success at training young people for leadership in the Jewish community. Whether through the Federation young leadership network, AIPAC, Brandeis Camp Institute, or the large national defense organizations like the Anti-Defamation League (ADL) and the American Jewish Committee, young Jews in their twenties and thirties could acquire skills and knowledge and build networks where they could begin to assume leadership positions. These young people went on to seek out opportunities for volunteer and professional leadership in agencies throughout the Jewish world. But as the focus of Jews shifts away from membership organizations, we must now identify and train a new breed of Jewish leaders.

With this in mind, Hillel has reimagined a student leadership model with increased focus on peer engagement and long-term commitment. Since 2006, Hillel has trained more than one thousand student interns who have connected more than sixty-three thousand previously uninvolved Jewish students to Jewish life on more than sixty campuses in the United States, helping them explore and connect to Jewish life on their own terms.[6] With a clear focus on our objectives, we have created a system to engage increasing numbers of young Jews in Jewish activity:

- Student interns are identified by their peers and selected for participation based on demonstrated commitment and charisma.
- Hillel trains and evaluates the interns based on objective benchmarks (e.g., engage sixty students from their social network over the course of the year).
- Hillel educators supervise and provide feedback to the interns in a consistent way, recognizing and rewarding their achievements.
- After a year in our program, we help transition the interns into volunteer leadership roles on campus and in the community.

Importantly, this relationship-based, peer-to-peer approach doesn't advocate any particular way of being Jewish, nor does it carry a hidden agenda to get the students to "come to Hillel." Instead, the student interns, mentored by Hillel educators of diverse Jewish backgrounds, explore, share stories, ask questions, and celebrate Jewish life with other students.

Jewish experiences range from Shabbat and holiday celebrations in dorms and off-campus apartments to women's spirituality circles, Jewish manhood discussions, Jewish-black dialogue groups, and social justice trips—all of which the interns create based on the interests of their peers. Students who were once minimally engaged are increasingly reporting involvement in Jewish activities, while the interns are honing their leadership skills in ways that will benefit the Jewish community, for now and for the future.

Every successful enterprise, be it corporate, professional, or nonprofit, pays attention to effective leadership recruitment strategies. In this regard, I have several questions:

- Will Jewish communal organizations provide meaningful volunteer roles on their boards and major initiatives to even a fraction of the thousands of Jewish students we have trained over the past few years and who are now graduating?
- Are Jewish organizations flocking to campus, like Teach for America, Google, and Wall Street, seeking to hire students as paid interns during school and summer breaks so as to attract them to Jewish communal service positions when they graduate?
- Do Jewish organizations have a strategy to hire recent graduates to help the Jewish community build an online presence and use social media to mobilize their peer group?

I'm afraid the answer to the above questions is "no," "no," and "no." We need to turn those "nos" into "yeses" so we can transform the Jewish community and make it compelling to the next generation.

Myth 4: The Younger Generation's Obsession with Individuality and Personal Choice Will Undermine Jewish Communal Solidarity and Will Weaken the Ability of the Jewish Community to Engage with Other Ethnic and Religious Communities in a Coherent Fashion

Reality: As the next generation begins to understand who *they* want to be as American Jews, as distinct from who their parents

117

want them to be, they will emerge as active participants in networks of their choosing. As they do, they will be well equipped to build bridges across sectors of the Jewish world as well as with outside organizations, networks, and initiatives.

Case Study: A few years ago I was visited by the head of faith-based recruitment from Teach for America (TFA). Their research on successful graduates from their program revealed a common success factor—leadership experiences in college (not grades, majors, or pedigree of school). Many of the Jewish students applying to the highly competitive TFA program referred to their prior *tikkun olam* or *tzedek* activities as formative experiences in college. I was then asked if I would endorse Teach for America, thus sending a not-so-subtle message of Jewish support for TFA. I was flattered but not sure why they thought my endorsement would matter and influence the students' decision to accept the offer to spend the next two years of their life in the TFA program. I was politely corrected and told that I was being asked to write not to the students, but to their parents.

I was extremely impressed with how thoughtful and strategic the TFA approach was. I could not think of anything like this being done in the Jewish world. We have built institutions, experiences, and programs—many of excellent quality—that are isolated and disconnected islands unto themselves. Where is the thread, the overarching strategy that would enable an individual to understand that each positive experience with a Jewish initiative is just one part of a greater, holistic Jewish journey? There is a desperate need for a coherent strategy to link these disparate immersive experiences so we can guide each young Jews' life journey in a direction that might plant the seeds for future engagement.[7] Attempts to actualize this vision are usually met with skeptical sighs born out of organizational mistrust and the fear of lawsuits for breach of privacy.

Let's try to think about this a little differently. Transitions have historically been understood as the handoff between one Jewish organizational affiliation and another or one Jewish community and another. The Jewish community must now create a model of Jewish adult free agency rather than narrowly focusing on a centralized, coordinated, or orchestrated "handoff." Transitions should result in capable, empowered Jewish citizenship. As much as it might seem valuable to pass participants from one activity to the next, we need to revisit the overall strategy and messaging. We need to create a new communal norm to promote pipelines and stewardship. Otherwise, each program spends enormous resources in marketing itself and then trumpeting the number of participants and the percentage of growth over the previous year. And then, more money is spent to evaluate the impact of a program on the participants in order to convince funders that the program provides a good return on investment. A handful of programs spend additional money to follow up with participants, although success in this regard is notoriously difficult.

Programs often tout participants who went on to do other great things like advanced Jewish fellowships, yet they do nothing to actively nurture these transitions. Little time or resources are spent on an effective handoff of participants so that they are more easily identified and recruited for other quality Jewish engagements. Why can't the Jewish community agree that the outcome of these activities should be a progression of Jewish learning and growth, not merely a head count of participants? Transitions require us to leverage our most successful Jewish experiences—from Taglit-Birthright to Jewish service-learning immersive experiences and from Jewish summer camps to youth groups—and develop a comprehensive model that fosters Jewish growth through these experiences to facilitate each person's unique Jewish journey.

> There is a desperate need for a coherent strategy to link these disparate immersive experiences so we can guide each young Jew's life journey in a direction that might plant the seeds for future engagement.

There are no shortcuts to meeting this challenge, no singular activity that will effectively ensure that our most meaningful and transformative Jewish experiences will result in ongoing Jewish learning and growth for the participants. We must create expectations of responsibility and continuity so that participants emerge with the motivation, confidence,

119

and capacity to pursue subsequent growth on their own. Next, we must change our language and protocols so that rather than hiring alumni coordinators, we train and hire stewards of Jewish journeys—preparing each one to become self-sufficient. Success in our endeavors will be measured by the number of Jews who continue their Jewish journeys rather than by the number that participate in a given experience or activity at one point in time.

If Teach for America has nine thousand corps members teaching six hundred thousand students in forty-three regions across the country and is able to share student leadership data and profiles of Jewish young adults with us, is it impossible to imagine a Jewish world in which such organizational sharing is the norm?

The Missing Piece

What is missing in Jewish life today for young adults is not another great program, idea, or organization. We need an engaging and welcoming framework that all or most of our children and parents can embrace, no matter which path they choose. Our upwardly mobile community has embraced college education as a rite of passage. The campus setting has become a laboratory for how Judaism can be experienced as a compelling option for American Jews in a society without barriers to full assimilation. We can and must think creatively and collaboratively about how we can leverage the campus setting and this stage of emerging adulthood to bring greater energy and passion to contemporary Jewish life.

As we shift the discussion and funding away from a narrow programmatic and organizational focus to one that best advances this new goal, we must encourage some new thinking and new behaviors. The recent books *Switch: How to Change Things When Change Is Hard* by Chip and Dan Heath and *The Power of Habit: Why We Do What We Do in Life and Business* by Charles Duhigg confirm that the challenge of changing behavior—both personal and organizational—requires more than giving people more options.[8] Ultimately, we will need to collaborate and coordinate in a manner that puts the individual and not the institution at the center and promotes common language and incentives to this end. Let's simplify our approach with three core principles:

1. Define objective benchmarks for emerging adult Jewish literacy, and reward innovative and collaborative efforts that help advance those objectives.

2. Find ways to mark the transition from college to communal Jewish life with meaningful ritual, public celebration, and incentives for fostering continued growth and leadership opportunities across the spectrum of Jewish offerings so that more young Jews can easily find their niche in the Jewish community after they graduate.

3. Empower next-generation leaders in communal decision making and stewardship through paid internships, innovation grants, and coveted roles in existing and future decision-making bodies.

In the eighteenth and nineteenth centuries, Jews responded to the dramatic changes brought on by the European Enlightenment with their particular form of Jewish Enlightenment (the Haskalah), which focused on new religious ideologies, the revival of Hebrew, and the creation of the Zionist movement. The changes taking place now, early in the twenty-first century, require equally creative visions of Jewish life. The time is ripe to partner with young adults in a new Jewish Enlightenment that will capture the imagination of the next generation as they migrate from campus life to creating Jewish life in communities all around the world.

Jewish Social Justice

Looking Beyond Ourselves

Rabbi Jill Jacobs

In my first year of rabbinical school in 1998, I began telling classmates and teachers at the Jewish Theological Seminary (JTS) that I wanted to be a rabbi who does social justice work. The responses were not encouraging: "Why not be a social worker or a public service lawyer? Why a rabbi?" "That's a Reform thing." "You'll never find a job doing that." On the flip side, Jews deeply involved with social justice organizing and advocacy were equally shocked that a Conservative rabbinical student cared deeply about human rights and economic justice: "I didn't think religious people were into that." "Social justice is part of secular Jewish culture."

As a young rabbinical student, I struggled to integrate my budding religious leadership with my growing interest in social justice. In the *beit midrash* (study hall), I was diving deeply into the Jewish textual tradition. In dialogue with the ancient Rabbis, my peers and I grappled with theology, ritual, and civic life. Outside of the *beit midrash*, I volunteered with a group organizing tenants squeezed out of Harlem by rising rents. I

Rabbi Jill Jacobs is the executive director of Truah: The Rabbinic Call for Human Rights, an organization of eighteen hundred rabbis who mobilize their communities to protect human rights in North America and Israel. She is the author of *Where Justice Dwells: A Hands-On Guide to Doing Social Justice in Your Jewish Community* and *There Shall Be No Needy: Pursuing Social Justice through Jewish Law and Tradition*. Rabbi Jacobs has been named three times to the *Forward*'s list of fifty influential American Jews, to the *Jewish Week*'s first list of "36 under 36," and to *Newsweek*'s list of "The 50 Most Influential Rabbis in America" every year since 2009.

spent a summer working with a labor union on a Justice for Janitors campaign. In these settings, too, the people I met were surprised to encounter a rabbinical student. In Harlem, I heard—heartbreakingly—"You're the first Jew I've ever met who's not a slumlord." In the union, the many self-defined secular Jews on staff came looking for confirmation that their work was "Jewish."

In the end, I got lucky. I graduated into a Jewish community in which social justice was making a comeback (much as Sidney Schwarz describes in his lead essay). I *did* find rabbinic work, first as the director of outreach and education at the Jewish Council on Urban Affairs in Chicago, then as the rabbi-in-residence at Jewish Funds for Justice (recently renamed Bend the Arc: A Jewish Partnership for Justice), and now as the executive director of Rabbis for Human Rights–North America. In the process, I discovered deep connections between social justice and Judaism. My explorations led me to write two books—first *There Shall Be No Needy: Pursuing Social Justice through Jewish Law and Tradition*, which looks at contemporary American economic and social issues through a Jewish lens, and then *Where Justice Dwells: A Hands-On Guide to Doing Social Justice in Your Jewish Community*, which argues that Jews should do social justice as Jews and provides guidance about how to do so.

The very name of my current organization (founded in 2002, the year before I graduated from JTS) speaks to a healthy shift in the culture of social justice in the Jewish community. In the past, social justice has been seen as the purview of secular Jews. To be a religious Jew meant to observe Shabbat, keep kosher, and obsess over the minutia of ritual practice. Now, the paradigm is shifting. More and more rabbis feel that their mission includes justice work. I receive regular calls from rabbinical students wondering how to carve out a space in the "social justice rabbinate"—something that certainly did not exist when I was in school. Synagogues have stepped up involvement in social service and even advocacy, and service learning has become hot.

Many of these developments parallel trends in the general American population. When I was an undergraduate at Columbia in the mid-1990s, the campus was uncharacteristically quiet. Student protests focused primarily on internal issues, primarily ethnic studies. Only a few years later,

United Students against Sweatshops, campus living-wage campaigns, and other broader social justice movements began gaining traction both at Columbia and across the country. Today, it is common for college students to spend their spring breaks volunteering, to participate in a gap-year service program, and to aspire to social justice and social service careers. It is no surprise that young American Jews resemble their peers in this regard.

The interest among young Jews in social justice responds to the "why be Jewish?" question that the Jewish community so often avoids asking. For too long, the presumed answer to this question has been the holy trinity of anti-Semitism, the Holocaust, and Israel. That is—be Jewish because other people hate us. Be Jewish as a tribute to those who lost their lives. Be Jewish to protect the State of Israel. Increasingly, these answers ring hollow for young Jews in search of positive reasons for identification. At the same time, the rise in multiculturalism has sent many Jews searching for their roots. This trend has resulted in an explosion of new Jewish expressions in everything from music to Jewish languages to public manifestations of Jewish pride. Identification with initiatives in the universe of Jewish social justice is one component of this trend.

> The interest among young Jews in social justice responds to the "why be Jewish?" question that the Jewish community so often avoids asking.

But this newly framed Jewish affiliation does not conflict with universalism. A young person might easily self-define as Jewish and Catholic and claim each as part of his or her heritage. Nor does Jewish affiliation demand making one's social group largely or exclusively Jewish. Surveys of Jewish affiliation tend to ask what percentage of one's social circle is Jewish. For young Jews, it is easy to feel proudly and fully Jewish without spending time primarily with Jews. This contrasts with my grandparents' generation, many of whom socialized exclusively with Jews, without actively participating in Jewish ritual or practice.

Schwarz is spot-on in his observation that "in contrast to tribal Jews, covenantal Jews see their identity less as a matter of group solidarity than as a spiritual legacy…. If covenantal Jews feel an affinity to Judaism, it is because of the ethics and values that Judaism has brought into the world.... Their loyalties are decidedly more global and universal." The continuity agenda, which appears to promote staying Jewish for the sake of the past, does not speak to these Jews. To be meaningful, Judaism must present a compelling vision of what Jews can contribute to the world.

To some extent, the Jewish community has supported the explosion of interest in social justice among young (and many not-so-young) Jews. Several major foundations fund local and national Jewish social justice groups such as Bend the Arc (national), Jews for Racial and Economic Justice (New York), Jews United for Justice (Washington, D.C.), and the Jewish Council on Urban Affairs (Chicago). The Union for Reform Judaism has put major resources toward Just Congregations, which helps congregations engage in community organizing. There has been a major communal investment in service learning through Repair the World and other organizations. It has become de rigueur for preteens to participate in a *mitzvah* project as part of their Bar and Bat Mitzvah preparations. Most synagogues and other Jewish institutions speak proudly about their social action and social justice work as a cornerstone of the community.

Notwithstanding these major investments, and despite the extraordinary success of some organizations and institutions, social justice is sometimes presented as the newest gimmick in the continuity tool kit. I regularly hear Jewish professionals describe social justice as an entry point to Judaism. That is to say, because young unaffiliated Jews are interested in social justice, we should show them that social justice is Jewish, and then they will graduate to "real" Jewish involvement.

What if, instead, we allowed ourselves, our Judaism, and our community to be transformed by social justice? I believe that if we took social justice seriously—that is, if we invested massive resources, time, and communal attention in justice work—we would create a more meaningful, appealing, and inspirational Judaism for the future. To take social justice seriously, we must first truly believe that justice work is good for Judaism and good for the Jewish community. Taking social justice seriously means integrating justice into our learning, our ritual practice, and our communal life in such a way as to make every aspect of our Jewish lives feel more powerful.

Why Should the Jewish Community Support Social Justice?

The Jewish community—including the mainstream Jewish organizations—regularly speaks the language of social justice. We talk about the obligation to the poor, the stranger, and the vulnerable. We hold up *tzedakah* (charity) as one of our highest values. We provide extraordinary social services that meet the day-to-day needs of people regardless of ethnic or religious affiliation.

But we sometimes become a little scared when talk turns to social change. By social change, I mean transforming policies and systems that create and maintain power inequalities. Such policies and systems include labor laws and practices, the criminal justice system, tax codes, the allocation of health care, the social safety net, and other areas of law and practice that affect our economic status and place within our community. Social change also takes on deeply ingrained racism, sexism, homophobia, and other prejudices, especially when these manifest in laws, policies, or practices that negatively affect certain groups.

Most individual Jews support progressive domestic policies, including immigration reform, health care for all, and strong anti-poverty programs.[1] Most major Jewish organizations are on record as supporting such policies as well. At the same time, many Jewish institutions tend to view social and economic issues through an "us-or-them" paradigm. Is this good for the Jews? Is it good for Israel? How do we balance Jewish and secular issues? Is this a Jewish issue?

I reject this "us–them" paradigm. Instead, I believe that social justice is good for Judaism and good for Jews. In the next few pages, I will explain what I mean.

Social Justice Is Good for Judaism

If young Jews are asking "why be Jewish?" or why they should affiliate themselves with a Jewish community (or not asking the question, but simply defaulting to nonengagement), then the response must be that Judaism matters. Judaism must speak directly to the most important issues of the moment and must do so in a deep and compelling manner.

As Schwarz correctly notes, young Jews are not looking for Jewish "lite." They are, in his words, "yearn[ing] for authenticity." This is why intensive learning programs such as Mechon Hadar in New York and Pardes and the Conservative Yeshiva in Israel have gained so much popularity among young Jews. This is why the independent *minyanim* scene has taken off and why more and more universities offer Jewish studies programs. These institutions and approaches make no apology for their seriousness. Instead, they offer meaningful learning and prayer opportunities that challenge participants to develop new skills and delve into theology, ritual, spiritual practice, and other complex areas of Jewish life.

Social justice, too, must be a challenging proposition. Taking on social justice as a Jewish community requires an intensive conversation about how Jewish law, thought, and practice influence our perspective on contemporary issues. This requires Jewish literacy, engagement with our tradition, and a willingness to enter into serious dialogue about the issues of the moment.

My own interest in this approach began when I was in rabbinical school. I spent time working with a tenant-organizing group in Harlem and then a labor union working with janitors in New Jersey. Along the way, I started wondering what Judaism might have to say about the issues that I was seeing on the ground. Until this point, what I knew of Jewish approaches to social justice mostly consisted of a few choice quotations: "Justice, justice you shall pursue" (Deuteronomy 16:20); "In the image of God, God created humanity" (Genesis 1:27); "You shall not oppress the widow, the orphan, or the stranger" (Jeremiah 22:3). I knew concepts such as *tzedakah, tikkun olam* (repairing the world), and *g'milut chasadim* (acts of loving-kindness) but had never seen these concepts addressed in a complicated and intellectually rigorous manner.

When I started studying Talmud and Jewish legal materials, I found a rich and complex conversation about the relationships between landlords and tenants, and employers and employees. How much notice must a landlord give before evicting a tenant? How much notice must a tenant give before leaving? Can a tenant be evicted when there is a lack of housing to be found? What if the landlord's own home becomes uninhabitable? What if the landlord's child marries and needs a place to live? What constitutes fair pay? What does a dignified and safe workplace look like? Can workers unionize? Can non-union workers break a strike? What if a worker shows up for work and finds that there is nothing to do? Can workers quit when doing so will cause economic loss to the employer? The discussions about these questions go far beyond simple declarations of a commitment to justice.

Much of my own writing has focused on exploring such questions through a three-way conversation among Jewish text and tradition, contemporary social policy, and the experiences of real people. In many cases, what I found surprised me. For example, in the course of writing a chapter on criminal justice for my first book, I found myself needing to put aside all of my assumptions about crime and punishment. I realized, for instance, that even the definition of crime is different in Jewish law than in American law. Whereas American law tends to lump together violent and nonviolent offenders, Jewish law maintains two systems of courts (each with its own rules) and types of punishments for capital crimes and noncapital crimes.

Especially interesting to me were debates about prisons in Jewish law. While the concept of prison does not exist in early Jewish law, communities in the medieval period and later began to experiment with this mode of punishment according to the needs of the moment. I became especially interested in a debate between two twentieth-century Israeli rabbis about whether to hang a mezuzah in a prison cell. Traditionally, Jews hang a mezuzah—a scroll with biblical texts—on every door of one's permanent home. One does not hang it on the door of a temporary home, such as a hotel. In the case of the prison cell, the debate centers on the question of whether a prison constitutes a permanent home. On the one hand, a person might be there for several years. On the other hand, everyone living in prison dreams of leaving. One rabbi ruled in favor of hanging the mezuzah, and one ruled against. What struck me, though, was not the conclusion of the debate, but rather the assumption—by both rabbis—that a prison stay is, by nature, short-lived—at most, a few years.[2] In contrast, when I think about prisons in America, I think first about people spending decades or even their entire adult lives in prison. While I am not prepared to advocate for a mass release of all prisoners, the Jewish legal texts challenged me to think of prison as a temporary solution, and not primarily as a long-term one.

I offer this example not to force conclusions about how to reform the criminal justice system in the United States or elsewhere. Rather, I believe that such discussions about current events will both enhance our understanding of these issues and deepen our connection to Judaism. For me, the various Jewish perspectives on crime and punishment forced me to reconsider assumptions that I have absorbed from American culture. At the same time, I gained new insight into my own tradition as I contemplated the multi-century discussions about how to create a fair justice system.

When I speak with young Jews who are committed to social justice but disconnected from the Jewish community, they often dismiss Judaism as having nothing to offer them. Many do feel proud of the Jewish traditions of *tzedakah* and justice and of the Jewish history of activism. But these same activists complain that when

> There is a disconnect between the Jewish social justice history that many of these young people want to claim and the religious expression of Judaism that they experience in their synagogues and elsewhere.

they go to synagogue, they hear sermons that don't jibe with their politics—especially when it comes to Israel—or they hear sermons that do not relate to their lives at all. There is a disconnect between the Jewish social justice history that many of these young people want to claim and the religious expression of Judaism that they experience in their synagogues and elsewhere. What if, instead, our communities offered rich and nuanced learning about the issues of the moment through the lens of Jewish text, history, and culture? What if our synagogues offered prayer services that linked spiritual fulfillment with action in the world? Certainly, some young people have found their way to rich Jewish experiences such as these through local or national social justice organizations or through *minyanim* or synagogues that tie together learning, justice, and prayer.

In Washington, D.C., a gathering of young Jews called Tikkun Leil Shabbat merges Friday night services with learning about social justice issues. Uri L'Tzedek, an Orthodox social justice organization, offers social justice *batei midrash* (study halls). At synagogues such as IKAR in Los Angeles, and B'nai Jeshurun in New York, social justice is always woven into prayer and communal life. Pardes in Jerusalem offers a social justice track for students studying there for the year. Multiple synagogue and campus rabbis have told me that their community is using one of my books to guide their study for the year. While such organizations and communities are growing in number and in influence, it is not yet the norm that Jewish communities engage with social justice in an intellectually serious and spiritually meaningful way.

Social Justice Is Good for Jews

Is health care a Jewish issue? What about prisons? Tax reform? I have heard multiple people argue that these issues and others like them are not "Jewish." Such declarations puzzle me. After all, American Jews use the same health care systems that other Americans use. We depend on the same criminal justice system to keep us safe, and to treat us fairly if we are charged with a crime. We abide by the same tax code as everyone else.

But when we refer to "Jewish issues," we most often mean issues that exclusively or primarily affect the Jewish community. These certainly include Israel and may also include support for the Jewish poor, protections against anti-Semitism, and funding for day schools. No wonder unaffiliated Jews, especially those in their twenties and thirties, often describe the Jewish community as insular. When we focus too much on issues within our own community, we send the message that we view our own needs as distinct from those of the rest of America.

The United States has welcomed Jews like no other secular country in the history of the world. Today, Jews can study in any university, pursue any career, and live wherever they want. Jews are leaders in every sector of business, public service, academia, and government. How do we respond to this unprecedented welcome? In some cases, we start to get a bit too comfortable. As our communities become wealthier, it becomes easier to self-segregate. We can choose to live where we do not have to see poverty on a daily basis, to send our children to well-funded schools, and to forget the immigration and workplace struggles of earlier generations. This complacency can lead to a loss of interest in maintaining the ties that have traditionally connected us to low-income communities, immigrant communities, and communities of color.

To compound the problem, there is a growing anxiety among many Jews about the interest that our liberal allies have taken in the Israeli-Palestinian issue. As campus activists, mainline churches, and the Occupy movement take up the banner of ending Israel's occupation of the West Bank, Jewish groups have largely responded by circling the wagons. Any criticism of Israel is branded as "delegitimization" of Israel or an expression of anti-Semitism. There is no doubt that anti-Semitism does play a role in the intense interest in the conflict among a certain segment of activists. However, labeling all criticism as anti-Semitism serves only to draw a wedge between the Jewish community and the minority and progressive communities that should be our natural allies on economic and social concerns.

> As campus activists, mainline churches, and the Occupy movement take up the banner of ending Israel's occupation of the West Bank, Jewish groups have largely responded by circling the wagons.

The history of anti-Semitism suggests that this breakdown in relationships between the Jewish community and other minority communities will come back to haunt us. Instead, we are better served by building strong relationships with these communities such that they will be there to defend us when needed. This relationship building entails working together on issues of common concern, or even on issues of primary concern to our partners. We do not have to give up on our commitments or values to do so, but rather should bring these to the table when we form partnerships with other communities.[3]

What Social Justice Can Look Like

Two of my most powerful prayer experiences happened in a single day, and in close proximity to tomatoes. In September 2011, I traveled to Immokalee, Florida, with a group of rabbis organized by Rabbis for Human Rights–North America to learn about slavery and other labor violations in the tomato fields. For two days, we sat with tomato pickers who had organized themselves into the Coalition of Immokalee Workers. We heard about cases in which employers held workers in chains overnight or prevented escape by seizing workers' passports and visas. Women told us of regular sexual harassment and even assault by bosses. We listened to workers talk about pesticides (some banned in every state but Florida) that cause birth defects, chemical burns, and probably cancer. We discovered that most tomato pickers do not earn minimum wage. And we learned about the courageous efforts of the workers to persuade retailers to buy tomatoes only from wholesalers with a zero tolerance policy for slavery, a zero tolerance policy for sexual harassment, safety protections for workers, and minimum wage guarantees.

And then we went to a tomato field.

The field we visited belonged to Pacific Tomato Growers, a Jewish-owned company led by Jon Esformes. A year before we arrived, Esformes had decided to sign an agreement with the workers' organization. He did it on the day before Yom Kippur. In his speech at the press conference announcing the agreement, he spoke about *teshuvah* (repentance/return). Now, workers at the farm wore safety equipment, received safety training, and received higher wages. Esformes pointed to the tree under which the press conference had been held, and we decided to daven *Minchah* (pray the afternoon service) there. This was, we decided, holy space. In the course of the service, we sang aloud a line giving thanks for the bounty of the land. We passed around a tomato as we offered blessings. We prayed for strength for ourselves and the workers.

After the service, we set out for a supermarket, where we kept praying. We visited a branch of a supermarket chain whose devout Christian owners refused even to meet with the workers. We encircled the tomato display, joined hands—rabbis and tomato pickers together—and prayed aloud. Before we left, we delivered a letter asking the management to purchase tomatoes picked under just conditions.

I mention these prayer experiences because they represent a powerful model for doing social justice as Jews. In this model, prayer and justice complement and enhance one another. We break out of the mold in which prayer and ritual take place in the synagogue and justice work assumes a purely secular character. In partnering with the primarily Latino tomato workers, we took on an issue of primary importance to another community. At the same time, the issue became personal for us rabbis as well—after meeting the workers, we knew that we could never again eat a tomato without worrying that it had been picked by a slave.

This campaign did not end with a few prayer services. Rabbis returned home, spoke to their communities about what they had seen, visited the national headquarters of a major grocery chain, and led groups of adults and children to rally at local grocery stores. We focused most of our efforts on Trader Joe's—and the company signed an agreement after several months of pressure.

> The paradigm for Jewish continuity has long depended on fear: fear of intermarriage, fear of anti-Semitism, and fear for Israel's survival. In contrast, social justice work builds on hope and strength.

Everywhere I travel, I hear about the impact that this campaign has had on Jewish communities. One rabbi told me that the best day of Hebrew school all year was the day that the eighth graders wrote and delivered letters to Trader Joe's. People of all ages and Jewish backgrounds told me that they put a tomato on the seder plate that year. Ministers of other faith traditions expressed admiration and gratitude for bringing the issue to the attention of the religious community.

At one point, a rabbi e-mailed me to complain about bringing rabbis to the tomato fields. He wrote, "Without diminishing the issues of migrant tomato pickers in America, what on earth do they have to do directly with the Jewish community? Can't Rabbis for Human Rights organize around issues that are demonstrably and directly Jewish?" I have already argued why I believe workers' rights and other American issues to be Jewish issues as well. I am interested, though, in the fear and anxiety evident in this e-mail. Why was the correspondent—whom I do not know personally—so angry that my organization would involve itself with migrant workers?

The answer, I think, points to the resistance that prevents social justice from gaining a greater foothold in the Jewish world. The paradigm for Jewish continuity has long depended on fear: fear of intermarriage, fear of anti-Semitism, and fear for Israel's survival. In contrast, social justice work builds on hope and strength. To take on justice work wholeheartedly, the Jewish community must embrace a new vision of itself as a powerful community with a mission of creating real change in the world.

The majority of Jews in their twenties and thirties have already cast aside the fear-driven approach to Jewish life and Jewish continuity. Members of this cohort have grown up feeling fully American, have encountered little anti-Semitism, and have experienced Israel as a powerful military force and not as a besieged refuge. The question for this generation will not be "Should I care about tomato pickers?" (or health care, or poverty, or any other justice issue), but rather, "Should I care about the particular needs of the Jewish community?" There is no question that social justice has taken off among this generation of Jews. The question is whether this generation will grapple with justice issues through a Jewish lens.

To address this challenge, we need a new breed of rabbi, cantor, educator, and Jewish professional prepared to prioritize justice issues, to weave these into all aspects of communal life, and to address head-on the question of what Judaism can bring to contemporary ethical dilemmas. My own organization, Rabbis for Human Rights–North America, has accordingly invested more and more heavily in training current rabbinical and cantorial students to be strong human rights leaders. Such leadership requires believing that justice work is essential to creating a strong Jewish community and having the knowledge and skills to help community members address moral issues within a Jewish context and a Jewish community. We need more and more such training, as well as training for up-and-coming educators and other Jewish professionals. Such training should immerse these future leaders in justice issues, involve them in learning about such issues from a Jewish perspective, and grant them the skills to engage their own communities and to partner with others.

Social justice can make the Jewish community stronger. Through engaging in social justice, we bring to life our tradition's wisdom about how to create a better society. And by doing social justice as a community, we create stronger relationships both internally and with other faith and ethnic communities.

Jewish Community Centers

Not Just a Gym and a Pool

Rabbi Joy Levitt

When I look back at the formative experiences of my early adult years, I can't help but be amazed (and perhaps somewhat alarmed) at how challenging the world seemed and how attracted to that challenge I was. The issues that Sidney Schwarz so clearly articulates—Israel's precarious place in the Middle East and the repression of Soviet Jews—and some that he did not—the position of blacks and women in America and the war in Southeast Asia—made my adolescence and emerging adulthood, well, if not simple, at least clear. My work was cut out for me. And I wasn't alone. Everyone like me, which is to say privileged, well educated, tribally connected (to borrow Schwarz's phrase), and looking for trouble (as most adolescents are) needed to look no further than the restricted country club in town or the boys-only track team in high

Rabbi Joy Levitt is the executive director at the Jewish Community Center in Manhattan. Prior to coming to the JCC, she served as a congregational rabbi on Long Island and in New Jersey for twenty years. She is the coeditor of *A Night of Questions: A Passover Haggadah*. Most recently, Rabbi Levitt founded the Jewish Journey Project, a new initiative designed to revolutionize Jewish education for children.

135

school. I remember arriving on the Barnard/Columbia campus in 1971 only to find it closed down in protest of our country's bombing of Hanoi and Haiphong Harbors shortly after the semester began. We were marching, shouting down the administrations on 116th Street in Manhattan and Pennsylvania Avenue in Washington. We were righteous, we were right, and let's just admit it finally—it was a lot of fun.

Not for everyone. Not for Andrew Goodman and his friends, who were murdered in the South trying to make it possible for more blacks to vote. Not for the countless young men whose lives were dramatically changed as they fled to Canada and beyond to avoid the war. And of course not for those who died in the 1967 war in Israel or who suffered in Soviet prisons. These really were dangerous and difficult times. But even as we were shaped by the events of our time, we also shaped them; we believed that our words, our actions, and our commitments mattered, and in fact they did.

> I find myself somewhat bemused and a little concerned about how worried we all are about "young people." I can't remember anyone worrying about us at that age. There were no resources poured into start-up organizations and *minyanim*, no free trips to Israel, no over-authorizing of our brilliance or entitlement in the world.

Mostly, though not exclusively, those words, actions, and commitments derived not only from my tradition and faith but also from the leaders who were calling us to action. Whether that was Abraham Joshua Heschel or my own rabbi, there was a certain connection between my journey in the world and that of my people. Did our institutions support our journeys? Frankly, I don't remember caring one way or another. Certainly the communal infrastructure that connected us to Israel and to Soviet Jewry worked well enough. And the synagogue, at least for me, was a place of social network, if not exactly spiritual inspiration.

I find myself somewhat bemused and a little concerned about how worried we all are about "young people." I can't remember anyone worrying about us at that age. There were no resources poured into start-up organizations and *minyanim*, no free trips to Israel, no over-authorizing of our brilliance or entitlement in the world. Don't get me wrong; we didn't have it so tough, either. Compared with the world of our parents, our road was mostly paved for us with only an occasional bump. But we also didn't expect or frankly want much from the older generation. We thought we knew better than they did, and we were willing to take the risks that came with the independence we craved.

Finding a Path

The world doesn't feel any less challenging to me now, and I worry about whether we have laid down enough roadways for our children to find their own way. It isn't as though nothing got accomplished. Certainly women and people of color are freer to live the lives they wish than before. The Soviet Union is no more, and Jews are, in most places in the world, safe. In Jewish life, there are more choices and less judgment, especially in the non-Orthodox world today. But as Schwarz notes, the economic instability, coupled with the challenges of Israel as it grapples with the reality of its power and powerlessness, the degradation of our environment, and the increasing gap between those who have and those who have not are real and present in the lives of this generation of emerging adults, as they are for us. There is no shortage of work to do.

And yet ... many of the institutions of Jewish life—synagogues, Federations, and JCCs—struggle to be places of meaning in Jewish life and places that offer people the opportunity or the context with which to explore these realities. Or worse, they do not struggle; they seem confused and uncertain about how it is that so few people want to engage with the very real and important work that they do. Schwarz has laid out some of the reasons this is so and has offered a series of strategies to address the challenges we face. From my vantage point in one of those institutions—the JCC—I see huge opportunities to strengthen Jewish life and provide multiple pathways for learning, social justice, and spirituality. Because our JCC is relatively new and had the benefit of very progressive lay and professional leadership early in its history, we have been less encumbered with the old models and more able to test new ideas. While this has not been easy and we have frequently found ourselves at the center of controversy within the community, we have learned several important truths along the way that serve as our guideposts.

It's about Community, Stupid

If newspapers have lost market share because they forgot that the business they are in is not print media but communication, then JCCs need to learn from their painful experience. We are not in the programming business; we are in the community business. As long as we focus on programs alone, we will run consumer-driven institutions that will struggle to compete in a marketplace of better resourced commercial facilities. An important corollary to this is that we make a huge mistake when we position ourselves as the "secular" alternative to the "religious" program of synagogues. Whatever "secular" used to mean, it's a word that has little currency today.

> We are not in the programming business; we are in the community business. As long as we focus on programs alone, we will run consumer-driven institutions that will struggle to compete in a marketplace of better resourced commercial facilities.

Certainly there are Jews who are not observant, whose faith is at best ambivalent, and who find prayer unhelpful. But they are searching for meaning and purpose in this world no less than regular synagogue attendees are, and the word "secular" doesn't begin to describe their journey. JCCs that take this journey seriously will be more successful than ones that only strive for the latest fad in fitness equipment. Jews can work out anywhere; in fact, they might even prefer to work out without having to go through a security ordeal at the front door or seeing babies have their diapers changed in locker rooms. But if the values that derive from our tradition are embedded in the places they work out, then people will soon notice that something more is happening to them than improving their muscle tone. They will feel respected, known, welcomed, and connected, not because it's good business but because our Jewish values require it.

When we widen the markers of Judaism, to borrow a phrase from Rabbi Irwin Kula, we increase the number of people who feel part of the community. Those markers include practically everything the JCC does, from teaching people to swim to helping them decrease the stress in their lives. All derive from Jewish values, and we need to do a better job of connecting those values to their lives.

Confidence Is Good; More Confidence Is Better

It never ceases to amaze me how fearful people are: of strangers, of ideas, of difference, of change. I'm not sure why I am not one of those people; perhaps it is how I was raised or the relative safety of my life. Regardless, good, strong institutions have confidence, and JCCs that back away from risk will find themselves speaking to fewer and fewer people. Nowhere is this more true than when we're talking about Israel. From its beginnings, the mission of our JCC has included a connection to the people of Israel. Because we wanted to avoid the food fights that occur when passionate lovers of Israel debate its present and future, and because we believed that our mandate was to reach the less-engaged members of our community who might more readily respond to cultural experiences, our Israel program was focused on the arts—music, film, theater, and dance.

But in recent years we have realized that our community has lost important muscles of conversation around difficult issues and that we need to become the living room for the serious debate that exists. What does this mean? It means we can regularly expect picketing outside our building, attacks on our program, threats and accusations, and potential loss of funding. It's not pretty. But when we do it well, thousands of people come and thank us, particularly young people. And what we've learned is not that they are more liberal but that they are more confident. They don't carry the same baggage we do about Israel's vulnerability. Rightly or wrongly, they see Israel as a strong military force in the region that can defend itself. They have been raised to be comfortable with multiple points of view, and they want our community to be an open, transparent place where they can listen, learn, and form their own opinions. They are less interested in advocacy than in education. When we can be that place confidently, we reach them and their friends in large numbers.

139

When we are not that place, when we shut down discussion and portray our community as unable to withstand the free exchange of different, even challenging views, our young people become confused and angry, and they tend to walk away. The dissonance between the way we raised them—to be open and thoughtful and respectful of difference—and what they see us doing is simply too great.

It Takes a Village

The JCC's biggest new initiative is the Jewish Journey Project (JJP), a collaborative effort among synagogues, JCCs, and a vast array of Jewish organizations that have come together to challenge one of the most basic tenets in Jewish life—that there is nothing that can be done to make Hebrew school an effective vehicle for engaging school-age children. JJP represents a big new idea about Jewish learning. It enables children and families to choose from a wide array of learning opportunities offered throughout the community in multiple venues and modalities. At its core is the assumption that synagogues cannot be expected to do this work alone.

Before I came to the JCC, I spent twenty years as a congregational rabbi bemoaning the mediocre state of after-school congregational Jewish education. There was no obvious solution. It was like the proverbial elephant in the living room; everyone, including rabbis, educators, and parents, knew it, but no one wanted to talk about it. Then, about ten years ago, some educators began to look at possible ways to strengthen Hebrew school, while simultaneously parents who could find alternatives began opting out. Today, all over the country, individuals, groups of families, and some forward-thinking synagogues are engaged in serious efforts to start the conversation.

When I first came to the JCC, I encountered a fair amount of pressure from parents to start a Hebrew school. Of course I encountered a fair amount of pressure from my rabbinic colleagues not to start a Hebrew school. Those who wanted us to start a Hebrew school argued that the JCC was born to be a catalyst in the community for change and that when institutions weren't working, we had an obligation to children and families to try to do something for them and our community as a whole.

Quite convincing. Those who were appalled at the idea argued that Hebrew school was the province of synagogues; that only within religious communities could quality Jewish education take place, and that the JCC had always maintained that it was born to strengthen Jewish life and that its synagogues were partners in this work, not adversaries. Fair enough. But the real reason I was loathe to start a Hebrew school was that I fundamentally don't believe that in the current structure they can be successful. I simply saw no way that the JCC could do a better job than the synagogues. It wasn't that the synagogues weren't trying; it was that the model was all wrong. Clearly they were stuck and had a hard time seeing a way out. As I began listening to parents and educators, rabbis and communal leaders, it became clear to me that the JCC might be able to play a role as incubator of new ideas and convener of the players who desperately want to find a new model. The Jewish Journey Project is the result of those efforts.

> When we shut down discussion and portray our community as unable to withstand the free exchange of different, even challenging views, our young people become confused and angry, and they tend to walk away. The dissonance between the way we raised them—to be open and thoughtful and respectful of difference—and what they see us doing is simply too great.

If we are right, then what we will have done is change the nature of the conversation among synagogues, JCCs, and innovative Jewish organizations and perhaps repurposed some places in the process. By asserting that Jewish education isn't about institutions but about dynamic, flexible, creative opportunities to engage with the tradition and the community based on children's passions and talents, we have moved the conversation away from turf issues (which never benefit real people and usually don't even benefit the institutions fighting) and toward the central challenge of preparing our young people for our community and the world. If we are right, our synagogues will be free of the burden of sustaining failed schools and able to discover new ways to connect with their children and families. Our JCCs, museums, and other Jewish organizations will all understand that they are partners in this work, and they will think harder about ways to participate in the education of our children.

Social Justice Is about Saving the World, Not Saving the Jewish People

At its core, the JCC considers improving our city as part of its core mission. Since its inception, we have had a vibrant literacy program in Manhattan's struggling schools and many programs for teens and families to support homeless families. When our building was built, we decided to dedicate Shabbat morning each week to underserved children in some of the city's poorest neighborhoods. Through organizations like the Children's Aid Society, hundreds of kids come each week to the JCC to swim, play basketball, study for their SATs, dance, do photography, and enjoy being together. It is one of our finest efforts and makes me proud every day.

There's a growing debate in Jewish life about the place of social justice. I agree with Schwarz when he applauds the number of organizations that have sprung up to respond to the community's desire to serve. But there is a caveat here. When we raise the value of social justice and encourage our community and particularly our young people to get involved, we need to be clear about our motive. It is about repairing the world. It's about acknowledging our privilege and connecting the words of our tradition to our deeds. Too often people view social justice programs as a vehicle to keep people engaged with Jewish life when other aspects, like prayer and even study, have failed. It may very well accomplish this goal, but not if it is the actual goal. People who are serious about service—and all of us should be—want and need the focus to be on those who need our help, not on ourselves and the strengthening of our Jewish lives.

A few years ago, a friend of mine who is a retired math teacher pointed out to me that there were no numeracy programs in the city helping underserved children with math skills. Because our literacy program was now in fourteen schools, with hundreds of volunteers working with thousands of children, it seemed like a natural next step for us. This year, we opened our first two numeracy programs with thirty volunteers, including high school and even some middle school tutors, whom we train. It is run by a former board member who several years ago decided to leave his career in the financial world and get a master's degree in education. Now a teacher at the Bank Street School, he jumped at the opportunity to create this new program for us. It doesn't get much better than that.

Stop Talking So Much and Listen

Those of us who became Jewish professionals usually think we know what people need. We certainly think we know what Judaism demands, suggests, hopes for, and wants of us. Some of us even believe that what people need and what Judaism demands are the same thing. This makes for a great deal of preaching and screeching and not a whole lot of listening. One of the great challenges and opportunities in a service-oriented business like a JCC is that you ignore people at your peril. More important, when you actually ask them what they want and need, you'd be amazed at the depth of their creativity, imagination, and dreams, along with their willingness to help make it happen.

For years, people were telling us that JCC programs were too expensive. While many in the community could afford it and more, there were others for whom it was simply priced out of their reach. We probably could have ignored this, because we are in an affluent neighborhood with thousands of Jews, but in so doing, we would have fallen short of our mission to celebrate the diversity in our community. R & R was born to provide high-quality programming that was open and available to everyone for free on Shabbat afternoons. In this way, we were making an important Jewish statement to our community—that Shabbat is a gift to the community and that this JCC was open to everyone. As a result, instead of our JCC looking like a private health club on Shabbat afternoon, with individual fitness and pool members coming in and out of the building, there are usually five hundred to six hundred individuals and families all over the building, studying and singing, watching movies and doing origami, meditating and listening to lectures.

There were ways that we could have gotten tripped up here. We obviously needed resources to make it possible, and we were fortunate to have a donor who believed in the value of openness and was willing to put her

143

money where her values were. We could have gotten pushback from the more observant members of the community who might be offended by various activities offered that are outside the bounds of the Jewish laws of Shabbat as they see them. As it turns out, many members of the traditional community choose to attend R & R. They are grateful that we provide Shabbat elevators and many programs that pose no barriers to their participation. Some rabbis with whom I have spoken feel that the JCC is providing a great service simply by encouraging people to stay out of the commercial culture on Shabbat.

More Questions

When we take a hard look at these lessons, we are still left with lots of questions. If it's all about community, in what ways might we be doing a better job building community? If risk taking is a fundamental truth about healthy institutions, in what ways are we still reticent, and how might we change our organizational culture so that we don't shrink from a challenge? If it takes a village to educate our children, then why are our community's collaborative efforts so fraught with conflict, and how might we reduce the level of anxiety around cooperative ventures? Finally, now that we understand the value of more listening and less talking, why is it still so hard to do?

Let's start with the last question, because if we can get it right, then everything else will follow. Here's a true story. I was once having a conversation with a congregational rabbi in our community who was upset that very few families were coming to services on Friday night. He decided to implement a rule that families must attend six Friday night services each year in order for their children to become Bar/Bat Mitzvah in his synagogue. With a fair amount of complaining, most complied—up until their child's Bar/Bat Mitzvah, after which they were never seen again. The rabbi was happy that at least he had managed to get them there some time.

What happens when we turn this story around and ask families why they don't come to Friday night services? As it turned out, many of them left the city on weekends. A particularly urban phenomenon, busy, hard-working (and yes, affluent) families enjoy the rest and relaxation that a country house can provide. The irony here should not be missed. These families are actually trying to have Shabbat. True, they are looking for something different than the rabbi had in mind. But what would it look like if the synagogue were a place that helped support your family's Shabbat whether that meant coming to services or providing you with materials to have Shabbat at home with your family? What would it look like if your synagogue encouraged you to find other families and join together in someone's home for a potluck dinner and discussion about the weekly Torah portion? The deeper question is: What is our goal here? Is it to strengthen synagogue life or Jewish life? Or is it, in fact, to strengthen family life, understanding Judaism as a technology rather than as an end product?

If we listen to people, what might they tell us? At the JCC, they tell us that it's hard to instill good values in their children in a city with so much wealth and so much inequity. They tell us that getting and staying healthy is a daily challenge, particularly for older adults. They tell us that they are lonely. They tell us that they don't have enough to do or that they have too much to do. They are worried about our country. They are worried about their parents. They are concerned about aging.

They also tell us that they want to learn. They feel ignorant about their tradition, and they want a deeper, more serious connection to it. They tell us they want to celebrate, to feel joy, to connect better to one another. They want to make friends, they want to be seen, and they want their lives to matter. By the way, they don't always use these words to tell us these things. Often they complain that the pool is too cold (or, too warm—my favorite weekly conundrum). They want a different teacher for their three-year-old, because he isn't being stimulated enough. They are unhappy with the noise in the lobby or the crowding in the elevators. The print in the program guide is too small. The programs cost too much. There aren't enough men (one of the great mysteries in Jewish life—where are all the men?). And while sometimes their comments are

> What is our goal here? Is it to strengthen synagogue life or Jewish life? Or is it, in fact, to strengthen family life, understanding Judaism as a technology rather than as an end product?

simply constructive criticism about small matters, I have learned to listen to the emotion behind the comment, the question behind the question, which usually boils down to only one question: Do you care about me?

Someone once told me that early in its history, B'nai Brith grew to be one of the largest, if not the largest, member organization in Jewish life. What was the key to their success? They offered health insurance in an immigrant community desperately in need of it. Everyone joined. They correctly understood that they were a service organization and that listening to and understanding their community was their responsibility and mission. It is no different today.

> We are not Jewish to be Jewish; it is not an end in itself, however much we may think so. We are Jewish in order to live better, healthier, more purposeful lives, taking the values of our tradition into the marketplace and sharing them as widely as possible.

Schwarz concludes his lead essay with a charge to leadership. He is exactly right about that. In no way am I suggesting that listening carefully to the needs of our community means that the professionals don't have to do their best to respond to what they have heard and shape it into a cogent program of Jewish living. That's what we are paid to do. But the last thing I am worried about is whether Judaism is up to the task. In its texts and traditions, its history and values, Judaism has grown and thrived best when its leaders appreciate its elasticity and its boundaries, its wisdom and its commitment to what people need. We are not Jewish to be Jewish; it is not an end in itself, however much we may think so. We are Jewish in order to live better, healthier, more purposeful lives, taking the values of our tradition into the marketplace and sharing them as widely as possible. When our institutions enable us to do that well, when they teach us and listen to us, when they care about us and make it possible for us to care about others, they are better places and we are better people. And the future will take care of itself.

The Orthodox Difference

Rabbi Asher Lopatin

L et me be candid with anyone starting to read this chapter: I am
Orthodox—modern Orthodox, progressive Orthodox, open Orthodox, but when it comes down to it, I'm Orthodox. That makes my experience as a synagogue rabbi for seventeen years and my understanding of
the needs of the community different from those of a rabbi of any other
denomination. A lot of the changes that Sidney Schwarz talks about in his
lead essay do not apply to the Orthodox community. On the other hand,
Orthodoxy is, in fact, in a state of transition, but the issues we are facing
are different from the issues facing the other denominations of American
Jewish life.

My synagogue membership is not entirely Orthodox. Most of the
young families in my congregation—about a quarter of the 425 households—would not classify themselves as Orthodox and do not observe
kashrut, Shabbat, and family purity laws in accordance with Orthodox

Rabbi Asher Lopatin is the spiritual leader of Anshe Sholom B'nai Israel
Congregation, a modern Orthodox synagogue in Chicago. On a Rhodes
Scholarship, he completed an MPhil in medieval Arabic thought from Oxford
University and did doctoral work at Oxford on Islamic fundamentalist attitudes
toward Jews. He was ordained by Rabbi Ahron Soloveichik, Yeshivas Brisk, and
Yeshiva University. He is the incoming president of Yeshivat Chovevei Torah,
succeeding Rabbi Avi Weiss.

standards. Almost half of the singles in the congregation—another third of the synagogue—also would not call themselves Orthodox. Thus, even though my synagogue faces different challenges than most non-Orthodox synagogues, much of my membership lives in the same marketplace described in Schwarz's lead essay. The contrasts between my experience serving an Orthodox congregation and what is happening in the rest of the non-Orthodox Jewish community may therefore prove instructive.

Let me list five areas in which the Orthodox experience is unique and differs from the non-Orthodox Jewish world, and then I want to suggest some lessons that the rest of the Jewish community can derive from the Orthodox Jewish experience in America.

1. Israel

Throughout the Orthodox Jewish world, everyone loves Israel—whether this means the State of Israel as a modern political entity or the Land of Israel as an embodiment of Jewish tradition. The ultra-Orthodox, while not embracing "Zionism," are sometimes the most vociferous and right wing when it comes to issues of dialogue with Palestinians or other Arabs, territorial compromise, and human rights issues in Israel. Yet all Orthodox Jews embrace *aliyah*, from *haredi* to the most modern of Orthodox Jews. Some wrestle with the question of where they can make a greater contribution, and others agonize about leaving family behind in the United States, but everyone admires those who make *aliyah*, those who fight for Israel, and those who are building up the Jewish state. Even among the least Orthodox of my congregants, Israel is important and a trip to Israel is an important personal religious experience. In fact, Israel is where many of my least involved congregants find their connection to Judaism and Jewish practice.

I do find that for most of my younger congregants (half of them are in their twenties and thirties), the politics about Israel (e.g., the threat from Iran, or from Hamas, and so on) does not interest them as much as talking about Israel from a social and personal point of view. They love to talk about their Birthright or junior high school experiences and to friends who have gone through the Israeli army. What draws people to Israel seems to be the sense of ownership they acquire for their Jewish

K
**********1770   11/09/16 03:17PM

Jewish megatrends : charting the course of the American Jewi

anf
3330522834 7963   Fri

Expires 11/18/16

heritage combined with a powerful social experience. The group experience works a special magic over both teens and young adults. I have seen this same magic at work with adults attending AIPAC conferences with more than ten thousand participants as well as at J Street conferences.

2. Adjusting to Demographic Changes

There are many Orthodox congregations that are aging just as seriously as Conservative and Reform congregations. Some of this is just about location. Neighborhoods change. Yet the majority of Orthodox congregations are filled with children and young members every Shabbat. It is typical to find in Orthodox synagogues young adult services that are bursting at the seams and multiple children's services for different ages every Shabbat and holiday. I remember when Rabbi Kenny Brander was building up the Boca Raton Synagogue from eighty members to more than six hundred members—each youth group got its own siddur and curriculum. My own synagogue, only two-thirds the size, currently has five distinct youth *minyan* groups every Shabbat. But even more significant than Orthodox synagogues with good children's programming are the many other Orthodox synagogues that are bursting with kids and teens even though they don't have good programs. There are just a lot of young people who show up at Orthodox synagogues. Shabbat is a happening.

Significantly, healthy Orthodox congregations are often more flexible and quicker than their Reform and Conservative counterparts to move to a different neighborhood where there are younger people or where younger families feel they can live. Members of Orthodox synagogues tend to live closer to one another and to the synagogue, because most want to be able to walk to Shabbat services. In Chicago, healthy Orthodox synagogues are constantly moving to better buildings, slightly north or slightly west. They are not wedded to their buildings, perhaps because they tend to be smaller and reflect a relatively lower investment of dollars than Reform or Conservative synagogue buildings do. Also, healthy Orthodox congregations learn to reinvent themselves as welcoming, *kiruv* (outreach) congregations. Both my own synagogue in Chicago and the National Synagogue in Washington, D.C., are in neighborhoods that no one would have expected to be hospitable to a homogeneous, Orthodox congregation. Yet both congregations experienced dramatic growth when people of many different levels of observance suddenly found the synagogue right for them. In turn, the two synagogues helped stabilize the neighborhoods, which might otherwise have experienced a decline.

3. Switchers

The worst-kept secret in the Jewish world today is the fact that both the Reform and the Conservative movements are losing some of their best and brightest young people to Orthodox synagogues and communities. Many are graduates of the Ramah or NFTY camp systems or those movement's most intensive Jewish programs. If they want to retain the intensity and passion of Jewish practice that they experienced in those settings, they often can only find it in Orthodox synagogues.

Many Conservative synagogues have long had library *minyanim* for the more serious-minded daveners who don't want to be trapped in a weekly Bar or Bat Mitzvah service, but the challenge for Conservative synagogues is that their communities, as a whole, lack the critical mass necessary to have a genuine Shabbat or a holiday atmosphere. Orthodox synagogues—even those with a heavy contingent of non-Orthodox members—*feel* like Shabbat and *yom tov* (Jewish holidays). People linger and then go to each other's homes for lunch or dinner, or to picnics on the holiday, or on Shabbat walks. Partly due to the fact that so many members of Orthodox synagogues live within walking distance, it is easy and natural to create a communal culture in which members spend extended time with each other, either before or after religious services. It provides the kind of communal bonding that is so hard to find in American society. Many Conservative leaders have bemoaned the ruling of the Committee on Laws and Standards that allowed people to drive to and from shul. Whereas Conservative culture gave in to what seemed to be a reality of

> The worst-kept secret in the Jewish world today is the fact that both the Reform and the Conservative movements are losing some of their best and brightest young people to Orthodox synagogues and communities.

suburbia—that if people couldn't drive they would never come to shul because they lived too far from the synagogue—Orthodox culture decided not to compromise. The result: all over Orthodox communities in Scarsdale, Boca Raton, and Berkeley, California, people find small *minyanim* in a house just a few blocks away for Friday nights and sometimes Shabbat afternoons where they pray, and then they take the fifteen- to twenty-five-minute walk to shul on Shabbat morning.

Of course there are people who drive to Orthodox synagogues as well. However, the atmosphere is one of observance, of celebrating the whole day, of being in a community where the world feels different on a holiday or Shabbat. People can eat in each other's homes because most people keep kosher or are at least trained to bring in kosher deli when friends from the synagogue are coming over. In many modern and centrist Orthodox synagogues, the rabbi produces a detailed list of supervisions that are acceptable or not, of procedures required for washing vegetables to remove all the bugs, and of which foods, drinks, and liqueurs require a kosher sign and which do not. Does everybody in the community keep these standards? No. But everyone respects the communal kashrut standards that enable robust socializing, and there is trust that if you go to someone's home you will be able to eat whatever is served. These are among the key ingredients that help Orthodox communities remain vibrant and attractive to so many.

4. Orthodox Transition

I can only imagine what it felt like being Orthodox in the 1940s and '50s, when it appeared that Orthodox Judaism was disappearing—or being totally marginalized—while the Conservative and Reform movements were growing by leaps and bounds. But by the 1970s and '80s, with the Orthodox Upper West Side of New York as its flagship, Orthodoxy was cool again, and there was a feeling that it was growing faster than the other movements were. During the past decade, it is somewhat ironic for Orthodox Jews to hear about the demise of Conservative Judaism and the contraction even of Reform Judaism.

There is tension between the modern Orthodox and the ultra-Orthodox sectors of our community. Twenty years ago, the ultra-Orthodox got the Glatt Yacht shut down, and we, the modern Orthodox, got a scare. The Glatt Yacht was a strictly *glatt* kosher boat that took people around the New York Harbor and featured wonderful music and mixed dancing. The ultra-Orthodox got the modern Orthodox rabbis who supervised the Glatt Yacht to pull the kosher supervision because mixed dancing is generally prohibited by Orthodox authorities. The incident signaled the power of certain rabbinic authorities to constrain practices that might help make Orthodoxy attractive to a wider cross-section of Jews.

But non-Orthodox Jews tend to have an exaggerated assessment of the power of the ultra-Orthodox. By virtue of the extremism of the ultra-Orthodox, their actions garner a tremendous amount of press coverage, even in the mainstream media. The opposition of most of the ultra-Orthodox to Zionism for theological reasons has generated media interest for decades. Just a few years ago several ultra-Orthodox rabbis turned up in Tehran and posed for pictures with President Mahmoud Ahmadinejad, even as he was being reviled by the rest of the Jewish world as Israel's public enemy number one. A second example was a rally of some fifty thousand Orthodox Jews at New York's Citi Field (formerly Shea Stadium) in May 2012 protesting the Internet and the damage done to society by electronic devices. Clearly, this brand of Orthodoxy stands in stark contrast to the values and ideology of modern Orthodoxy.

If the rabbinic leadership of ultra-Orthodoxy had its way, modern Orthodoxy would not exist. If you are Orthodox and live in the great strongholds of modern Orthodoxy—Teaneck, New Jersey; Newton, Massachusetts; Skokie, Illinois; Pico-Robertson in Los Angeles, California; and the Baka neighborhood of Jerusalem—you will often be kvetching about how the ultra-Orthodox are trying to wrest Judaism away from those of us who are modern Orthodox. Nonetheless, after your kvetch, you can get into your SUV, go to the modern Orthodox class of your choosing, sip a latte from the kosher coffee shop around the corner, and listen to a recording of the Maccabeats sing about Rosh Hashanah and repentance (filmed at Yeshiva University).

Modern Orthodoxy has also recently benefited from two important infusions of intellectual support. In the 1990s it came from Edah: The Courage to Be Modern and Orthodox, which held numerous well-attended conferences (of course in New York) and published an influential halachic journal that helped create a learned response to attacks on modern Orthodoxy. Then, in 1999, Rabbi Avi Weiss founded a new rabbinical seminary called Yeshivat Chovevei Torah Rabbinical School (YCT). Rabbi Weiss is a religious progressive even as he remains politically conservative, and YCT was firmly committed to supporting a more open and modern approach to Orthodox Judaism in America. YCT challenged Yeshiva University's role as the primary training ground for American Orthodox rabbis. YCT's graduates have had no problem finding positions in the Jewish community, particularly in the world of Hillel, where openness to all expressions of Judaism is especially welcomed. YCT graduates will, for years to come, become outstanding spokespersons for modern, open Orthodoxy.

Clearly the strength of the ultra-Orthodox is their passion and the loyalty of their adherents. In contrast, the strength of modern Orthodoxy is its willingness to collaborate with other sectors of the Jewish world. One of the best examples of this commitment to pluralism took place some ten years ago. Rabbis from the Orthodox, Conservative, and Reform synagogues founded the Chicago Jewish Day School as a pluralistic, multidenominational, halachic, and inclusive school. It has grown from 7 students to 180 students, and there is a waiting list for the kindergarten. The school is roughly 40 percent from my Orthodox synagogue (not all of whom are Orthodox), 25 percent Conservative, and 35 percent Reform, Renewal, or those unaffiliated with a movement. The local Conservative day school in the suburbs has been shrinking considerably over the past ten years, and Chicago is not alone in the trend that has seen the growth of pluralistic, diverse schools and a contraction in homogeneous, non-Orthodox schools. So, if done right, pluralistic communities of prayer and learning are even more attractive today than they were in previous times.

Even as there are occasional episodes of the modern Orthodox being put on the defensive from more traditional elements, both within their own communities and from the outside, the triumphalism of the ultra-Orthodox is tempered by a sense that their insular world is coming to an end. The challenges to ultra-Orthodoxy are many: intermarriage (think

Clinton and Mezvinsky); the growing acceptance of gay lifestyles and gay marriage; the ubiquitous Internet, which easily penetrates the walls that the ultra-Orthodox have built around their communities; women in *tallitot* praying at the Kotel (Western Wall); women singing in the Israeli army. We will continue to see efforts by segments of the ultra-Orthodox world to combat these unwelcome incursions of modernity on their world, but a struggle against society and history is a hard one to win.

The most interesting amalgam of modernism and traditionalism in the Orthodox world is Chabad-Lubavitch, who are ultra-Orthodox in ideology and practice but quite liberal in how they work with any Jew they encounter. More than a decade after the Lubavitcher Rebbe passed away, Chabad is thriving, and they understand outreach and nonjudgmental behavior (if not philosophy) better than any other Orthodox or non-Orthodox group in America. People who feel uncomfortable in a Reform temple go to a Chabad House and feel totally at home. Chabad Houses differ from community to community, but they can be found in nearly every state in the United States

> What is being discovered is that with some good marketing and a little bit of chutzpah, traditional Judaism can be attractive to highly secularized American Jews.

and half the countries in the world. The most successful ones tailor their approach to what the local Jews are looking for: *B'nei Mitzvah* for families with kids, parties with booze for college students or recent graduates, spirituality or individualized learning for seekers. Some Chabad outreach rabbis pray in regular Orthodox synagogues or *minyanim*, and others start their own services; some keep a small house, and others build a big "shul"—frequently calling it "The Shul," which makes all the other existing congregations angry. Many parts of the Orthodox world have borrowed freely from this very successful playbook of Chabad. What is being discovered is that with some good marketing and a little bit of chutzpah, traditional Judaism can be attractive to highly secularized American Jews.

5. The High Cost of Orthodox Jewish Life

One challenge that middle-class Orthodox Jews are feeling more and talking about more than other Jews is the challenge of paying for day school tuition. It is hard to imagine, but with day school tuitions averaging $20,000 per year in many cities—and up to $30,000 a year in New York—a family either needs to be on significant tuition assistance, which is available, or earning a lot of money to afford to send two, three, four, or more kids to day school. In the ultra-Orthodox community, as in Catholic communities, day schools are cheaper, and they raise significant sums from donors to keep tuitions affordable. Some parents have decided to have fewer children than they would like in order to afford day school. Other parents—but not many—are opting for public schools supplemented by several hours a day of Judaic studies. One new trend that families are exploring is Hebrew charter schools, where Hebrew and Jewish history are offered as part of the curriculum, often supplemented by optional Judaic courses after school.

The Orthodox Union, along with other organizations, is working hard to tackle the expense of day school education. Some in the education community feel that it is an unaffordable model. A few schools have gone out of business. Many friends of mine have used unaffordable day schools as another good reason to make *aliyah*. In Israel even "private" religious schools are heavily subsidized by the government and cost a pittance compared to American day schools. Personally, my wife and I depend upon financial aid to enable us to send our four kids to the pluralistic day school in our neighborhood, which we were involved in founding. Some in New Jersey have attempted to create bargain-basement day schools, stripping away administrative positions and having bigger classes. Around the Shabbat table, in the *kiddush* club, and even in the back of the shul, Orthodox parents discuss, debate, and strategize about how to afford the kind of day school that will provide the intensive Jewish education that is expected in the Orthodox community.

Nevertheless, from the anecdotal and empirical evidence that I have gleaned over my seventeen years in the pulpit, it seems to me that Schwarz is correct in his counterculture theory that the high cost of being Jewish is not the real problem. I believe his arguments apply to the Orthodox day school world as well. If a school is good enough and special enough, people will come forward with money, with tuition aid, and parents will stretch enough to get their kids into the school. It does require self-assured parents to apply for financial aid and reveal their incomes, sometimes to committees made up of their peers. Paying day school tuition, even after financial aid, also requires giving up fancy vacations and perhaps that new kitchen. Yet day schools are subject to competitive consumer forces: is the day school so much better than suburban public schools that it is worth giving up the skiing trip this winter?

I have met parents who have gone in both directions. Some take their children out of expensive day school to go to a free suburban public school known for its outstanding education. Others make a sacrifice in lifestyle and register their child in a day school that better reflects their family values. On the other hand, when a day school deteriorates in quality—either real or perceived—parents look at public schools, especially ones that might have even more variety and opportunities for their children than day schools, as an attractive alternative. Over the next few decades we will hopefully see the better day schools thriving, attracting more donations, and successfully making the case to parents that day school for their children is well worth the sacrifice.

Beware of Complacency, Oh Ye Orthodox Jews!

Even as times are good for Orthodox Jews, it would be dangerous for the Orthodox world to become complacent. The fact that the Orthodox community has a higher percentage of first- and second-generation members than do the other movements may buffer the movement from some of the social and cultural trends that Schwarz identifies in his lead essay. Yet it may well be that the increased communal cohesiveness evident in the Orthodox world today is a temporary phenomenon.

Only time will tell whether Orthodox Jews can withstand the draw of an American culture that presents few, if any, barriers to the full participation of Jews. Consider the implications of a society in which the children of a recent president (Bill Clinton) and vice president (Al Gore) marry Jews. In my synagogue it is perfectly normal for Orthodox young adults to start dating non-Jews assuming, of course, that their partner will convert before getting married. Frequently, these converts—usually women—are the ones that bring their spouses back to a fully observant Orthodox life, but it is just as possible that these congregants may opt for an "easier" Conservative or Reform conversion. Now it is true that there are some couples in my synagogue, and many in non-Orthodox synagogues, where the non-Jewish spouse is even more committed than the Jewish spouse to raising their children as Jews. But these are uncharted waters, and I wonder whether any religious subculture can keep its unique identity in the face of an alluring and accepting American culture. Certainly the Amish have gone down this road, and the ultra-Orthodox seem prepared to do the same.

But most of the Orthodox Jews I know are not prepared to turn their back on the educational, professional, and cultural opportunities that America offers. As America becomes increasingly multicultural, there is less of a stigma to a person wearing a turban, a beard, or a *kipah* in the workplace. Ironically, by being accepting of observant Jews, American culture is both making it possible for Jews to be more explicitly observant *and* subtly seducing Jews into a powerful secular vortex. Who knows how many Orthodox Jews have the commitment necessary to remain observant Jews? How many will continue to take off all the holidays, leave early on Fridays so as not to work on Shabbat, and keep strictly kosher? Despite all the gains of feminism, women now understand that the "mommy track" will prevent them from keeping up with their male counterparts in the workplace. Might the realization that the "Ortho track" entails similar sacrifices start to impact the choices made by the next generation of Orthodox Jews?

Bowling Alone

Robert D. Putnam's book *Bowling Alone* argues that American culture is not very hospitable to the kind of community that I am describing here. He suggests that too many Americans simply want things "their way." It is true, as I have experienced in synagogue life, that some people do have a need for their own clique within the congregation. Every successful Orthodox synagogue has various niche groups: *kiddush* clubs where men sneak out during the Torah reading, haftarah, or rabbi's sermon (or all of the above) to drink a little and bond with each other; *hashkamah* (early morning) *minyanim* where men get to synagogue about thirty minutes earlier than the main service (sometimes more), daven really quickly so they are out almost two hours before the main service, and then kibitz with each other about whatever strikes their fancy; and learners' services, young adult services, or some other kind of specialized *minyanim*. In my synagogue, the *hashkamah minyan* wanted to meet only every other week; in other synagogues, it may be every week. Ideally, everyone shows up at the main *kiddush* and eats *cholent* together. And ideally there is some overlap between those who go to the different services or *kiddush* clubs.

It may be that the appeal of Orthodoxy is that it defies the trend that Putnam portrays in *Bowling Alone*. As Schwarz points out in his lead essay, if Americans are suffering from a breakdown in community and social capital, then religious communities may be the antidote. Whether it is the two hundred regulars who come to our main service or the twenty who go to the smaller *minyanim* that take place in our building on Shabbat, people want to pray together, to schmooze at *kiddush* together, and to celebrate Shabbat and holidays together. People want to fast together on the Ninth of Av, break their Yom Kippur fast together, stay up all night learning on Shavuot—together. Synagogues, prayer groups, and larger organizations such as Federations and JCCs have to find out how to provide people with opportunities for breakaway moments and for together moments. But as a recent study of Synagogue 3000 notes, it is all about relationships. People want relationships—real ones, not just virtual ones. People want to belong and to be together with other people—whether they are the same or different.

> If our institutions can be flexible and nimble and offer people opportunities to create relationships, high-quality activities, and a deep sense of community, then Jews will come.

One of the simplest activities we have at our synagogue is the Shabbat Afternoon Windy City Happy Hour. Congregants who say that they are from Anshe Sholom get a free scoop of ice cream at a local ice-cream shop. All the flavors are kosher, and no money is exchanged (the store bills the shul a dollar a scoop later), and people just hang out for an hour schmoozing—twentysomethings and thirtysomethings, singles and couples, kids and eighty-year-olds and everyone in between. For the incentive of one free scoop of ice cream some kids scooter on Shabbat from two miles away or more! But it's not the ice cream, of course. It is to be together with their friends and new friends—from Anshe Sholom and from the Conservative synagogue up the block. People will use any excuse when they feel that there is potential for building a relationship.

I'm optimistic. If our institutions can be flexible and nimble and offer people opportunities to create relationships, high-quality activities, and a deep sense of community, then Jews will come. As a committed Jewish pluralist, I am the first to acknowledge that there are wonderful programs and activities being offered by the growing range of non-Orthodox Jewish denominations and institutions that make Jewish life stronger. But it may well be that the non-Orthodox world could learn a thing or two about how to create sustainable and committed Jewish communities from the Orthodox world. In the end, the American Jewish community is only as strong as its weakest link.

Interreligious Collaboration

American Judaism and Religious Pluralism

Rabbi Or N. Rose

O ver the past decade, I have spent a significant part of my work as a rabbi engaged in interreligious educational and activist initiatives. I was motivated to do so because of both positive and negative experiences. On the one hand, I was raised in a vibrant Jewish home, rich with Jewish learning and ritual observance, in which my parents were also actively engaged in a variety of interreligious activities. These included hosting non-Jewish religious leaders at our Shabbat table, visiting Christian and Muslim houses of worship, and planning and participating in various public programs about religion. These experiences showed me that engagement with people from different religious traditions can help Jews deepen their Jewish

Rabbi Or N. Rose is director of the Center for Global Judaism at Hebrew College and codirector of the Center for Interreligious and Communal Leadership Education (CIRCLE), a joint venture of Hebrew College and Andover Newton Theological Seminary. He is the coeditor of *Jewish Mysticism and the Spiritual Life: Classical Texts, Contemporary Reflections; God in All Moments: Mystical and Practical Spiritual Wisdom from Hasidic Masters;* and *My Neighbor's Faith: Stories of Interreligious Encounter, Growth, and Transformation.*

identities, as well as learn about the richness of other spiritual paths, and can lead to collaborative social and environmental justice efforts.

On the other hand, I have been deeply disturbed by the ways in which religion has been used to foster or justify bigotry, hatred, and violence. We can turn on the TV or open a newspaper on any given day and read about the role of religion in situations of conflict around the globe. Spurred by the devastating events of 9/11 and its aftermath, I felt compelled, in the words of the writer Gustav Niebuhr, to participate in the quiet but growing "countertrend" of interreligious cooperation flourishing in the United States and elsewhere in the world.

In the past ten years, I have been blessed to meet and work with remarkable people from many religious traditions (including my own) who are dedicated to creating an alternative interreligious narrative to the antagonistic one we often see in the headlines. These individuals are working with children, youth, and adults on dialogue, study, service, and advocacy efforts large and small. Although these projects differ in many respects, what they share in common is that the people leading them are all committed to building religious alliances among religions that work to heal and transform the societies in which they live.

As a person whose interreligious work is focused largely in the United States, I greatly appreciate that our society is, relatively speaking, highly tolerant of religious differences. This is a remarkable feat given that the United States is both the most religious civilization in the Western world and the most religiously diverse country on the planet.[1] The ability of people from different religious communities to coexist peacefully (by and large) in this society should not be taken for granted, given the state of affairs elsewhere in the world. I, like others in this burgeoning field of interreligious education and activism, want to help strengthen the existing culture of religious tolerance and maximize the civic and spiritual benefits that can emerge through intentional interreligious engagement. This proactive approach to religious diversity is what Diana Eck of Harvard University calls "religious pluralism." It involves a deliberate and "energetic engagement with diversity," with the goal of creating mutually enriching relationships in which commonalities and differences can be explored honestly and productively.[2]

In the context of this volume, which is dedicated to exploring possibilities for the spiritual and cultural renewal of Jewish life in the United States, I wish to share why American Jews should be involved in interreligious initiatives and how these efforts can both strengthen our community and contribute to the health and vitality of our country and the world. It is worth noting here that many Jews do not identify as religious per se, but as primarily secular or cultural—one way in which Judaism differs from other religious groups or "faith" traditions. But whatever our relationships to belief and practice, Jews across the religious-secular spectrum have much to contribute to and gain from interreligious collaboration in a society that is highly religious, is religiously and culturally diverse, and has a growing secular population.[3]

Meeting the Stranger, Overcoming Prejudice

Some readers may be surprised to learn that according to a recent national survey, Jews are now one of the "best liked" religious groups in the country.[4] After suffering from centuries of prejudice and oppression—including periods of pronounced anti-Semitism in America—we have gained widespread acceptance and respect in this country. Our newfound status does not mean that anti-Semitism is a thing of the past, but it does mean that we have a particular responsibility to work to ensure that other minority groups can enjoy the same freedom and security that we experience in this society. The ancient biblical injunction to welcome the stranger has taken on new meaning for American Jews, who are now very much at home in the United States.

This work involves several interrelated elements, including personal and communal reflection, study, relationship building, and advocacy. Of these different forms of activity, I want to stress the importance of the interaction of people across religious lines, because I have repeatedly witnessed how such encounters have helped people address their prejudices, led them to learn more about other religions, and take action with and in support of others. Recent social scientific research indicates that "religious bridging" through personal contact is the most significant factor in fostering peaceful and cooperative relations among religious and secular people in our country.[5] Imam Abdullah Antepli, Muslim chaplain at Duke University, speaks personally and candidly about the importance of meeting people from other religious traditions: "I consider myself a recovering anti-Semite. I use the term 'recovering' because I am still working to cleanse myself of the hateful images of Jews I was taught as a child in my native Turkey. Meeting with Jews and hearing their stories has been the most powerful antidote to this virus." The work of untying the knots of prejudice and working with others to create an inclusive, educated, and just society requires an ongoing effort like other forms of *avodah* (holy service).

Imam Antepli's comments should also remind us that while anti-Semitism has decreased significantly in our society, it has not disappeared—and it remains a much stronger force in other places in the world. Although it is unwise to assume an overly defensive posture, this issue still clearly requires our attention, particularly in a global age when people are encountering one another in new ways and when events in one part of the world can rapidly impact life in another. In such an environment, it is crucial that we work with partners from other communities to help educate people and create opportunities for meaningful dialogue.

One particular challenge that we face as contemporary Jews is how best to engage with Muslims in respectful and productive ways. Given the ongoing Israeli-Palestinian and wider Arab-Israeli conflict, the events of 9/11, and other acts of terror carried out by Muslim extremists, it is important that we resist the

> Jews across the religious-secular spectrum have much to contribute to and gain from interreligious collaboration in a society that is highly religious, is religiously and culturally diverse, and has a growing secular population.

temptation to discriminate against (or stand by idly as others mistreat) the countless number of innocent Muslims—or those mistakenly identified as Muslim or Arab—in our society and elsewhere in the world. The anti-Islamic behavior that emerged around the building of Park51 in lower Manhattan (the so-called "Ground Zero Mosque") and elsewhere in the country in recent years is shameful and should serve as a reminder of the need for us to actively work to overcome such prejudice. We have an obligation to help ensure that the United States is hospitable to Muslims, who continue to struggle for acceptance in this country.[6] This work is obviously made more difficult because of tensions over Israel/Palestine and other historical and political issues. Nonetheless, our ethical teachings, our history, and our standing as a powerful minority group in America make it imperative that we help the Muslim community feel welcome in our shared society.

Over the past fifty years the Jewish community has done significant work to heal relations with Christians—both Catholics and Protestants. Although there is certainly more work to be done in this area, we can apply relevant lessons—positive and negative—from these efforts at reconciliation while applying new and different strategies to create more harmonious relations with Muslims. This work requires more people from *both* communities to learn about the other (beyond the headlines), to engage together in study, dialogue, and action for the common good—sharing our stories, listening to the questions and concerns of the other, and building trust. We must also commit ourselves to address the prejudice that exists within each of our communities and in the broader society.

Sharing Our Wisdom with Others

Interreligious collaboration is important not only as a strategy to counter prejudice but also because it offers us the opportunity to share with non-Jews some of the richness of our heritage. We have unique spiritual and cultural contributions to offer our dialogue partners. The goal is not to convert the world to Judaism but to contribute to a vibrant dialogue among people from different communities, knowing that none of us has all of the answers to life's great challenges and that we need to help one another in our pursuit of meaning and goodness.

One powerful example of this type of interreligious sharing was the request made by His Holiness the Dalai Lama in 1989 (just prior to receiving the Nobel Peace Prize) to meet with American Jewish leaders to discuss the issue of exile. This great spiritual master has been leading his community of exiled Tibetan Buddhists for the past several decades from their adopted home in Dharamsala, India. As a relative newcomer to this work, the Dalai Lama wanted to learn how the Jewish people survived as a distinctive community in exile for so many centuries. At his invitation, a delegation of religious and secular Jewish leaders met with the renowned Buddhist leader to share their insights about the importance of text study, home-based rituals, and the creation of local synagogues and community centers. In inviting these Jewish representatives to teach him about Jewish life and thought, the Dalai Lama modeled for us what it means to be, as Sidney Schwarz calls it, a true seeker of *chochmah* (wisdom), even when it requires exploration far from home. In so doing, the Dalai Lama—one of the most celebrated religious figures on the planet—also demonstrated that *anavah* (humility) is a key element of wisdom.[7]

Moving from the global to the local and from the communal to the personal, in his brief essay, "What the Rabbi Taught the Reverend about the Baby Jesus,"[8] Rev. Gregory Mobley of Andover Newton Theological School describes how the Jewish mystical concept of *tikkun olam*, in which human beings play a decisive role in bringing healing and wholeness to both God and the cosmos, became an important theological resource for him and how a conversation about it with a rabbinic colleague helped him understand his own tradition in a new way. Mobley was deeply moved by the kabbalistic model of "dynamic mutual interdependence of Creator and creation." It had both "a poetry and a physics" that rang true for him. In reflecting on this subject with Rabbi Rim Meirowitz, Mobley said that he regretted that this theme of God's need for human sacred action in the work of redemption was not a part of Christian theological discourse as he knew it. "What about the baby Jesus?" asked Rabbi Meirowitz. A light went on for Mobley. He immediately thought about all of the textual and artistic images of the infant Christ and the many people—starting with Mary and Joseph—who nurtured and protected him.

> The goal is not to convert the world to Judaism but to contribute to a vibrant dialogue among people from different communities, knowing that none of us has all of the answers to life's great challenges and that we need to help one another in our pursuit of meaning and goodness.

What I find particularly interesting about this story is that Mobley did not simply learn something valuable about Judaism; his encounter with Meirowitz helped him uncover a new layer of meaning in his own sacred texts. As these men both know, the teachings of *tikkun olam* and the baby Jesus are not the same, and neither was suggesting that these ideas were interchangeable. Because Judaism and Christianity share important textual and cultural roots and a long and complex history of interaction with each other, they have points of theological commonality and significant differences. This is further complicated by the fact that both are multi-vocal traditions with significant differences of opinion within each community.[9] Mobley and Meirowitz were seeking not to create a simplistic theological equation but to help each other deepen their particular understandings of God through an honest and generous personal exchange.

Of course, in order to serve as teachers of Judaism in the wider world, we have to develop the knowledge and skills to communicate effectively with people outside of our community. While I am not suggesting that interreligious activities should be limited to experts, it does require us to delve into our religious and cultural legacies and to reflect on how we have come to make various Jewish choices. In our effort to overcome our ignorance of other religions, we cannot neglect our own heritage. While each of us needs to be wary of speaking on behalf of Judaism or the Jewish people, we need to be able to contextualize our ideas and experiences and offer our dialogue partners a rich and nuanced portrait of our tradition. This is one of the responsibilities we bear in engaging in interreligious initiatives.

I recently co-taught a course on Jewish, Christian, Muslim, and Unitarian Universalist approaches to revelation for adult learners from local houses of worship. Each week a scholar from a different tradition offered a forty-five-minute presentation, and then the participants broke into small groups for text study and moderated conversation. At the end of one session, a Jewish woman in her late fifties came over to me and explained how embarrassed she was by her ignorance of the subject. She also said that she was the first woman in her family to go to college and the first female doctor in her town. "I know something about doing my homework," said the woman, "and I have a lot of Jewish homework to do." This was but one of many conversations I have had with Jewish participants in interreligious programs who have successful careers and extensive secular education, but who lack a basic Jewish education. Interreligious activities can serve as powerful contexts for us to explore our Jewish identities and clarify our values and commitments, but this is difficult to do if one has only limited knowledge of Judaism and involvement in Jewish life. Jewish educators involved in interreligious activities have both a responsibility and an opportunity to help Jewish participants think about how to continue learning about their own tradition and how they might deepen their own Jewish engagement.

Learning from Others

Interreligious learning is a two-way street; we must all play the roles of both teacher and student, and we have much to learn from other religions and from practitioners of these traditions. In my own development, I know how profoundly I have been shaped by the teachings—in words and deeds—of such luminaries as Mahatma Gandhi, Dorothy Day, Dr. Martin Luther King Jr., Mother Theresa, and the Dalai Lama. Nor is it just from the work of these exceptional public figures that I have learned, but also from my interactions with many other less celebrated individuals of a variety of faith traditions.

In the winters of 2005 and 2006 I had the privilege of serving as a scholar-in-residence for the American Jewish World Service's Rabbinical Student Delegation to El Salvador (once co-leading with Rabbi Sid Schwarz). This weeklong service-learning trip included twenty-five students from various Jewish seminaries across the country. Our experience included living and volunteering in a small village, meeting with local families for meals and with activists for discussion of various social and environmental justice issues. We also

> These priests served as important teachers to me in my growth as a Jew and as a rabbi, stimulating me to look more closely at my own beliefs, religious resources, and vocational responsibilities.

spent time as a group studying Jewish sources related to the on-the-ground work we were doing and creating a short-term, pluralistic Jewish community, including celebrating a Shabbat together. We were reminded that intra-Jewish dialogue can be just as challenging as interreligious efforts!

Among the elements of the trip that I found most powerful was meeting with several older Catholic priests who spent their entire careers ministering to poor and disenfranchised people in this turbulent, developing country. There were three aspects of the work of these religious leaders that particularly moved me. First, while I had engaged in various social justice efforts as a young Jewish leader and worked with some very courageous mentors and allies, I had never spent time with a circle of clergy who had put their lives on the line in the name of justice. Second, inspired by the teachings of liberation theology, these men committed themselves to the poor and marginalized in remarkable ways. Their reading of the biblical prophets and of Jesus as champions of the poor and the oppressed convinced them that in a country so ravaged by economic injustice, they had to stand, unequivocally, with the poor. This meant that they not only ministered to and advocated for the disadvantaged—providing a "voice for the voiceless"—but also sought to empower the poor to be leaders in the movement for justice, believing that the people most deeply affected by injustice had spiritual and practical insights that were essential to solving sociopolitical issues.

Finally, I was inspired by the ways in which the men spoke about their personal relationships with Jesus. Throughout our conversations they referred to Jesus in a variety of ways, including as a friend or companion, who walked with them through their struggles, providing them with spiritual support in their hour of need. As a theologically oriented person, I found it inspiring to contemplate the image of God (or a dimension of God) as friend. Although various metaphors are used in the Jewish tradition to describe God's immanence, friendship is not a common one. More frequent are images of God as parent—father and mother—teacher, redeemer, and even lover. So while "friend" was not a part of my theological vocabulary (nor has it become a central metaphor for me since), hearing these men use this term with such passion and commitment challenged me to think more deeply about my own experience and understanding of God.

Meeting with the priests in El Salvador helped me strengthen my commitment to social justice and, specifically, to issues of global economic justice. It also challenged me to consider both the Jewish sources that inform my activism and God's role in this part of my life. This experience also led me to ask how I, as a rabbi, could help others in my community engage in the sacred work of *tzedek* (justice) as Jews and as global citizens. Although there were obviously elements of their theological and political worldviews that I could not share, these priests served as important teachers to me in my growth as a Jew and as a rabbi, stimulating me to look more closely at my own beliefs, religious resources, and vocational responsibilities.

Precedents and New Horizons

Although the vision of religious pluralism I present here is a distinctly contemporary phenomenon, it is important to recall that people of different religious traditions have been learning from one another for centuries, adopting and adapting teachings they found compelling from various "external" sources. Consider the figure of Maimonides—one of the greatest minds in Jewish history—and the fascinating ways in which he sought to integrate elements of Greek and Muslim thought into his writings. His ideas then influenced Jewish, Christian, and Muslim intellectuals of his generation and of generations to follow. Today, we have much more freedom than in medieval times to openly discuss the multiple sources that shape our Jewish identities, without (for the most part) the fear of being branded heretics by fellow Jews. Nor do we need to defend the legitimacy of our religious tradition against hostile Christian or Muslim authorities. In the United States in particular, we can engage in interreligious dialogue as full and equal members of society.

Although interreligious programming is not yet a widespread phenomenon in the Jewish community, there are a range of opportunities for youth and adults. Some of these programs are organized by local or national Jewish institutions (in partnership with other religious groups) and others by interreligious (or interfaith) entities. Here are four examples of noteworthy initiatives:

- Interfaith Youth Core (IFYC): Founded in 2001 by Eboo Patel and others, IFYC works primarily with colleges and universities to engage students in interfaith service-learning projects. It also works with administrators to assess the religious and spiritual climate on their respective campuses. IFYC is one of the largest and most influential interfaith organizations in the country. In 2010, IFYC helped launch the President's Interfaith and Community Service Campus Challenge, sponsored by the White House, with support from the Department of Education and the Corporation for National and Community Service. Now entering its second year, this program has galvanized more than 250 colleges and universities to create year-long service-learning projects.

- Greater Boson Interfaith Organization (GBIO): This thriving social justice organization was created by a group of forty-five clergy and community leaders in 1996. GBIO works to train and organize the communities of Greater Boston across religious, racial, ethnic, class, and neighborhood lines for the public good. In 2005, GBIO played a lead role in expanding access to quality affordable health care to approximately 430,000 people across the Commonwealth. Several local rabbis, Jewish community relations professionals, and lay leaders played key roles in the creation and growth of this faith-based community organization. There are similar interreligious organizations in other cities across the country; like GBIO, many of them are affiliated with the national Industrial Areas Foundation. Additionally, Rabbi Jonah Pesner, a leader in GBIO for several years, went on to create the national Just Congregations initiative of the Reform movement (in partnership with the Jewish Funds for Justice—now part of Bend the Arc—and with major support from the Nathan Cummings Foundation), working on community organizing efforts with more than seventy-five synagogues in more than twenty states since 2006.

- NewGround—A Muslim-Jewish Partnership for Change: Originally developed through a partnership of the Progressive

Jewish Alliance (now part of Bend the Arc) and the Muslim Public Affairs Council in Los Angeles (2006), NewGround has since become an independent organization (2011) with offices at Los Angeles City Hall provided by the City Human Relations Commission. NewGround offers a broad range of activities—dialogue training, arts programs, text study, and fellowships—for middle and high school students, young professionals, and adult learners. It has partnered with more than thirty Muslim and Jewish organizations to reach a broad cross-section of the two communities in the Los Angeles area.

- CIRCLE: Founded in 2008 with a generous grant from the Henry Luce Foundation, the Center for Interreligious and Communal Leadership Education is a joint venture of Andover Newton Theological School (mainline Protestant) and Hebrew College, immediate neighbors in Newton, Massachusetts. CIRCLE works both locally and nationally to help prepare religious leaders for service in a multireligious society. This includes jointly taught academic courses by Jewish and Christian faculty; regional and national conferences for academics, clergy, and graduate students; and the publication of the scholarly *Journal of Interreligious Dialogue and State of Formation* for emerging religious and ethical leaders. CIRCLE is part of a growing national movement that includes many other seminaries, divinity schools, and related institutions incorporating interreligious training into their curricula. In addition to Hebrew College, several other Jewish seminaries house interfaith centers or sponsor interreligious programs for professionals and laity.

These models of interreligious cooperation raise important questions about pedagogy. In any of the wide variety of interreligious programs being offered in American houses of worship, on college campuses, online, and in other settings, educators and clergy need to think carefully about goals, implementation strategies, and measures of success. What are the best practices and best settings for engaging people in meaningful interreligious programs—text study, service learning, political advocacy, and so on? Which of these activities might be best suited for a particular life stage? When might conversations between two faith communities be preferable to convening many faiths in dialogue? These and other salient questions must be considered for our work to be effective. It is also crucial that we conduct research to map Jewish engagement in interreligious initiatives and the impact of this work on participants and our community as a whole.

The Need for Honesty

It is important to note that the work of interreligious cooperation requires that we carefully investigate those teachings in our respective traditions that can help us develop a pluralistic agenda as well as examine those teachings that present the religious "other" in negative and prejudicial ways. We need to explore the historical contexts in which these sources were framed, the theological and ethical assumptions of our forebears, and the way we use these texts in our communities today. Each of our faith traditions includes texts that should make us acutely uncomfortable. Some can be explained in ways that stretch our ethical and religious imagination; others call for refutation. This honest reassessment of our sacred texts is a necessary component of interreligious cooperation if we seek to engage in a process of healing and growth, both within our own faith and across religious boundaries.

Another challenge of interreligious engagement is learning how to name the commonalities *and* differences that we discover in our interactions with people from other religious groups. Judaism is a tradition that views *machloket*, disagreement, as a key part of religious and ethical life. From the ancient sages Hillel and Shammai to modern Jewish discourse, we value passionate debate carried out for the betterment of our community and the world beyond us. We need to bring this same sensibility to our interreligious encounters. Frankly, there are too many interreligious programs where people make superficial pronouncements about our commonalities without allowing for any discussion of difference. Not wanting to rock the boat, participants avoid questioning or challenging one another on any substantive issues. The result is a polite exchange, lacking in depth. We would do well to remember that the Hebrew word *kadosh*, which is commonly translated as "sacred," also carries with it the connotation of "separate." We need to take seriously the particularity of our individual and communal ideals and practices and bring these proudly to our interreligious encounters. Learning both how to open ourselves to the wisdom of others and how to disagree with them productively is at the heart of this work.

Finally, the American Jewish community now includes many Jewish families that are interreligious in their very makeup due to intermarriage. This is a fact of contemporary Jewish life, especially in liberal religious communities, and all signs indicate that this trend will continue. This makes it even more important for rabbis, educators, and communal leaders to learn about other religious traditions and communities. Interfaith families need help making informed religious choices and navigating the complexities of interfaith marital and family life, and Jewish professionals cannot do this effectively unless they are knowledgeable about the other faiths present in these mixed households. Additionally, as people shaping the culture of Jewish institutions, our leaders must help educate their communities about other religions and carefully consider how their synagogues, schools, and community centers approach such complicated issues as dual religious belonging and other questions of inclusion and boundaries.

Religion continues to play a pivotal role in our world and in American life. The Jewish community can and should be a catalyst in promoting peaceful and constructive relations among different religious groups. To do so, we must consciously engage in educational and activist initiatives that promote a commitment to both the particular and the universal, to the health and vitality of one's own religious community and to the welfare of others. We need Jewish participants in interreligious programs to serve as dedicated and knowledgeable bridge builders who are committed to moving between these realms. The vision of religious pluralism outlined in these pages is demanding and ambitious to be sure, but one that holds great promise for the American Jewish community and the increasingly diverse range of people we are encountering daily in this country and throughout the world.

On Tribes, Food, and Community

Nigel Savage

Sidney Schwarz's lead essay provides a compelling framework to reflect on the state of the American Jewish community and its prospects for the future. I want to comment on his distinction between tribal and covenantal Jews and then use the Jewish food movement as a framework to talk about the kinds of trends that need to be encouraged and supported if we want the Jewish community to continue to grow and thrive.

The Tribal and the Covenantal

Even more than his proposed solutions—which I broadly endorse—I want to focus on the distinction that Schwarz makes between tribal Jews and covenantal Jews. This distinction is real, and at the sociological level, it accurately describes the growing gap between what are increasingly two very different camps.

Nigel Savage, originally from Manchester, England, founded Hazon in 2000. Since then Hazon has grown to be a nationally significant organization, both renewing Jewish life in profound ways and working to create a healthier and more sustainable world for all. Before founding Hazon, Savage was a professional fund manager in London. He has a master's degree in history from Georgetown University and has learned at Pardes, Yakar, and Hebrew University. Savage is infamous in the United Kingdom for his cameo appearance in the cult Anglo-Jewish comic movie *Leon the Pig Farmer*. He is also believed to be the first English Jew to have cycled across South Dakota on a recumbent bike.

Tribal Jews are actively committed to Israel and to a sense of Jewish kinship. They are comfortable exhibiting Jewish distinctiveness, are in favor of giving overwhelmingly to Jewish causes, and have a profound sense of Jewish history (including a strong awareness of the trauma of Jewish persecution through the ages). In the other camp are the Jews that Schwarz calls "covenantal." These Jews are universalists. They are uncomfortable arguing for Jewish distinctiveness. Tribal Jews understand the importance of marrying someone who is Jewish even if they don't always find someone Jewish to marry. Covenantal Jews, by contrast, don't really understand the argument for in-marriage. Tribal Jews are committed to giving to Jewish causes; if covenantal Jews give to Jewish causes, it is because doing so advances universal goals.

One of the reasons that Schwarz's distinction is so useful is that it lets us drill down to a question that he doesn't explicitly pose. Can these two camps be reconciled? And if so, how might we do it?

In principle I believe that the answer to the first question is "yes," and I think that the Jewish food movement gives us some insight into how we might do it. But I am not unaware that the gap is significant and widening. If we don't find ways to bridge this gap, the American Jewish community will become weaker and more fragmented.

It is important to note that from the 1950s to the early 1980s the tribal and covenantal camps were not so polarized. The Orthodox world was smaller than it is now and less confident in itself; the non-Orthodox world was larger, and within it, there still existed a more tribal sense of Jewish identity. The recent (2012) survey of New York Jewry makes clear that the gap is widening. Increasingly the fault line in Jewish life is not between the Orthodox and non-Orthodox; rather, the fault line runs down the middle of Orthodoxy. On one side are the liberal Orthodox, Conservative, Reform, Reconstructionist, Renewal, and unaffiliated Jews. Despite denominational, doctrinal, and theological differences, these groups share many values. They socialize with each other. Their children attend the same schools and universities. They tend to vote for the Democratic Party. And on the other side is the right-wing of modern Orthodoxy, plus the *haredi* world. This group is inherently tribal, less committed to engagement in American society, and much more Republican. In the non-Orthodox Jewish world, even those with strong Jewish educational backgrounds are far less inclined to think and behave along tribal lines.

It is important to remind ourselves that Jewish tradition is both tribal and covenantal. I celebrate the particular in Jewish tradition just as I celebrate the universal. I am part of the Jewish people, and I am part of a religious culture that has bequeathed to the world certain values that are now widely embraced.

Many people would think of me as being on the covenantal side of Schwarz's divide. This would be especially true of *haredi* Jews, who would see me as liberal and universalist in many ways—which indeed I am. But as a liberal Jew, I'm uncomfortable with the sometimes selective ways that liberal Jews read Jewish texts. Many liberal Jews don't like to dwell on the particular in Jewish life. Yet the Jewish heritage is tribal. We are a people, a family, indeed a tribe. Lord Sacks, the chief rabbi of the British Orthodox community, has consistently, and I believe rightly, argued that the Jewish understanding is that universal goals are best accomplished through particular channels.

Schwarz asked the contributors to this volume to reflect on personal influences in relation to the questions he is raising, and that reminded me of a wonderful, modest Dutch philanthropist whom I met as a Jewish student leader in the 1980s. He made an argument then that helps us navigate this challenge today. His name was Oscar Van Leer, and it was his family that created the Van Leer Institute in Jerusalem. I was among a group of European Jewish students whom he hosted at two conferences in his hometown of Amsterdam on the topic of preference and prejudice. He asked us, "What's the difference between the two?" Thinking about this difference is critical to untangling some of the issues around tribalism and covenantalism.

Let's agree, for starters, that it's wrong to be prejudiced against someone—for being black, gay, Jewish, Palestinian, Muslim, wearing a *streimel* or a *hijab*—whatever. But does being against prejudice mean that one cannot express a preference for something or someone? Too few liberal American Jews and too few young Americans in general have thought through this distinction. Because they are against prejudice, they naturally recoil at preference. But the two are not the same.

Human life has always been about positive preferences. If a member of my family were to be killed, that would feel different to me than the killing of a human being in a remote part of the world—even though I believe, as Jewish tradition teaches, that every human being is made *b'tzelem Elohim*, in the image of God. I recently agreed to be a guarantor for the student loans of my cousin's son, who is applying to university in the United States. Why did I agree to do this? I hardly know my cousin's son. He grew up in Manchester long after I left there. The answer is "family." The bonds of family establish preferences in my life. Without being prejudiced against people who are not members of my family, I hold this preference that gives my cousin license to ask for the favor. In turn, my acceptance of preference as healthy and natural led me to respond positively to my cousin.

We can all agree that family ties allow preference and that the same preference can't be shown to all seven billion inhabitants of the planet—I can guarantee only so many college loans. But where do the thirteen million Jewish people stand, between my family on the one side and the entire human family on the other?

Hazon sponsors a Cross-USA bike ride. For its participants, one of the most remarkable and unexpected aspects of the ride is experiencing the nature of Jewish community in small-town America. In Spokane our riders were hosted and fed by members of the Jewish community—people we had never met until they opened their homes to us. This has been true in every community we've passed through. In River Hills, Wisconsin, my host—a remarkable eighty-year-old named Richard Goldberg, whom I met for the first time as I rode into the temple there—drove me home, drove me back to the synagogue, then got up at 5:30 the next morning to get me back in time for our early-morning departure. We told all of our hosts that night that we'd send our van around to pick up our riders, because it was so early in the morning. Not one of them accepted our offer; they all got up themselves at the crack of dawn to get our riders back to the synagogue by 6:00 a.m. In Aberdeen, South Dakota, we were hosted by members of this tiny Jewish community. In Madison, Wisconsin, over Shabbat, members of the Reform community fed us for Friday night dinner, the Conservative shul hosted us for Shabbat lunch, and the Chabad House gave us *se'udah shlishit*, the third meal.

I want to be clear: we could ask, and occasionally have asked, non-Jewish communities to host us. The goals of our ride are universal—covenantal, in Schwarz's terminology. We are riding to support sustainable food systems for all. But the connections along the way are mostly tribal. We are not prejudiced against the non-Jewish communities that we pass through, nor they against us. But the ties of preference that bind us to other members of the Jewish community are tangible and substantial. It is precisely these ties that are less well understood and less well accepted, especially among our young people and most especially in the big coastal cities of the United States.

So prejudice is wrong, but preference is not. For me, such preferences lie at the heart of my Jewishness and, indeed, of who I am. My tribal preference for the Jewish people influences me in ways small and large. I visit Israel. I read Jewish and Israeli newspapers. I feel shame when Jews act badly. I'm interested in Jewish history, Jewish thought, Jewish art, Jewish culture. In all of these spheres my preference is just that—a preference, but not a prejudice. I drink wines from around the world, but I have a preference for Israeli wines. "Jewishness" is my existential/cultural/familial/religious "language" for understanding the world. I don't believe that it's necessarily better than Catholicism or being a Quaker or a Buddhist or a Hindu. But it is who I am; it explains how my values are formed. It gets to the heart of how I see and interact with the world.

> Just as covenantal Jews need to grapple with tribalism and the expression of positive preferences, so too must tribal Jews reengage the universal that lies within Jewish tradition.

Just as covenantal Jews need to grapple with tribalism and the expression of positive preferences, so too must tribal Jews reengage the universal that lies within Jewish tradition. Our tribal history gave us a preference for settling legal issues within our community and not reaching out to local non-Jewish governments. That was legitimate in the Middle Ages, when surrounded by anti-Semitism. It is not appropriate, though, in relation to sexual abuse in the twenty-first century. Orthodox leaders need to make clear that tribalism doesn't excuse protecting one of their own in a situation where a child may have been sexually molested. The radical heart of Jewish tradition is the idea expressed at the very beginning of the Torah that every human being is made *b'tzelem Elohim* (in the image of God)—black, brown, straight, gay, rich, poor, Jewish or Sikh, Israeli or Palestinian. This provides some insight into the persecution of Jews throughout history. Totalitarian and despotic regimes have had to take on the Jews—from the ancient Romans to the Nazis, Stalin, and radical Islam today. If you believe that some people are better than others and that others are inferior, then sooner or later you'll run up against Jewish people who, from the core of our tradition, reject such an idea.

So I think Schwarz's distinction is right, and it's important that we address it. The gap between tribal and covenantal Jews has become a critical fault line in the Jewish community. In the coming years we need to create learning contexts whose central focus is bridging the gap between these two camps. We need to work in liberal Jewish settings to make the case for preference in Jewish life. In turn, leaders in Orthodox and right-wing communities would do well to reemphasize the universal underpinnings of Jewish teachings to counter some of the prejudicial attitudes that are becoming increasingly evident in their ranks. If we succeed, we may be able to reweave the threads of connection that enable us to think of ourselves as a single Jewish community, as a single Jewish people. If we fail, then intra-Jewish misunderstandings and even enmity will increase. It is hard to imagine a community thriving when it is so badly polarized.

The Jewish Food Movement

The Jewish food movement, which has been nurtured and catalyzed by Hazon, is a wonderful example of a healthy integration between the tribal and the covenantal in Jewish life. Within the Jewish food movement we can see what is possible and what is necessary as we build the Jewish future. As I think about the Jewish food movement—including organizations such as Adamah, Eden Village, Jewish Farm School, Urban Adamah, and others—I realize that a significant part of our success and impact is due to the fact that we have been both tribal and covenantal. Even as we have been rooted explicitly in a Jewish framework, the wider goals that we promote are powerfully covenantal. And for the twenty-somethings in programs such as Adamah and Urban Adamah and the twenty- and thirtysomethings who teach at Teva and at Eden Village, there is a daily interweaving, in powerful ways, of Schwarz's four central motifs: wisdom, justice, community, and sacred purpose. Let me give two examples of what I mean by this.

Hazon's network of Community-Supported Agriculture programs (CSAs) is both tribal and covenantal. We're now the largest faith-based CSA network in North America. On the one hand, we're pursuing a covenantal goal—putting Jewish purchasing power behind local organic farms (whose farmers, overwhelmingly, are not Jewish). On the other hand, we're using the CSAs to do serious Jewish educational work and to redefine what it means to be a Jewish community. We not only come together to celebrate Shabbat on Friday nights; we also get together on Wednesday nights to pick up our vegetables or meet the farmer.

The same is true with the Adamah program at the Isabella Freedman Jewish Retreat Center in Falls Village, Connecticut. The Adamahniks are from a wide range of Jewish backgrounds. They are driven by a desire to learn farming and to connect to land. Yet the fact that the participants are living, working, and studying together during the three-month program is inherently tribal. Adamahniks are Jewish. The land they work is Jewish-owned land. Their days start with *Shacharit*, the Jewish morning liturgy. Their week is built around Shabbat. The rhythm of their fellowship year intercalates the seasonality of place with the cadences of Jewish time. Both Adamah and its more recent offshoot, Urban Adamah in Berkeley, California, involve *chochmah* (learning farming skills and learning Jewishly), *tzedek* (doing justly in the world), *kedushah* (sanctifying time together on a daily and weekly basis), and *kehillah* (living in a profound sense of intentional community—living, learning, working, and eating together).

I recently visited Pushing the Envelope Farm in Geneva, Illinois. Different members of the Margulies family, who run the farm, learned with and from the Teva Learning Alliance, Hazon, and Adamah. In their hometown of Geneva, they started their own educational farm. They do extraordinary programming—teaching kids and adults about wild edibles, farming, working with animals, cheese making, composting, and brewing.

They also provide members of the local Jewish community with a range of programming that connects to Jewish life: text study, making Chanukah candles, a Tu b'Shvat seder, building a sukkah, learning the Jewish agricultural laws. Pushing the Envelope Farm serves both the local non-Jewish community in Geneva and the wider Jewish community stretching to Chicago.

The Jewish food movement is informed by and brings to life something I learned from the late Reb Shlomo Carlebach, something that has become Hazon's theme quote. He said, *"The Torah is a commentary on the world, and the world is a commentary on the Torah."* I take this to be both prescriptive and descriptive. The explosion of interest in Jewish farming around the country is evidence of what happens when we allow our ancient tradition to engage with one of the most vital and complex issues of our time. How should a person eat? That is both a Jewish question and a twenty-first-century question. It is a question that connects to kashrut, to Jewish food traditions, and to *b'rachot*, the way we offer thanks and gratitude for our food. It is also about teenage obesity and land use and organics and the treatment of animals and many other issues. What the Jewish food movement demonstrates is that when we apply the Jewish tradition to one of the central issues of our time, Jewish tradition comes alive in powerful and unexpected ways.

> What the Jewish food movement demonstrates is that when we apply the Jewish tradition to one of the central issues of our time, Jewish tradition comes alive in powerful and unexpected ways.

Yet what has happened thus far is just a prelude. We need to develop a master's degree program in Jewish food education. The Adamah and Urban Adamah programs could and should be scaled up tenfold. Every Jewish child in this country should have the chance to participate in a Teva program. We need to change the food that is served in Jewish institutions. We need to put *sh'mitah* (biblical laws that govern practice during the sabbatical year) firmly on the agenda of the Jewish world so that we ask in all our institutions: What does it mean to eat Jewishly? What does it mean to keep kosher in the twenty-first century? How might we use the coming *sh'mitah* years—starting in September 2014 and September 2021—as a frame to reimagine our understanding of what it means to live healthy and sustainable lives?

Liberal institutions need to readdress traditional categories of kashrut. All of our institutions need to ask: Can or should we serve soda in two-liter bottles given that we know that sugar is bad for us and the bottles will take a thousand years to biodegrade? Where does our food come from? Do we grow any of it ourselves? How are the workers treated? How were the animals treated? How do we respond to hunger in our communities? Do we compost any of our food? How might our new, emerging ethic related to land and food make common purpose and connect us with other faith communities?

A growing number of local communities, in many cases helped and encouraged by Hazon, are now asking these questions. At Ekar in Denver and Kayam in Baltimore, new Jewish urban food-growing programs are revitalizing Jewish life in incredible ways. The Leichtag Foundation is trying to do something similar in San Diego. Young Jewish farmers and activists are organizing in Amherst, Boston, Seattle, and Toronto, to mention only a few cities. Over the coming years we need to ask the big questions about food, ethics, ecology, and sustainability more thoroughly and more systematically, and we need to have the courage and discipline to follow through on our answers to those questions. If we do so, we will increasingly find that, at one and the same time, we are renewing Jewish life, strengthening our institutions, and being a blessing to the wider community.

Toward Intentional Community

I founded Hazon in late 1999 in a burst of idealism. Hazon was intended to be inspirational and empowering, and to a very considerable extent, it continues to embody that ethos. But the political world in which Hazon was formed ended on 9/11, and the economic one ended with Bernie Madoff and the fall of Lehman Brothers. Idealism does not preclude truth telling, so it must be said: Much of organized Jewish life is, if anything, in even worse shape than many people think. A high proportion of the Jewish communal leaders whom I see are overworked, exhausted, demoralized. Rabbis face challenges in all directions. Donors are skeptical and/or burned out. We have too many well-staffed, pretty buildings with too few people stepping through the door.

The fundamental assumptions of contemporary American life—individualism, hyper-choice, rapid mobility—stand in deep tension with core Jewish values. Ours is not a society that easily engages notions of obligation and responsibility. William Rapfogel, the leader of New York's Metropolitan Council on Jewish Poverty, recently wrote a sharply worded op-ed in which he disparaged Jews who cared more for sexy new Jewish projects than for the seemingly boring and prosaic task of helping local Jews in need. In 1917 the great American journalist Walter Lippman wrote, "We have changed the world more quickly than we know how to change ourselves." What was true then is even more true a century later. As Schwarz writes, the institutions of twentieth-century Jewish life are failing, and the new institutions of twenty-first-century life are as yet too small and too weak to replace them.

> Much of organized Jewish life is, if anything, in even worse shape than many people think.... We have too many well-staffed, pretty buildings with too few Jews stepping through the door.

As the number of Jews engaged in intensive Jewish life decreases, it becomes ever more important to create immersive Jewish experiences. Temporary retreats of all sorts are vital to Jewish life. I include in this category Birthright trips; summer camps; multiday Limmud conferences; Hazon's bike rides and food conferences; service missions, both in the United States and in the developing world; synagogue retreats at conference centers all around the country; and family trips to Israel. The list could go on. The common denominator in all of the above-mentioned experiences is the creation of a real Jewish community over the course of several days (or more) in which the participants are in close proximity to each other and can experience a sense of Jewish space and Jewish time.

If there is one area ripe for investment by Jewish Federations and foundations, it should be in these types of Jewish immersive experiences. We should do the research to create a baseline of how many people participate in multi-day immersive Jewish experiences each year, and then figure out how to raise that number by at least 10 percent each year for the next decade. This would include supporting retreat centers, providing matching funds to institutions to do their own retreats (e.g., synagogues and day schools, for their own populations), and providing support staff and materials to help organizations run high-quality retreat programs of all sorts.

Retreats are vital precisely because Jewish life is not simply or not only a "religion" in the Protestant sense. We are a maximalist tradition, interested not only in religion, narrowly defined, but also in food, time, music, history, culture, family, ethics, politics, land, art, literature, and so on. Jewish life was lived in an immersive 360-degree Jewish bubble until modernity at the end of the eighteenth century exploded it. Temporary immersive experiences are vital to enabling the organic elements of Jewish life to be put back together.

> We are a maximalist tradition, interested not only in religion, narrowly defined, but also in food, time, music, history, culture, family, ethics, politics, land, art, literature, and so on.

If the Jewish community made this kind of serious commitment to temporary immersive experiences, then it would set the stage for an idea that Schwarz mentions briefly in his essay—intentional communities. Under the radar of organized Jewish life, interest in intentional communities is starting to grow. The phrase may not be familiar to most people, but an intentional community is one in which people who share a certain practice or set of commitments choose to live together. (The best-known intentional community in recent Jewish history is the kibbutz.) Schwarz suggests that intentional community might well be an antidote to the spiritual poverty of contemporary American life. I strongly agree.

The past few years have seen the development of four key experiments in short-term intentional community in American Jewish life: the Adamah and Urban Adamah programs, in which roughly a dozen Jewish twentysomethings live together for three months at a time and study farming and Jewish life; the Avodah program, in which roughly a dozen

Jewish twentysomethings live together for an academic year, working on social justice programs in an urban setting; and the Moishe Houses, an international network of more than sixty urban Jewish houses for twenty-somethings whose rent is subsidized and who, in turn, host a range of Jewish programming. Moishe House estimates that the self-directed programs in their houses touched fifty thousand people last year.

All of these programs focus on postcollege, premarriage, young adults. It is a niche, but a critical one. These young adults have left the orbit of their families and college communities. A person who spends an extended time in such an intentional community is changed forever. The intensity of the Jewish experience that they have in such settings is significant. Many of these young adults will become Jewish leaders in the decades to come. Some of them may be at the forefront of new models of Jewish living that we cannot today even envision. If in coming decades we can foster new, Jewishly inspired intentional communities, then we will plant the seeds for creating sustainable, multifaceted Jewish communities in urban, suburban, and rural environments. I believe that such communities will embody the four core values that Schwarz believes are keys to a vibrant Jewish future—*chochmah*, *tzedek*, *kehillah*, and *kedushah*—wisdom, justice, community, and sacred purpose—and they will do so in ways that will expand our understanding of what it means to be Jewish in the twenty-first century.

> Temporary immersive experiences are vital to enabling the organic elements of Jewish life to be put back together.

Spreading the Gospel

There is one further challenge that we should think about if we're serious about renewing Jewish life in the future—the challenge of evangelizing for Jewish tradition in public space. One of the reasons that the tension between the tribal and the universal in Jewish life isn't addressed directly is because most Jews lack confidence in their knowledge of Jewish tradition to talk about it in the public square. But the faith communities that have grown the most rapidly in this country in recent years are those that have the self-confidence to go into public space and proclaim: You should

185

be a Mormon! You should be a Christian! If we learn anything from living in a free-enterprise society, it is that if you have a good product, the key to growth is strong marketing.

The word "evangelism" sits uneasily with Jewish people. We have been at the wrong end of it for too many centuries. Too many of our people have died at the hands of those who believed that their God and their religion was the only true way. But we entered the world as a proselytizing religion. Maimonides includes converting people to Judaism as one of the 613 *mitzvot*. I think that it is time for the Jewish community to start to invite people, publicly, to become Jewish.

> One of the reasons that the tension between the tribal and the universal in Jewish life isn't addressed directly is because most Jews lack confidence in their knowledge of Jewish tradition to talk about it in the public square.

This need not mean—and should not mean—evangelizing in inappropriate ways. It doesn't mean saying, "If you don't become Jewish, you're condemned to hell and damnation." But we should say something like the following: *"If you are happy in the religion that you grew up with, we hope that you will grow and flourish in it and be a good Christian, a good Muslim, a good citizen. But if you find that it doesn't speak to you, if you have always had Jewish friends or you've been interested in Jewish tradition, or if you would simply like to learn more about what it means to be Jewish, then we warmly invite you to start to learn with us. And here's a website in which you can find rabbis of every Jewish denomination who would be willing to welcome you, learn with you, and perhaps help you on the first steps of your Jewish journey...."*

Doing something like this shouldn't be owned by a single stream of Jewish life. To be most effective, it needs to be trans-denominational. And there will be one significant side effect of such a process: in making the case for Jewish tradition in public space—focused on non-Jews—we will also make Jewish tradition accessible to the most universal of our own young people, who are more comfortable in the public spaces of American life than in the Jewish spaces that are the focus of so much Jewish programming.

At the root of this lies a core tension: either we believe in Jewish tradition or we do not. For me, Jewish tradition is wise, humane, ancient, contemporary, vibrant, ethical, challenging, and exciting. The Torah really is a commentary on the world—and the world is a commentary on the Torah. I reject the false distinction between the universal and the particular. I believe that this country would be a better country and the world a better world if there were more Jews in it.

Standing up for Jewish tradition in public space—actively inviting people to consider becoming Jewish—would be a blessing to the many non-Jews who are interested in becoming Jewish. It would also be the clearest possible signal to our own young people that we are proud of being Jewish. May our ancient tree of life grow and flourish for generations to come.

The Federation System

Loving Humanity and the Jewish People

Barry Shrage

Even at the beginning of the twenty-first century, at a time when "umbrella charities" seem to be losing influence, local Federations and our national Federation system still embody the hopes and dreams of many Jews. To the extent that we fulfill these hopes and dreams and position ourselves at the leading edge of Jewish history, we will attract the best and brightest leadership, raise needed resources, and receive the blessing of future generations. If we don't, we will disappear from history, and future generations will curse our failure. But we will not be easily replaced. As even our most ardent critics might say, "If the Federation didn't exist, we would have to invent it."

I don't think they say this because they admire our process or the way we spend the community's money or the amount of money we raise.

Barry Shrage has served as president of the Combined Jewish Philanthropies of Greater Boston since 1987 and has worked in the Jewish community since graduating from the Boston University School of Social Work in 1970. His passion for Jewish education and strengthening Jewish identity has been at the heart of his work throughout his professional career.

They do not necessarily believe that the Federation per se is required, but they do yearn for leadership, vision, purpose, unity, opportunity, and hope at a time that seems, for many caring Jews, to be filled with both enormous danger and unprecedented opportunity. On the one hand, we continue to face the possibility of massive assimilation at home and physical annihilation in Israel. On the other hand, we have an unprecedented opportunity to help ensure that Israel remains a prosperous and creative nation, secure in its own land while also taking a leadership role in an international renaissance of Jewish civilization. This civilization, inclusive of culture, learning, spirituality, and caring, will help the Jewish people become a beacon of justice for all humankind.

The Federation is not primarily a fundraising organization. It is an organization that has the power to mobilize enormous financial, intellectual, and human resources in the service of the Jewish people and Jewish meaning. To serve the Jewish people in a time of rapid change, great opportunity, and newly emerging danger requires a clear vision of the Jewish future, the capacity to quickly mobilize community energy and resources, and the ability to change as circumstances require without losing sight of the future that we are trying to build.

> We are seeking to create a Federation that is focused on change and on a compelling vision of a Jewish future characterized by purpose and spiritual grandeur.

Many Federations seem to be looking backward to the 1960s and '70s, the golden age of the Federation movement, when financial support for Israel and "sacred survival" became "the civil religion of American Jewry." All too often the pressure to raise more money than the previous year using some vague appeal to Jewish peoplehood obscures the very real challenges of the present as well as the opportunities of the future.

In Boston, we are trying a different approach. We are seeking to create a Federation that is focused on change and on a compelling vision of a Jewish future characterized by purpose and spiritual grandeur. We have developed ideas, found partners, secured significantly increased funding, and seen some success flow from our efforts. Attitudes are changing. Jewish education and Jewish learning are viewed with greater seriousness

189

among the community's elites and throughout our community. Nearly 60 percent of interfaith families are choosing to raise their children as Jews in Boston, compared to around 30 percent in most other cities. More Jews are engaged in serious Jewish learning. Congregations are vibrant. Money is being raised for new program initiatives at home and for our partner communities overseas. Change seems possible. There is room for optimism and hope, and both are required if we are to succeed. But if we are to succeed, we must be able to communicate a vision of a meaningful Jewish life, and we must believe deeply in our work and in the value of Jewish life. And we are not alone. Other Federations are developing their own models with the potential to change the future.

The value added of the Jewish Federation movement in the twenty-first century lies in its ability to help generate such visions and then find the human and material resources to make these dreams come true, for the sake of our children and grandchildren and for the sake of the Jewish future.

The Millennials: Tribal, Covenantal, and Communal

All of this seems entirely consistent with Sidney Schwarz's proposals. I find myself in general agreement with Schwarz on goals and the dreams we share for the Jewish future. But I believe that Schwarz's megatrends distort reality, and even if his predictions are more accurate than I think they are, I am not prepared to allow those trends to determine our communal destiny. If the next generation turns out to be insular and "tribal," our community needs to cry out for justice for all humankind. If the next generation turns out to be largely "covenantal," we need to teach love of the Jewish people. If the future belongs to the Internet, we need to create space for face-to-face communities of caring and love. If the next generation is utterly uninterested in Jewish learning, we need to prioritize making Jewish learning compelling and meaningful and as "viral" as Birthright is.

In my experience, the radical differentiation of "covenantal" and "tribal" Jews that Schwarz describes is inaccurate and represents a stereotype of young American Jews that serves some organizational and ideological agendas at the expense of a far more nuanced and rapidly changing picture of a generation. Jewish millennials are certainly different from my generation (actually, as a child of the sixties, I think we were far more "covenantal"!), but they are complex and defy easy categorization. They are universal *and* particular; tribal *and* covenantal; interested in culture and art and music *and* rabid sports fans; deeply committed to volunteerism *and* deeply committed to success in their own careers and to material success; concerned about world hunger *and* aficionados of gourmet food. Some may love Moishe House and progressive politics, but some don't care much for the current president, and some don't care much for politics at all. A small number may be deeply concerned about the plight of Palestinians, but others are far more concerned with Israel's security and the world's hypocrisy.[1] I'm afraid that many barely know that Israel exists. And of course, like each generation, their politics may well change over time. More significantly, Birthright Israel has already made a measurable impact on the next generation's connection to Israel, with Birthright participants 46 percent more likely to feel "very close" to Israel than non-participants (those who applied but weren't able to go due to lack of space).

> In my experience, young adults respect adults who actually believe in something and offer compelling beliefs. An older generation that crafts its beliefs based on market research of the next generation isn't worth following.

Moreover, I'm not sure that communal strategy should be based on market research or what any expert thinks the next generation is looking for. If we believe that Israel's survival or well-being depends on our political support or, for that matter, constructive criticism of Israel's government, we are ethically bound to argue our position. In my experience, young adults respect adults who actually believe in something and offer compelling beliefs. An older generation that crafts its beliefs based on market research of the next generation isn't worth following.

I would certainly be wary of having our communal policy shaped by assumptions made about young Jews becoming increasingly "distant" from Judaism, Israel, and organized Jewish life because Israel is now a "badly tarnished brand" due to its alleged oppression of Palestinians. Peter Beinart has gotten a lot of media play for this argument, and Schwarz seems to be convinced of it as well. Yet Beinart now concedes that for most young American Jews, "distancing" is caused by alienation from Judaism itself due to poor Jewish (and particularly the lack of widespread day school) education rather than Israel's "bad" action.[2] Yet many demographers, Leonard Saxe of Brandeis University most prominent among them, now believe that "distancing" is exaggerated, and some assert that the next generation will be closer to Israel (thanks in part to Birthright) than the last. Moreover, the most powerful voice for distancing, Steven M. Cohen, believes that distancing is related not to the perception of Israel's behavior but rather to the effects of widespread intermarriage and the failure of Jewish education among America's Jews.[3]

Nor am I convinced that young Jews are lining up to identify as covenantal Jews. While many young Jews will say that being Jewish only requires them to "be good people," it is unclear what this really means to them or how their stated interest in volunteer service or social justice is embedded in their Jewishness. In fact, according to a 2010–11 study by the Corporation for National and Community Service, between 2008 and 2010 the U.S. average national volunteer rate for millennials was 21.4 percent per year, the lowest of any other age group. Generation X (aged twenty-nine to forty-five) had the highest volunteer rate at 29.2 percent, followed by baby boomers (aged forty-six to sixty-four) at 28.8 percent for the same period.[4] It has also been suggested that the apparent interest in volunteering may simply be an artifact of the desire of high school students to build their resumes and the fact that increasing numbers of high schools make service a requirement for graduation. Let me be clear: it is our goal to strengthen the covenantal commitment of the next generation, but that need not happen at the expense of our "tribal" commitments.

Interestingly, many of those Jews most committed to "universal" and "covenantal" values are also committed to encouraging full cultural, religious, national, and linguistic pride and cultural rights for every minority. Schwarz seems to believe that these commitments don't extend to their own—the Jewish people. In my experience, this is not generally the case. A trip to Israel often reveals for them the beauty, meaning, and importance of their own cultural, religious, national, and spiritual heritage.

In fact, the alienation of young American Jews from Jewish identity and Jewish institutions is not a mystery. American Jewry is largely a fourth-generation community living in freedom. Sociologists have long predicted the complete assimilation of such communities. Schwarz gets it right when he observes that "for more than a century, American Jewish identity has been driven more by ethnic affinity and a concern for survival than it has by faith and religious observance." But ethnicity's importance as the tie that binds American Jews to Judaism really has developed in two distinct phases and may well be entering a third. In the first era, ethnicity was rooted in the Jewish neighborhoods and *landsmanschaften* (social/cultural clubs for immigrants who came from the same village in Europe) groups. Israel became the civil religion of American Jewry in the second era, only after the Six-Day War (1967), which had a profound impact on Jewish identity here, in the former Soviet Union, and throughout the world. In fact, it's not unusual to hear a person who came of age during this time say something like, "Until our victory in the Six Day War, I never held my head up high as a Jew." As such, 1967 brought American Jews fully into the American cultural phenomenon of assertive group identity (e.g., blacks, women, Hispanics). Israel's unexpected victory against all odds restored pride to the American Jewish community and slowed for a time the powerful slide toward complete assimilation.

It is fair to critique the Federation movement for its failure to use the development of an electrifying new ethnic Jewish identity to build something deeper and even more powerful. By 1990 a national population study revealed that levels of assimilation were far worse than any of us could have imagined. It wasn't an overemphasis on ethnicity that was driving away a generation of young Jews. It was a lack of decent Jewish education, the absence of authentic spirituality, the lack of a serious encounter with peoplehood (something more than ethnicity), and a failure of imagination on the part of synagogues and Federations to rethink their respective programs and message. Even the American Jewish community's emphasis on love of Israel was (and to an alarming extent still is) rooted in fundraising pitches, the "empty generosity" that Rabbi Abraham Joshua Heschel was already warning Federation leaders about at the General Assembly of the Council of Jewish Federations in 1966.[5] The

193

result was that by 1990 many young American Jews were connected neither to Jewish life nor to Israel in any serious way.

The Third Era of American Jewish Identity

The third era of Jewish identity can and must be radically different. Jewish identity in the third era must be based on *ahavat Yisrael* (love of Israel and of the Jewish people), but it needs to be filled with the kind of content that Schwarz sets forth in his essay—*chochmah*/wisdom, *tzedek*/justice, *kehillah*/community, and *kedushah*/sacred purpose. In Boston we have used a comparable set of values: *Torah*/learning and wisdom, *tzedek*/justice, and *chesed*/loving-kindness, which build strong face-to-face communities out of which *kedushah*/holiness may ultimately grow. Federations can and must play a crucial role in helping communities engage in the core values of Jewish living.

This agenda incorporates a strong dose of tribal identity without apology. Rejection of our tribal identity would be a betrayal of the generations that came before us who fought against all the temptations of assimilation and withstood all manner of persecution and discrimination. Not only is a "tribal-free" Judaism inconceivable, but it is also not necessary to attract the next generation of Jews. Judaism can and must be deeply connected to the Jewish people and to Israel, and it must be filled with spiritual meaning, learning, and a commitment to social justice. This is Jewish peoplehood with a mission.[6]

At the Boston Federation, our commitment to promoting lives of *Torah*, *tzedek*, and *chesed* is backed by millions of dollars invested in programs supporting formal and informal Jewish education and by a clearly stated vision for our future: adult learning, outreach to

> Not only is a "tribal-free" Judaism inconceivable, but it is also not necessary to attract the next generation of Jews. Judaism can and must be deeply connected to the Jewish people and to Israel, and it must be filled with spiritual meaning, learning, and a commitment to social justice. This is Jewish peoplehood with a mission.

interfaith families, social justice, and community organizing (mostly synagogue based) in the context of love of the Jewish people and love of Israel. But this commitment and this investment are not based on market research or on our perception that any one of these will attract the next generation of Jews. Rather, they are based on our belief that all these are at the heart of a meaningful Jewish life that we believe in and that reflects the life that God (or Jewish history) mandated for us. We view social justice not as an outreach technique but rather as something that lies at the heart of the Jewish enterprise, along with learning, community, and peoplehood.

What we have learned over the past decade is that the more we focus on raising money as our core objective, the fewer dollars we will raise. Yet the more we focus on our vision and the programs that will make our vision real, the more money we will raise and the more we will truly become central to the lives of the Jews who live in our community. If a Federation cannot articulate a compelling mission for Jewish life, it will fail. Our experience with the Federation in Boston provides evidence of a bold new path that may provide important new alternatives to the Federation movement. Interestingly enough, the particulars parallel much of Schwarz's prescription for the American Jewish future:

- We have vastly increased our commitment to formal and informal Jewish education, investing tens of millions of dollars in partnership with local family foundations and national foundation partners, like the Avi Chai and the Jim Joseph Foundations, in day school education, Jewish education for children with disabilities, intensive Jewish summer camping, travel to Israel, and the complete redesign of after-school Jewish education. We have built new day schools, dramatically increased their quality, and developed creative approaches to the high cost of day school education. We have also offered incentives (with our synagogue partners and funding from the Foundation for Jewish Camp) and significantly increased the number of families choosing intensive Jewish summer camping for their children.

- Beyond individual programs, we have sought to change the zeitgeist of our community though a multimillion dollar investment in adult learning and universal adult Jewish literacy. Through programs like Me'ah and Ikkarim and in partnership with Boston-area synagogues, we have helped drive Jewish learning viral, making it a much sought-after experience for thousands of Jewish families. Expanding Jewish adult education is key to the overall goal of building broad communal support for Jewish education. Only a community filled with adults who love Jewish learning and who find meaning for their own lives in Jewish knowledge will create great institutions of Jewish learning for their children and grandchildren. Only a community that sees the literary beauty of the Bible as clearly as it sees the beauty in Shakespeare will raise a generation of Jews who are Jewishly literate as well as masters of Western civilization and culture.

- We have made congregations into full partners in our effort to build real community and strengthen Jewish identity and commitment. Congregations already educate most of our community's children, and they can do much more. They can become real "face to face" communities and, in Isa Aron's words, "congregations of learners" and the central transmitter of culture and learning for us and for our children. By filling our congregations with sophisticated and comprehensive adult education, we can change the norms of Jewish life and the attitudes we convey to our children. The process of learning together itself creates community. For the Jewish people, learning can be an intimate act of self-discovery that strengthens the ties that bind us together.

- In conjunction with our Jewish Community Relations Council (JCRC) and several partner family foundations, we have worked to make our synagogue communities into "communities of justice." In partnership with the Union for Reform Judaism's Just Congregations project and the Jewish Organizing Initiative (recently named JOIN for Justice), we have made volunteer service and targeted social justice initiatives into an integral part of the program of many synagogues. Several years ago our efforts bore fruit when the JCRC joined with a coalition of local synagogues to play a major role in forging Massachusetts's comprehensive health care law. As with adult learning, our congregations can inspire a commitment to social justice, just as engagement in social justice itself creates community.

- We have made young adults a high priority. In conjunction with Birthright and local Hillels, we created IACT (Inspired, Active, Committed, Transformed) to ensure real follow-up for every Birthright returnee so that the full potential of the experience can be realized. Full-time IACT coordinators (paid for in full by our Federation) recruit students, travel with them to Israel, and then interview and engage them on their return, providing intensive Birthright follow-up to thousands of Jews on twelve local campuses. We also invest $700,000 a year to vastly increase post-campus young adult programs in partnership with local family foundations, PresenTense, and organizations like Moishe House.

- We have invested heavily in outreach to special populations, including interfaith households, gay and lesbian Jews, and people with disabilities. At least a third of Jewish children are already being raised in interfaith households, and our work with interfaith families seems to be making a difference. According to a 1995 population study of Boston's Jewish community, 60 percent of children being raised in interfaith households are being raised as Jews, and most of their families belong to synagogues.[7] While demographers are still contesting the meaning of these comparisons, 60 percent is nearly twice as high as most other community surveys report. We are thus engaging thousands of non-Jewish spouses and children of interfaith marriages in Jewish life and Jewish community. An intermarriage rate approaching 50 percent itself constitutes a megatrend that will have a massive impact on our Jewish future. Our work in Boston and the work of emerging

> organizations like InterfaithFamily.com and the Jewish Out-
> reach Institute show that Federations can and must engage this
> critical population.

- We have built a new fundraising model for our Federation that
  augments the traditional unrestricted campaign with restricted
  gifts from donor and foundation partners aimed at our highest
  strategic priorities. The value added of the Federation lies in its
  ability to create powerful networks of donors, agencies, foundations, and synagogues linked to great dreams and opportunities. It is this new model and the strength of these partnerships
  that have provided the resources for our new initiatives and
  our increased investments in creating a community of meaning and purpose.

The Most Powerful Megatrend: The Impact of Birthright Israel on Jewish Identity in America

One cannot talk about megatrends in the American Jewish community without taking account of what has been called "Generation Birthright." Boston is not alone in seeing the early fruits of one of the most ambitious Jewish philanthropic undertakings of the past one hundred years. I believe that the Taglit-Birthright Israel experience will dramatically change the nature of the next generation of American Jews.

There is something magical about Israel. Something transforma-tional. There is something about a first Israel visit that has the power to touch Jewish souls and strengthen Jewish identity as nothing else can. Birthright's power to build Jewish solidarity among Jews of every kind and from every part of the world has emerged with surprising power. Birthright takes full advantage of the magic of a first trip to Israel to cre-ate a unique cultural island for its young Jewish participants. Through touring, effective informal education, a *mifgash* (face-to-face encounter) with young Israeli soldiers, and just plain fun, Birthright gives young Jews a real sense of what it means to be part of the Jewish people and part of Jewish history.

Even beyond Israel's raw spiritual power, there is something about sharing a new experience with your entire generation that enables you to transcend past experience and see yourself and your generation in a new and special way (as was the case with the "transformational" sixties generation). The power of Birthright is therefore not just in individual stories of lives changed and Jewish connections made. It is in the power of an experience that has had a serious impact on three hundred thousand young Jews and that touches thirty thousand to forty thousand more every year. This may well represent close to *half* of the entire generation over time! Because it touches so many lives, it has the power to reshape the story of a generation and change the very zeitgeist within which Jewish life exists and changes. It is a "tipping point" experience for an entire generation, a moment of revolutionary change, though this new reality may not yet be clear to some observers.

Many of the young adult participants on Birthright have little previous connection to Judaism or to Israel. Some of them may have had a Bar or Bat Mitzvah, but many did not. Many come from interfaith households. This is a profile that is ripe for a wholesale abandonment of tribal Jewish identity, much as Schwarz predicts in his lead essay. Yet we already have data from several cohorts of Birthright participants, and it shows that young people who might have been resistant to a Jewish message for any one of a dozen reasons come back open and eager to learn more about Jewish life and community. In fact, I believe that Birthright Israel creates the ultimate response to those who suggest that Israel is the source of distancing for young American Jews. Ironically, it is now Israel (through Birthright Israel) that is the source of a great returning to Jewish life for the next generation.

We need to acknowledge that Birthright has the power to change the face of the next generation of American Jewry in ways that can lead to a more vibrant Jewish future than we might have ever dared imagine. When one young adult goes to Israel, one life is changed forever. When a thousand go, an entire community may be changed. But when three hundred thousand go, an entire generation can be changed forever, and who knows how many leaders and contributors, scholars and defenders of Israel, Jewish fathers and Jewish mothers, Jewish children and grandchildren, and perhaps even Jewish prophets three hundred thousand changed lives can produce? It can change the future.

From Jewish Continuity to Jewish Renaissance

Birthright has given the Jewish community a second chance to engage a generation that may have experienced Judaism and peoplehood as empty and meaningless or as ethnocentric and racist. If Birthright helps make participants more open to Jewish experiences, then it is the responsibility of the Federation movement to turn that openness into full engagement. We have started to do this in Boston through Federation-funded full-time follow-up staff on twelve of our most populous campuses. We have also dedicated new funding for second trips to Israel, interesting volunteer and internship opportunities, and a grants program for innovative programs in partnership with PresenTense, an Israel-based organization that encourages social entrepreneurship among young adults. But we still have a long way to go. Unfortunately, the broader American Jewish community and many Federations have barely begun to address the challenge of converting the Birthright experience into something deeper and more durable.

> Faith and optimism are in short supply these days, but if we are to succeed, we must believe deeply in our work and provide answers when our children ask us why they should choose Judaism.

Faith and optimism are in short supply these days, but if we are to succeed, we must believe deeply in our work and provide answers when our children ask us why they should choose Judaism. We have good reason to believe in our work, in our people, in our culture, in our values, and in ourselves. Federations can and must play a critical role in securing our future and answering our children's most important questions.

The Passover Haggadah has the wicked son ask, "What is this service to you?" How shall we answer the challenging question? Here is my humble attempt at a few responses:

- In a time that lacks vision and prophecy and that yearns for meaning, we are carrying an ancient faith in an ancient God so that our children and grandchildren will have spiritual options to fill their lives with light and joy.

- In a time of greed and selfishness, we are part of an old—a very old—tradition of caring for strangers—love of the poor and oppressed—and responsibility for widows and orphans, the elderly and handicapped.
- In a time of forgetfulness, we are part of the oldest living chain of learning and literature in the world, inheritors of an ancient and hauntingly beautiful culture.
- In a time of anomie and loneliness, we are part of an international network of Jewish caring and peoplehood that will welcome us to communities from Jerusalem to Buenos Aires to Dnepropetrovsk with real love and affection.
- In a time of rootlessness and alienation, we are connecting to a thirty-five-hundred-year-old history and a future of infinite possibilities.
- In a time of religious intolerance, murder, and terror, we represent a faith that recognizes (in the words of Rabbi Jonathan Sacks) the "dignity of difference." Our faith may be particular in its spiritual core, but it is universal in its concern for the oppressed of all humankind.

These, I think, are principles worth working for. They are the kind of principles that make Jewish life worth living. And these are visions and goals worthy of the Federation movement for the twenty-first century.

Jewish Education

From Continuity to Meaning

Dr. Jonathan S. Woocher

In his lead essay, Sidney Schwarz makes a powerful case that the frameworks, both institutional and ideological, that characterized twentieth-century American Jewish life no longer work for growing numbers of twenty-first-century Jews (especially younger ones). He argues that to reverse the visible trends of disaffiliation with mainstream Jewish communal organizations like synagogues, JCCs, and Federations, the Jewish community needs to seize the opportunities that flow from recognizing what *does* appeal to younger Jews: Jewish wisdom, the opportunity to make a difference in society and the world, meaningful connections and relationships, and spirituality, sanctity, and purpose in their lives—all delivered at the highest levels of quality.

Twentieth-Century Jewish Education's Successes ... and Its Failures

This is a road map that can serve Jewish education well as it moves through a period of dynamic change. Despite a public image that is often

Dr. Jonathan S. Woocher is chief ideas officer of JESNA and heads its Lippman Kanfer Institute: An Action-Oriented Think Tank for Innovation in Jewish Learning and Engagement. He served for twenty years as JESNA's president and chief executive officer before assuming his current position in 2007. Dr. Woocher is the author of *Sacred Survival: The Civil Religion of American Jews* and many articles on Jewish education, community, and religious life.

mixed, Jewish education is actually one of twentieth-century American Jewry's success stories. Even as Jews worked eagerly throughout this period to make their way into the mainstream of American society, large numbers sought simultaneously to maintain a sense of Jewish identity and to transmit this identity to their children. They did so largely through Jewish education. Without government support and often without the backing of major philanthropists, these Jews created and populated an impressive set of educational institutions and programs: thousands of synagogue schools, hundreds of day schools, dozens of summer camps, myriad other learning programs for literally every age group from infants to senior adults, and a support structure of institutions of higher learning and service agencies across the continent. Though no one knows the exact figure, the "gross Jewish educational product" of North American Jewry—the amount of money spent to maintain these institutions and run these programs—is in the billions of dollars annually ($5 billion is a reasonable estimate).

These expenditures have produced results. Despite the predictions of some that the disappearance of American Jews as a distinctive religious and ethnic group would be assimilation's inevitable end, this did not happen. The Jewish educational system surely deserves some credit for this outcome. Numerous studies confirm that Jewish education makes a significant difference with respect to Jewish identity: the more of it one has had, the more likely that one will score high on a wide range of measures of Jewish engagement and activity. On a collective level, mobilizing to educate successive generations of children served as a focal point around which American Jews built a wide range of other activities and frameworks that helped create a vibrant, multidimensional Jewish community.

Even now in the new century, trend lines in Jewish education are actually more positive than in many other sectors of Jewish life. There is vitality and growth across much of the Jewish educational landscape, including summer camp, travel to Israel (thanks to Birthright Israel), Jewish learning on campus, adult Jewish learning, and learning online. Although day school enrollments appear to have plateaued and perhaps declined slightly among the non-Orthodox, and supplementary program enrollments are declining, both sectors are benefiting from a wave of innovation. That innovation, as Schwarz notes, is not limited to traditional institutions. Much of the exciting action in Jewish education today is coming from entrepreneurial forces that are broadening the canvas of Jewish education, bringing Jewish learning into settings, from workplaces to the wilderness, and using creative approaches, from moot courts to multiplayer games, that expand its reach and spread its impact. But traditional institutions are not remaining static. Many are trying to "up their game," embracing technology and other new modes of learning and engaging in systemic change efforts.

Yet, despite this "good news," all is far from ideal in American Jewish education. Indeed, the very prominence of recent efforts to innovate and improve what exists bespeaks a growing recognition that, for all its achievements, the Jewish educational system inherited from the twentieth century is inadequate for the challenges—and opportunities—of the twenty-first. The flaws of twentieth-century Jewish education have been well chronicled over the past quarter century: the limited time that many families are willing to devote to Jewish learning; the inadequate support and training provided to educators; the overemphasis on Bar/Bat Mitzvah as the "pinnacle" educational experience, with an attendant overconcentration on a limited range of knowledge and skills and a huge drop-off in participation during the adolescent years.

New Challenges for a New Century

But these weaknesses are not the main challenge for Jewish education today. The main challenge emanates, rather, from the forces that Schwarz describes. Twentieth-century Jewish education largely succeeded in transmitting and preserving a Jewishness that allowed American Jews to assimilate without a total loss of group identity. Yet this success is no longer sufficient, because the question Jewish education is being asked to answer has changed. Twentieth-century Jewish education was designed to answer the question, "How can we ensure that individuals remain 'good' Jews, even as they become good (and successful) Americans?" Today's Jewish education must respond to a subtly, but significantly, different one: "How can we help Jews draw on and use their Jewishness to live more meaningful, fulfilling, responsible lives?"

To answer the question posed to it, twentieth-century Jewish education focused largely on encouraging a number of manifestations of group identification and belonging: having a minimal level of basic Jewish literacy (including being able to decode, but not necessarily understand, Hebrew); engaging in periodic Jewish observances, especially in synagogue; fighting anti-Semitism and remembering the Holocaust; supporting Israel; and being an ethical and charitable individual. In Schwarz's terms, this is a Jewish education designed to inculcate and reinforce a largely "tribal" identity. Even among those who sought more from Jewish education than the modicum provided by most supplementary programs by sending their children to day school or Jewish educational camp, the basic parameters of the Jewish education received did not differ significantly from this model—there was just more of it.

This type of Jewish education is fundamentally about "continuity"— socialization to a historical group identity and a set of norms associated with it. "Judaism," in this approach, consists of a definable set of contents and practices that mark one as a "Jew," and the intent is for the student to learn about and adopt as many of these as is considered reasonable and desirable, consistent with other desiderata (such as being a "modern" person or a patriotic American). (What was considered reasonable and desirable did, of course, differ depending on one's religious ideology.) This educational approach fits well with a preservationist mind-set in the face of a perceived threatened loss of Jewish identity. To be sure, educators, rabbis, and many parents wanted more than a merely prophylactic education. They wanted

> The new question that Jewish education must answer is not about group preservation, but about personal meaning. And, the question is being asked in a world that is quite different than the one that we knew even a quarter century ago.

children to feel positively about their Jewishness, to be proud and happy Jews, and for Judaism to be a guiding force in their lives. But, the fundamental underlying concern, as Schwarz describes (and as I have written about elsewhere[1]), was for Jewish survival and continuity.

We live now in a different time, a time of hybrid identities and multiple communities. For most younger American Jews, the issue is not whether or not to be Jewish—they are Jewish, and their Jewishness is in no sense a burden or a barrier. But with many identities intermingling in their self-definition and with many communities available within which to pursue the things they value in life, the *significance* of their Jewishness is very much up for grabs. The new question that Jewish education must answer is not about group preservation, but about personal meaning. And, the question is being asked in a world that is quite different than the one that we knew even a quarter century ago. The pace of political, social, cultural, religious, and technological change over that period has been dizzying. American Jews, precisely because they inhabit this world so fully, have been thoroughly exposed to these changes, changes well described in Schwarz's lead essay. What they seek for their lives are the same things others seek: a modicum of security amidst turmoil, a sense that their lives matter, satisfying connections with others, a feeling of being in control, pride in accomplishment. The big question is, Will their Jewishness contribute substantially to any of this? Can Judaism, Jewish community, Israel, the Jewish people, Jewish culture, and Jewish learning be a powerful resource for them as they seek to construct meaningful, fulfilling, purposeful, and responsible lives?

The Response: Learner-Centered Jewish Education

This is the question that Jewish education must answer today. To do so it must be different than it has been, different in its content and in how that content is organized and delivered. Even more important, it must differ in its understanding of its mission. Jewish continuity can no longer be Jewish education's goal. Rather, its goal must be to provide learners with the tools and resources to construct meaningful Jewish lives—understanding that these lives may not correspond to a preconceived image or norm, but will instead be unique "remixes" of materials drawn from the multifarious storehouse of Jewish history and tradition and from other sources. If Jewish education is successful in this mission, Jewish continuity will indeed result, but as an outcome, not the objective. The implications of the shifts required are profound and, for some, troubling. But, there is no avoiding the reality that Jewish education today must start from a different set of premises and end with a different set of practices than were enshrined in Jewish education throughout most of the twentieth century.

The pivot point in this redesign of Jewish education is the learner. Instead of being seen as Jewish education's "objects"—those who must be guided and steered (for their own good and the good of the collective)—learners must be recognized as its "subjects"—as active agents in shaping their own learning and using that learning to construct their identities. This does not mean that educators or educating institutions have no role in designing and selecting the experiences that learners undergo or the content they are exposed to. Rather, it means that education is practiced from the beginning as a partnership, with the learner gradually assuming a growing role in choosing her or his own educational path. (Some might see in this an analogue to humans' growing role and responsibility over time in our covenantal partnership with God in the work of *tikkun olam*, "repairing the world.") The more we learn about children as natural learners (and see this ability put to work in settings like Montessori schools), the clearer it becomes that a learner-centered approach to education is pedagogically sound. But this is about more than pedagogy. It is about empowering learners and their families as co-designers, and in some instances even co-producers, of their Jewish learning journeys. Ultimately, it is about trusting learners to construct ways of being Jewish that work for them and accepting that these ways will be diverse and evolving.

This model of learner-centered Jewish education will not (at least initially) be appealing to everyone. In religious education, even more than in other educational contexts, many will argue that the goal ought to be—indeed, must be—to educate individuals so that they will adopt a particular pattern of belief, understanding, and behavior. Such education need not be simple indoctrination—there is room for questioning, exploration and discovery, debate, and varying conclusions, though within certain boundaries. Nor is the motivation for what we might think of as "traditional" religious education in any way malevolent. It is understandable and even admirable to want others to find meaning and satisfaction in a set of beliefs and practices that have proved effective with many others over time, especially when these are also understood as "true." Some go further and argue that education that is *not* guided by a vision of what the product of such education should be, know, feel, and do (or at least be able to be, know, feel, and do) is unsound and ineffectual.[2]

It is certainly possible to structure the educational process in a way that maximizes the likelihood of a favored outcome. We know that the power of social environments to influence individual choice is enormous. The combination of a carefully constructed curriculum (one designed, as current jargon has it, with "the end in mind"), good teaching, and a strong supportive context (a "plausibility structure," in Peter Berger's language[3]) can often produce individuals who do manifest desired attitudes, values, behaviors, and commitments (in this case, a strong "Jewish identity" as defined by those responsible for the education).

Nonetheless, this model of Jewish education is likely to prove less and less successful (and may already have proved so) in a world where individual choice is seen as a sacred right (Cohen and Eisen's "sovereign self"[4]), where "prosumers" expect to have a say in designing a growing number of products and experiences they consume, and where exposure to a wide range of information, perspectives, and alternative meaning-systems is virtually unavoidable. There is both a moral and a practical case to be made for learner-centered Jewish education. We want Jews to embrace their Jewishness and the values and behaviors that reflect this identity as an affirmative choice, not merely a default condition. And, increasingly, for the vast majority of Jews, these are the only terms under which they will embrace these.

Learner-centered Jewish education is already being practiced in many ways. Constructivist pedagogies are becoming more common, and choice is being built into the curricula of a growing number of programs, even for children of elementary school age. Adolescent education in particular is being reshaped as a domain in which teens increasingly are seen as and being treated as active agents choosing their own involvements from among a multiplicity of options, many of which they are creating themselves. Hillel has made student empowerment a linchpin of its approach on campus. Parents too are being empowered—or are assuming the power—to play a greater role in shaping the learning for their children and themselves, in some cases even initiating programs in which they themselves take on a teaching role, in keeping with the Torah's vision and command *V'shinantam l'vanecha*, "You shall teach them to your children" (Deuteronomy 6:7). Technology has made it possible for unprecedented numbers of Jews to seek out Jewish knowledge and guidance from myriad sources when and how they want it. In none of these examples is the vital role of educators being lost, but it is being changed from a traditionally didactic one to a more nuanced and multidimensional one as a guide, facilitator, framer of experiences, expert resource, and partner. Moving to a mind-set that begins consistently with learners—their needs, their aspirations—and seeks to engage them as cocreators of their own learning experiences will be something of a Copernican shift for an educational system used to a much more "top-down" approach. Yet it is a step that is inevitable and one that will be an important part of the major shift in orientation for Jewish institutions that Schwarz rightly calls for in his lead essay.

The Power of Relationships

There is a second key component to the transformation needed for Jewish education to thrive in the new world that Schwarz describes: an increased emphasis on relationships as the driving force for Jewish engagement and commitment. We live today with an ironic juxtaposition: never have our capacities for connecting with others been greater (thanks to technology), yet we live in many ways farther apart from one another than ever before. (Think of the iconic image, now so prominent, of dozens of people walking past each other, each plugged via an MP3 player and earphones into her/his own world.) Humans seek relationships just as they seek autonomy and a sense of efficacy in their own lives. And we are all deeply influenced, consciously and unconsciously, by those relationships, by the groups we are part of and the people we identify with and seek to emulate or please.

In Jewish life today, there is a growing appreciation, as echoed in Schwarz's lead essay, that one of the flaws of our institutionalized Jewish community has been that amidst all the programming, all the activity taking place, relationships have often taken a backseat. In his work with synagogues, Dr. Ron Wolfson—the guiding spirit, together with

Rabbi Lawrence A. Hoffman, for much of the contemporary movement for synagogue revitalization—has come to emphasize relationship building, rather than programming alone, as the key to engaging individuals, especially young people, who are "institution shy."[5] The same is true for Jewish education. A panoply of educational programs is available to individuals and families today in myriad settings—all to the good when it comes to affording individuals and families multiple options from which to choose. But, unless there are also opportunities to forge real relationships with others who can serve as guides and with whom one can travel on the learning journey, that very multiplicity of options is as likely to prove bewildering and inaccessible as it is enticing and satisfying.

Relationships have always been part of Jewish education. Martin Buber, perhaps the twentieth century's prime proponent of relationships as constitutive of our very humanness, viewed education as a form of dialogue, with the relationship between teacher and student, even more than the content transmitted, serving as the animating force for learning.[6] Many of us, recalling our own educational experiences, would agree: what we remember best is often not the content of what we studied, but the teacher, counselor, or friend who inspired us and together with whom we learned. Indeed, two of the great success stories of twentieth-century Jewish education—Jewish camping and youth movements—made building relationships among peers and between participants and near-peer role models (counselors and youth leaders) a centerpiece of their work. We know too that relationships forged among families whose children are learning together can often become long-lived attachments that spill over into other dimensions of Jewish and general life. But, in the twenty-first century, when the very concept of Jewish community seems to have become problematic for many, infusing Jewish education with relationship building along multiple dimensions will be even more vital. Nurturing strong relationships between educators and learners and among learners themselves creates a rich social and interpersonal context within which the meaning making that is at the heart of the educational process is anchored and can take root.

The efforts being made today to increase the "relationship quotient" in Jewish education range from providing concierges to guide individual families toward the most appropriate educational programs and settings for their needs and interests to creating mega-events to bring thousands of participants on Birthright Israel trips together for an intensive experience of Jewish peoplehood in action. Although there is no substitute for the personal relationships that can grow from spending time with others face-to-face in a classroom, camp bunk, or *mifgash* between young American travelers and Israeli counterparts, the power of communication technologies to connect people instantly, frequently, and over any distance has the potential for both widening and deepening these relationships. Commentators often draw a distinction between the "real" world and the "virtual" world of technologically mediated communication. They frequently couple this with expressions of concern about the latter displacing the former, with an attendant loss of genuine human connection. This concern is not without merit. Still, for young people today, communicating via technology (e.g., texting, social media) is as natural as getting up in the morning. The challenge, therefore, is to tap into this dimension of their lives in ways that enrich their learning experiences, not only by making information more accessible (which technology clearly does) but also by making the experiences themselves more social and collaborative.

> In the twenty-first century, when the very concept of Jewish community seems to have become problematic for many, infusing Jewish education with relationship building along multiple dimensions will be even more vital.

This is already happening. "Community" comes in two forms: "intensive" community involves immediate, face-to-face relationships and a sense of closeness and familiarity; "extensive" community involves a sense of being connected to a large collective that spans time and space. Jewish community values—indeed, depends on—both of these forms, and technology can strengthen both. Technology is allowing and Israeli young people to share ideas and experiences with c in real time; it is keeping bunkmates and counselors conne the winters between camp sessions; and it is enabling parer and teachers to communicate beyond school hours. Technology makes it easier to feel part of an extensive community (the Jewish people) not merely in theory, but in reality, and to maintain and renew intimate connections with family, friends, and mentors even when physically separate.

Still, it is important to remember that technology is not a guarantor of strong and meaningful relationships, only a tool in sustaining these. At the end of the day, what will matter most is whether those who are shaping and implementing Jewish educational experiences recognize that effectively transmitting Jewish knowledge, skills, and values in today's world depends on fostering the kinds of relationships that make these beliefs and behaviors attractive and compelling because of whom they connect us with, not just what they consist of.

From Life to Torah and Back

Nonetheless, though content is not everything in education, neither is it inconsequential. Jewish education must be about something, and there is a great deal to choose from! What should the organizing principle for this selection be? What material is most important for learners to encounter; what experiences are most important for them to have? These questions bring us back to the central one that Schwarz's lead essay poses: what kind of Judaism are twenty-first-century American Jews likely to embrace? His thesis—with which this response agrees—is that Jews today are seeking a Judaism that provides guidance and direction for the lives they are living today as full participants in the contemporary world. The four categories that Schwarz proposes as pillars of this Judaism—wisdom, social justice, community, and lives of sacred purpose—can also be core elements in a Jewish education that will be genuinely life shaping, that will be able to answer the question of meaning that gives Jewish education its raison d'etre today.

We are ready for the "new Jewish learning" that Franz Rosenzweig envisioned nearly a century ago: one that begins with "life" in its lived fullness and complexity, that brings this life to Torah, to the accumulated wisdom of Jewish teaching and tradition, in order to be illuminated, enriched, sometimes challenged, and perhaps even transformed by that teaching, and then sends us back into the world to apply and test what we have learned.[7] As with empowering learners (rather than placing educational decision making in the hands solely of "experts"), seeing the content of Jewish education as being responsive to real questions emanating from life experience, instead of as a body of material that must be mastered because it has always been such, represents a profound shift in perspective. It requires us to ask why we are teaching what we are teaching and whether what we are teaching is geared to the real lives of our learners or only to the imagined lives we would like them to lead. If we are truly confident in the wisdom and relevance of Jewish teaching, then we will be more willing to trust in the "meeting" we arrange between empowered learners and Jewish tradition and more diligent in ensuring that this meeting is one in which both parties can give authentic and candid voice to what they have to contribute to that encounter.

This conception of Jewish education is broad and bold. It implies an approach to learning and teaching that, as Rosenzweig argued, includes everything: not just what is obviously "Jewish"—traditional texts, observances, the Jewish calendar, Jewish history (i.e., the stuff of which most Jewish educational curricula are made)—but the full range of experiences, issues, questions, and developmental tasks that define us as (Jewish) human beings. It also argues for an organizing principle for the content of Jewish education that uses the totality of our life experience as a springboard for introducing and exploring Jewish ideas, values, and ways of living in the world. We need not entirely reject conventional ways of organizing Jewish curricula around "subjects" or particular texts (e.g., history, Bible, Rabbinics, Hebrew language, Jewish holidays) to recognize that there are countless other models for connecting Jewish content to individuals' and groups' experiences,

> The four categories that Schwarz proposes as pillars of this Judaism—wisdom, social justice, community, and lives of sacred purpose—can also be core elements in a Jewish education that will be genuinely life shaping, that will be able to answer the question of meaning that gives Jewish education its raison d'etre today.

interests, and concerns, some of which may speak far more powerfully and directly to today's learners.

As noted earlier, one of the most exciting developments in Jewish education today is the dramatic broadening of the educational landscape beyond traditional forms of schooling. This is not only creating new venues and forms of Jewish learning—Jewish learning via the arts, travel, nature, service, media, athletics, meditation, professional activities—but also focusing attention on content areas—food, the environment, *tikkun olam*, aesthetics, communication, business ethics, spirituality—that are authentically part of the corpus of Jewish teaching, but that have been generally neglected in an education focused narrowly on the knowledge and skills associated with twentieth-century synagogue and Jewish institutional life.

Naturally, it would be impossible for every educational institution to encompass the totality of this type of life-relevant, life-shaping Jewish learning in its educational offerings. This is especially so when we recognize that different individuals will inevitably take different pathways into the vast world of Jewish teaching and resonate with different aspects of a multifarious tradition. Although many Jews will see themselves among the seekers of wisdom, social justice, community, and lives of sacred purpose that Schwarz describes, they will do so to different degrees and with differing emphases. What is more, each individual is likely to find different answers in and beyond what Jewish life has to offer to the fundamental questions they are asking: What constitutes wisdom for my life? How can I best pursue social justice in a complex world? Whence and with whom will I find true community? What purpose or set of purposes gives my life ultimate meaning? The practical implication of this reality is that diversity in Jewish education is indispensable if we are to engage deeply the largest number of potential learners.

Beyond Silos: Collective Impact

But diversity alone will not serve learners or the Jewish future well unless it is coupled with greater coordination and collaboration. Precisely because no institution can realistically hope to meet the learning needs and desires of even a single individual over a long period of time (individuals change), much less those of a substantial group, Jewish education must embrace better mechanisms for helping learners identify opportunities that respond to their needs, access these, and move readily and thoughtfully from one opportunity to the next in a continuous Jewish learning journey. In recent months, both the American institutional and philanthropic communities have been talking about the concept of "collective impact initiatives," introduced by John Kania and Mark Kramer.[8] Kania and Kramer argue that there are societal challenges that by their very nature cannot be solved by single organizations acting on their own, no matter how effective these are in their own work. Educating all children successfully, they suggest, is one such challenge, and it requires the combined efforts of multiple actors coordinated around shared goals and in active, ongoing communication with one another to meet this challenge.

The same is true in Jewish education. If our goal is to develop a community of passionate, lifelong Jewish learners who use their learning to live more meaningful, fulfilling, responsible Jewish lives, then this can only be achieved through the linked efforts of synagogues, day schools, camps, early childhood and youth programs, and myriad other actors, including many who are relatively new to the scene and are bringing fresh ideas and approaches into the field. In addition to the other shifts proposed above to make Jewish education more learner centered, relationship infused, and life relevant, a new operating culture will be required that rejects Jewish education as a zero-sum game (your gain is my loss) and instead treats it as an arena for "co-opetition": competing to provide more and more compelling learning experiences, and cooperating to maximize participation in all of these.

"*Lo Bashamayim Hi:* It Is Not in Heaven"

None of what has been outlined here as the agenda for twenty-first-century Jewish education will be easy to implement. But, neither is it "in heaven" (Deuteronomy 30:12). Examples of all of the thrusts called for already exist, and many are thriving. Increasingly, educators, institutional and communal leaders, and families are recognizing that the Jewish education of the twentieth century is inadequate for the challenges and opportunities of the twenty-first, and they are receptive to the call for change. As Schwarz suggests, the pace of change in contemporary life can at times throw us back on our heels. We are tempted to cling to the old because it did work (at least up to a point) and because new directions always carry risks and uncertainties. But, like Nachshon of Jewish legend and the *chalutzim* of the recent past, there are pioneers out there today who are taking action despite the risks and uncertainties. They are creating a new Jewish education that is at the same time deeply rooted in Jewish education's past. Their success will pave the way to the vibrant, vital Jewish community of the twenty-first century that we all wish to see.

Part 3

The Way Forward

Toward a Jewish Renaissance

Rabbi Sidney Schwarz

I am, by no stretch of the imagination, an accomplished chess player. Yet I have had the experience of walking through a city park and watching one chess master play against three or more opponents, each of whom was singularly focused on his or her particular chessboard and game. This was the image that came to my mind in the development of this book. The contributors used my lead essay as a prism through which they addressed emerging trends in their respective fields. I had the pleasure of engaging with each of the authors and their ideas over the course of many months. In many ways, each of their chapters serves as a case study that tests my assumptions and observations.

In this summary chapter, I want to highlight three themes that appeared in multiple essays and then focus on a thesis that turned out to be the one that elicited the most comments by the contributors—the relationship between tribal and covenantal Jewish identity among the next generation of American Jews. I will use those themes to fine-tune the analysis provided in the lead essay and to underscore the lessons that can be drawn about the prospects for the American Jewish future.

Authenticity

Jewish immigrants to America, and often their children, were consumed by their desire to acculturate. They wanted to shed the habits of dress, speech, and culture that identified them as "other." If America was the land of opportunity, then they thought, why not fully embrace the American way of life? Believing that Old World religion and customs were a barrier to that new American identity, they were quick to shed the particularities of their ethnic roots.

The younger generation of American Jews is now mostly third and fourth generation, which means that even their grandparents were American born. As Sharon Brous observes in her Los Angeles community, many in this age group have cut their ties to their Jewish roots, but those who do seek engagement are interested in the real thing. No longer looking over their shoulder to prove how American they are, these Jews have a level of confidence in their social standing that allows them to explore their cultural/religious roots quite seriously.

Like Brous, I too was the founding rabbi of a congregation—Adat Shalom Reconstructionist Congregation in Bethesda, Maryland—whose organizing principles were different from most of the congregations in our area. Our ability to attract a high percentage of young spiritual seekers who were unlikely to join any other congregation was due to the fact that we made Judaism accessible without dumbing it down. All too many non-Orthodox congregations today seem to believe that the only way to attract marginal Jews is to lower the expectations and offer some form of Jewish-lite fare. My experience has been quite the opposite, and it seems to parallel the experience of Brous in growing the IKAR community on the other side of the country. The more demands that we made on members—in terms of attendance, commitment to voluntarism, and even creating a hierarchy based on Jewish growth and learning—the more the community grew and thrived.

Will Herberg's classic book *Protestant, Catholic, Jew: An Essay in American Religious Sociology* was published in 1955. He observed that as Jews entered suburbia, many joined synagogues to mimic the religious behavior of their gentile neighbors. Joining a church or a synagogue was an "American" thing to do. I know of few Jews who join synagogues today just to "fit in." In my own experience, I find that Jews today are ready to be serious about their engagement with Judaism. If institutions offer Jewish lite, they will get "lite" commitment. Those institutions that offer authentic Jewish learning, practice, and culture will be rewarded with Jews who will take being Jewish seriously. Jews are increasingly using "authenticity" as a code word suggesting an expression of Judaism that is serious and that reflects the core values and practices of a tradition that has been preserved for thirty-five hundred years.

Asher Lopatin's synagogue in Chicago has been the beneficiary of this phenomenon, as young people raised in Reform and Conservative synagogues are now joining his Orthodox shul. This also explains the great appeal of the Chabad-Lubavitch movement and other outreach Orthodox groups like Aish HaTorah among non-Orthodox Jews. Thousands of Jews who have no intention of adopting an Orthodox lifestyle will spend enormous amounts of time (and money) in the orbit of these groups because they look and feel like "authentic" Judaism.

The quest for authenticity on the part of younger American Jews extends beyond synagogues and religious practice. Elise Bernhardt notes the phenomenon among young secular Israelis who are eager to engage with the classical sources of Judaism, and given the influence of Israeli behavior on Jewish life in the Diaspora, I predict that we will begin seeing secular or non-Orthodox yeshivot emerge in America and elsewhere that will have significant appeal to younger Jews. Jill Jacobs has been at the center of several organizations that have succeeded in drawing Jews back to the Jewish community because they have made social justice the top priority of how one walks the talk of Jewish values. Barry Shrage realized that Federations can no longer effectively raise money just on the basis of nostalgia and group solidarity, and he has pioneered a new brand of Federation in Boston that champions "purpose and spiritual grandeur." Jonathan Woocher notes how dramatically the key question of Jewish education has changed. In the twentieth century the question was "How can we Jews fit into America?" In the twenty-first century, he argues, successful Jewish education will have to answer the question "How can we live more meaningful lives?"

Because so many of the themes of twentieth-century American Jewish life no longer resonate with twenty-first-century Jews, my lead essay proposes four themes that can and should be the centerpiece for a renaissance of the American Jewish community: wisdom/*chochmah*, social justice/*tzedek*, community/*kehillah*, and lives of sacred purpose/*kedushah*. Although the formulations may differ slightly, I am encouraged to hear that key to Boston's success at their Combined Jewish Philanthropies (the Federation) were guiding principles that are quite similar to the ones that I proposed. Similarly, Woocher suggests that my four principles would be an excellent starting point for the kind of twenty-first-century Jewish education that he is advocating.

One of the challenges facing the non-Orthodox denominations of Jewish life is whether they are able to shape an approach to Jewish living that does not feel like watered-down versions of traditional Judaism. To a generation that sought acculturation into American society, that may have been a workable formula. But to a generation that seeks authenticity, it is a turnoff. The communities described in Nigel Savage's essay give us a glimpse of what a maximalist, non-Orthodox Jewish lifestyle can look like, and he offers a specific strategy of how we can begin to seed such communities around the country, starting with some focused foundation funding of intensive Jewish retreats. Clearly, Brous has used a similar maximalist formula in her successful building of the IKAR community in Los Angeles.

> Any Jewish institution that hopes to appeal to next-generation Jews needs to strive to raise the bar and not lower it.

Any Jewish institution that hopes to appeal to next-generation Jews needs to strive to raise the bar and not lower it. A good starting point are the principles that I propose, each deeply rooted in Jewish sources and experience: wisdom/*chochmah*, social justice/*tzedek*, community/*kehillah*, and lives of sacred purpose/*kedushah*. These are the principles that trumpet "authentic Judaism" to a generation of Jews who want the real deal.

Relationships

I am a bit surprised that discussion about technology, the Internet, and social media does not emerge as a major theme in the essays of our contributors. Each was asked to speculate about the future of his or her respective field, so I assumed that the tech theme would be more prominent. I have attended more conference panels than I care to count at which some tech guru chastises the Jewish community for lagging behind other sectors of American society in its adoption of the latest social media innovation. It always strikes me a bit like the studies that drug companies underwrite to prove why a drug that they manufacture is essential to good health. Everybody is pitching something. The question is whether the antidote is worse than the disease.

I'll admit to a bit of bias here. My periodic experiences with distance learning, both as a teacher and as a student, have left me cold. I similarly have started and aborted my blogging career more than once because of a distinct preference for in-person learning environments. In retrospect, it may not be a coincidence that I founded a program that I named *Panim el Panim*, "Face to Face," which offers Washington-based leadership seminars for teens, integrating Jewish learning, values, and social responsibility. But I am not unaware of the power of the Internet to expand the reach of what we do. When I first heard that a rabbi had started an online synagogue called OurJewishCommunity.org, I rolled my eyes. But I later reached out to its founder, Rabbi Laura Baum, and was much impressed when she told me that her website had reached three hundred thousand people in 180 countries since its founding in 2008.

Indeed, it is impossible to begin to strategize about ways to reach the next generation of American Jews without utilizing the power of social media, and I know that every one of the book's contributors is making use of such strategies in his or her respective institutions. Yet what hit me in reflecting on the essays is the extent to which so many of the contributors see relationships as the key to creating transformative experiences for Jews. Wayne Firestone has adapted the Hillel model so that it no longer makes "joining Hillel" the focus of outreach to Jews on campus. Nor is membership the primary yardstick of Hillel's success, as it was a generation ago. Most of the energy of Hillel's national strategy revolves around "engagement," and most of it is done in one-to-one meetings, with staff who are ordained rabbis, with trained Jewish educators, and, even more extensively, between one student and another.

Barry Chazan and Anne Lanski believe that more than any other strategy that might engage young Jews with Israel, none is as powerful as the personal visit to the land of our ancestors, the birthplace of the Jewish people. And during a short-term visit, no part of the travel experience is as powerful as the *mifgash*, the personal encounter during which young American Jews can meet and get to know Israel through the experience of their peers who were born and raised in the country. Joy Levitt understands that what makes her JCC vibrant is not its "programs" but the community that is built around the programs that the institution sponsors. Or Rose sees the great interest that Jews have in the wisdom and practice of other faith communities in America and is structuring programs where Jews can meet with Christians, Muslims, Hindus, and others. Not only do such encounters explode stereotypes and reduce prejudice, but they also open up new perspectives on our own faith and pave the way to collaborative efforts to address injustice in the world.

David Ellenson addresses the issue of social media more directly than anyone else when he observes that it has had the effect of making Jews far less dependent on rabbis and synagogues. My generation was introduced to do-it-yourself Judaism (DIY) with the publication of *The Jewish Catalog*, which came out in 1973. It was subtitled *A Do-It-Yourself Kit*. But the wealth of information now available at the touch of a keyboard or smartphone is DIY Judaism on steroids. Ellenson rightly observes that Jews now coalesce around interests and values, not institutions. Synagogues can do nothing to reverse this trend. The question is whether synagogues can find a way to capitalize on the trend to make themselves more central to the DIY phenomenon and not marginalized by it.

It is important to note that, as with every social phenomenon, we are now seeing some of the earliest champions of the age of the Internet raise questions about its impact on people and on society. Sherry Turkle, a professor of psychology at MIT, wrote one of the seminal books on the power of cyberspace in 1995, *Life on the Screen: Identity in the Age of the Internet*. In the book, not only does she argue that computers are changing the way people think and understand themselves, but she is also quite taken by the way that cyberspace allows human beings to step into virtual worlds that they never could previously access and interact with people they never would have otherwise met. Yet in her latest book, *Alone Together: Why We Expect More from Technology and Less from Each Other* (2011), Turkle shares deep reservations about the consequences of the age of the Internet. She notes that we are raising a generation of children who are unable to have a conversation and who mistake a Facebook "friend" for true friendship. Even for adults, the Internet has offered an illusion of companionship but without the quality of intimacy. The sheer volume of communication between people and the addictive nature of e-mail and texting has crowded out the time for deep relationships where people can take emotional risks and enjoy the fulfillment that comes from human interaction. The net result is a society filled with people who are much lonelier than those of previous generations, even as they feel increasingly overwhelmed to keep pace with the volume of superficial contacts.

There is, of course, the more mature embrace of technology that recognizes it as a tool to make our jobs easier and more efficient and not designed to replace face-to-face contacts. Yet because I see so much evidence of what Sherry Turkle now fears, my mind goes to a different place. I think that one of the strategies that the Jewish community has not fully leveraged is to have the courage to announce itself as countercultural. Jewish community should be the place where you don't have to simply be a cog (or a byte) in the cultural phenomenon known as cyberspace. Jewish community should be the place where people and relationships count. Do we not think that in a society where we are besieged by robo-calls, where we are expected to make appointments to call colleagues, and where our computers seem to anticipate our every consumer urge (and who knows what other urges our computers will predict in the near future) that people would be drawn to settings where they are actually treated in the spirit of the Jewish value of *b'tzelem Elohim*, that they are images of the Divine and need to be seen, heard, and respected as such?

> I think that one of the strategies that the Jewish community has not fully leveraged is to have the courage to announce itself as countercultural. Jewish community should be the place where you don't have to simply be a cog (or a byte) in the cultural phenomenon known as cyberspace. Jewish community should be the place where people and relationships count.

I am reminded of how much of the genius of Judaism throughout history has been its ability to offer a perspective that runs counter to the conventional wisdom of the day. David Polish developed a whole theory of Jewish history based on this idea in his book *The Eternal Dissent: A Search for Meaning in Jewish History*. Along these lines Reboot, an organization that engages young Jews in redefining Jewish life and tradition, came up with a brilliant project in 2010 called the Sabbath Manifesto, which they launched with a National Day of Unplugging. The Manifesto had ten principles that they asked people to observe for twenty-four hours, one day a year. The principles included the following: avoid technology, connect with loved ones, nurture your health, light candles, drink wine, avoid commerce, and give back. The movement, now going on its third year, is so appealing and hip that Reboot took the project to one of the most plugged-in places on the planet, the South by Southwest Music Festival in Austin, Texas, where they sponsored an Unplugging Party. Talk about ways to repackage Shabbat! And the appeal goes far beyond just the Jewish community.

Judaism can be the ultimate countercultural movement. It offers a way of being in the world that stands apart from the way that others in society think and behave. I think that the concept has particular appeal for our own day. For all of the gifts that America has offered Jews, there is much about the ethics and values of this society that stand in deep contrast to Jewish teaching. The rampant corporate greed and the worship of wealth violate the Jewish concept of *histapkut*, the ideal of a life of simplicity. They also violate the concept of *tzedakah*, the idea that we are but temporary custodians of our wealth and that a portion of it needs to be shared with those who have less. American media and popular culture are awash in obscenity and the sexual objectification of both women and men. It makes it hard to raise children who understand the Jewish value of *tzniut*, modesty in dress and in speech. The emerging habit of tweeting one's every daily activity and

> Judaism can be the ultimate countercultural movement. It offers a way of being in the world that stands apart from the way that others in society think and behave. I think that the concept has particular appeal for our own day.

sharing details of one's personal life on Facebook runs counter to the Jewish teachings around *anavah*, humility and discretion. The rampant individualism of American society that goes back to the days of the American frontier but has accelerated with the new cyberspace culture runs counter to Judaism's stress on *kehillah*, community, and on *achrayut*, our notion of taking responsibility for others who are in need.

American Jews, who are among the most avid spiritual seekers in American society, spend vast amounts of money and time in search of spiritual alternatives to the vapid and crass consumerist/corporate culture that America has become. Why shouldn't the Jewish community try to attract these Jewish seekers? For those Jews who want an alternative to a society that has become overly enamored of superficial friendships via the Internet, why not offer models of true community (*kehillah*)? For those Jews who are tired of being judged by the size of their flat-screen TV, why not model what a life of sacred purpose (*kedushah*) looks like? Both of these principles, the third and fourth principles that I suggest as the focal points of the Jewish community of the twenty-first century, are key to creating a Jewish experience that puts relationships at the center of our communal culture.

A House with Many Doors

This book is filled with many harsh critiques of the Jewish community. Yet let us not lose the forest for the trees. I was recently invited to address a gathering of the Hindu-American Seva Charities, which was being hosted by the White House Faith Office. Hindus have great admiration for Jews. They are mostly a first- and second-generation immigrant community eager to be integrated into American society. They hope to do so as successfully as have American Jews. From their perspective, the American Jewish community serves as a role model for how a religious/ethnic group can maintain its identity but become fully integrated into American society.

Indeed. Consider the very scope of this book. There isn't another ethnic subcommunity in America that has the range of organizations and services that Jews enjoy—a central fundraising and allocation system (Federations); community centers; social justice organizations; a national network on college campuses (Hillel); a network of day schools, afternoon religious schools, and summer camps; programs that connect Jews to the State of Israel; philanthropic foundations; arts and cultural institutions; synagogues and seminaries to suit a wide range of religious practice. And this list is not even complete, because it is limited to the sectors of the American Jewish community represented in this book. We are indeed a very rich and blessed community, and I am not talking about money.

Each of these sectors represents another way that Jews can express their identity. The fact that it can take the form of religious practice, philanthropy, music, dance, art, cinema, literature, theater, connection to Israel, sports, study, social justice, and much more reveals why it is so hard for Jews to explain to non-Jews why Jewish identity is not just about religion.

Just a generation ago, the Jewish community could assess its effectiveness with some simple, quantifiable data. Surveys would ask how many Jews were members of synagogues, how many were members of secular Jewish membership organizations, or how many made annual gifts to the local Federation campaign. As noted earlier, each of these measurements is currently in a serious state of decline. But the nature of the market (generational) and marketplace (American society) are changing so rapidly that it is easy to mistake weakening institutions with a weakening community. The operative word for the American Jewish community is thus not "decline," but "transition."

Those who are stuck in twentieth-century paradigms of Jewish identity and affiliation will track the disconcerting demographic data and rush to declare the Jewish community at great risk. But those who have had a glimpse of the many areas of emerging Jewish renaissance that have been cited in this book will see that we are living at a time of great opportunity. Sandy Cardin, the president of the Schusterman Family Foundation, which is helping to fund so many of the most exciting new approaches to Jewish life and community, makes a compelling case for how the old-line, established Jewish communal institutions can and should work with the nascent experiments that have been emerging over the past two decades. In fact, both need one another. Although

> The operative word for the American Jewish community is thus not "decline," but "transition."

the fledgling programs are capturing Jewish millennials more successfully than are the more established institutions, Federations, JCCs, and synagogues have infrastructure, facilities, expertise, and access to financial resources that the younger Jewish organizations have no ability to replicate. If Cardin is right, we should celebrate the fact that there is an emerging collaborative spirit among Jewish foundations so that new ventures can get the resources necessary to take their experiments to the next level. Clearly, the more the Jewish communal establishment explores ways of supporting and partnering with the robust Jewish innovation sector, the more exciting the Jewish future will be.

Not so many years ago, there were a few doors that one could walk through to enter into the Jewish communal house. One could join a synagogue, be active in a local Jewish Federation, perhaps join a JCC or membership organizations like Hadassah or B'nai Brith. These were the ways that Jews were counted. These were the totems of American Jewish affiliation. Today, those doors still exist, but there are many more doors available to next-generation Jews, who are not all prepared to follow in the footsteps of their parents. In fact, one of the most impressive features of the new face of the American Jewish community is that many Jews whose parents were not even marginally involved in Jewish life are finding doorways into the

> There is a growing and eclectic array of ways that one can "do Jewish" in America today, totally unimagined just a generation ago. This is a trend that is worth celebrating.

Jewish communal house. There is a growing and eclectic array of ways that one can "do Jewish" in America today, totally unimagined just a generation ago. This is a trend that is worth celebrating.

Tribal versus Covenantal Identity

In my lead essay, I draw a distinction between tribal Jews and covenantal Jews. The former identity is highly particularistic and focused on Jewish group survival, whereas the latter identity is more universalist, seeing Judaism as a legacy of values that could be applied in many settings beyond the Jewish community. Covenantal Jews might well be engaged in more parochial Jewish activities under the right conditions, but by nature, their identity is more global than it is ethnic. I argue that the Jewish community we have today was created by tribal Jews for tribal Jews. To the extent that the next generation of Jews is more heavily covenantal than it is tribal, the Jewish community cannot conduct business as usual and expect that the Jewish community will still be around in one hundred years.

Several of the contributors comment on this thesis. Barry Shrage challenges my analysis, not convinced that younger Jews are any less interested in tribal affiliations than were the previous generations. He sees significant numbers of Jewish millennials eager to connect with the Jewish community. He goes on to say that even if his assessment is wrong and mine is correct, he is not willing to sacrifice the elements of tribal Jewish identity—those behaviors that are central to Jewish communal life today—to accommodate the needs of covenantal Jews. In contrast, Nigel Savage concurs with my analysis, seeing it as "a critical fault line in the Jewish community." He goes on to make the case for why "preference" need not be prejudicial. In other words, Savage understands the bias of the younger generation toward a global ethic, and he is eager to frame Jewish identity in a way that does not violate the values of Jewish millennials. Jonathan Woocher juxtaposes the twentieth-century challenge of Jewish education—"How can we be good Jews and good Americans?"—with the twenty-first-century challenge—"How can we draw on Judaism to live a more meaningful life?" Woocher, correctly understanding my categories, calls the first question a tribal one, whereas the second question is a covenantal one.

> So here is the challenge: Can we transmit a tribal Jewish story in a way that the next generation of American Jews can hear it?

So here is the challenge: Can we transmit a tribal Jewish story in a way that the next generation of American Jews can hear it? Or, put another way, what would it take to get younger American Jews to have a strong enough affinity to their Jewish identity that the Jewish community will continue to be vibrant and relevant to our children and grandchildren?

Classical Jewish formulations were often organized around the triad of God, Torah, and Israel. If one wanted to understand the distinctions between the various religious denominations of American Jewish life, each could be explained using those classical categories. Even before I was ordained, I worked my way through college teaching Hebrew school and leading Jewish youth groups. I realized then that the Jewish kids I worked with cared not a whit about what their particular synagogue thought about God, Torah, and Israel, even though all of the educational materials I was given used that as the framework. The approach was "inside-out"—start with what Judaism has to say about these important concepts and then go into the world equipped with this framework to guide you on your way. It didn't work then and it still doesn't work today.

Some twenty years later, when we launched PANIM, I described the educational philosophy that was key to our success as "outside-in." We didn't assume that the teens we worked with started off with any great commitment to Jewish learning (the "inside"). We assumed that they cared about how they could make a difference in the world (the "outside"). By exposing them to the most critical issues facing our communities, our country, and our world—issues like poverty, war and peace, the crisis facing our environment, and human rights—we helped them understand how American democracy made it possible for them to be change agents on the issues that they cared about most deeply. Our programs were boot camps for political activism, community service, and civic leadership. Once the kids were hooked—and it happened routinely—our educational program was designed to give them a tool kit to be effective activists. That tool kit included a heavy dose of Jewish wisdom, texts, the Jewish historical experience, and the example of how the contemporary Jewish community was a role model for deep engagement on the full range of domestic and international issues on our agenda. It worked.

My prescription for a Jewish renaissance in America is informed by my experience. The Jewish community does not need to spend a dime to get Jews to my starting point. The vast majority are seekers of wisdom (*chochmah*), seekers of justice (*tzedek*), seekers of community (*kehillah*), and seekers of lives of sacred purpose (*kedushah*). Even if a Jewish person only cared about one of these elements, to the extent that a Jewish institution or a Jewish program can fulfill that need, it becomes a portal into Jewish communal life. Once in the tent, there is a greater likelihood that such an individual will find other elements of Jewish life of interest as well. This is the only way we will succeed in engaging next-generation Jews.

A Story

In order to take this out of the realm of theory, I want to illustrate my point with a story. In January 2011, at the invitation of an Israeli organization called Tevel B'Tzedek, I spent a week in Haiti working with a team of Israeli volunteers who were doing amazing work within weeks of the earthquake that devastated the country. During that trip I forged a relationship with Pastor Johnny Felix, a young, charismatic minister who had started his own congregation and a school serving kindergarten through the sixth grade. Upon my return home to my synagogue, Adat Shalom, I told my stories, showed my pictures, and, with my urging, the congregation launched a fundraising campaign to help pay for teacher salaries, computers, and the tuitions of the children who could not afford the annual tuition of seventy-six dollars.

It wasn't long before I was approached by members of Adat Shalom who said that they wanted to organize a service mission to Haiti if I agreed to lead it. Thus it was that a group of eighteen of us, evenly divided between adults and their children, ages fifteen to thirty, went to Haiti in December 2011. We stayed in Leogane, near the center of the earthquake and close to Pastor Johnny's New Christian School. During the days we worked side by side with Haitians, helping build houses that would enable them and their families to move from one-room wood huts with no plumbing to these new homes. In the evenings, after our physical labor was done, we explored the teachings of Judaism to understand how our work was a fulfillment of Judaism's core commandments about *tzedek u'mishpat*, doing righteousness and justice in the world without regard to race, religion, or nationality.

It was clear to me that the adults were more taken by the study of Jewish sources than the young people were. Although they were respectful, my sense was that to the teens, the Jewish study was some nice window dressing offered by their rabbi to fill the evenings. These were classic, post-tribal Jews: "What's Judaism got to do with it?" The important work was happening during the day.

Then on Sunday we went to Pastor Johnny's church. It became abundantly clear in that setting that our being Jewish mattered a great deal.

The church was in a tent with a dirt floor. The benches people sat on were castoffs. Some were broken. It was clear how poor these Haitians were. Most did not even have permanent homes. Yet they were dressed exquisitely and had been there for two hours when we arrived for the last ninety minutes of the service. As we walked in, we were greeted by "Shabbat Shalom," a Hebrew song that I taught when I first visited the congregation a year earlier. Our visit fell during the festival of Chanukah. Pastor Johnny had invited me to preach the morning sermon, so I chose to use the lessons of Chanukah to offer words of hope and encouragement to people who had endured, not just the devastation of a natural disaster, but whose families had also endured decades of brutality, oppression, and corrupt rule by a string of dictators. And when our makeshift Adat Shalom choir got up to teach some Hebrew songs, the congregation joined with passion to the words: *Hinei mah tov u'mah na'im, shevet achim gam yachad,* "How good and beautiful it is to be in this space, a gathering of sisters and brothers sitting together in the spirit of friendship and in unity."

At the close of the service I invited everyone to get up and form a circle around the perimeter of the tent. We joined hands and I taught the song: *Shalom haverim, le'hitraot,* "We say goodbye to our friends but we will meet again." I introduced it by saying that this song was our commitment that our Jewish congregation would stay in relationship with our new Haitian friends.

The service was transformational for us Jews. I knew it when I saw my congregants tearing up as we joined our hands and voices with the Haitians. And I knew it based on the conversations over the next few days. Our group came to understand that being more compassionate human beings made them better Jews and being better Jews made them more compassionate human beings. The Haitians helped us learn that lesson.

The Haitians we were with were devout Christians who live on next to nothing. Most had not finished high school. They were simple people but beautiful souls. They had never met a Jew before and they treated us like we walked straight out of the Bible. During the week we were just a bunch of white folk with some hammers. But in church we were God's

233

chosen people who had come to worship with them, to support their pastor, and to provide financial support to the school Pastor Johnny built to educate their children. To them we were the children of Israel on a mission from God, just as had been written in Scripture. Because our Haitian hosts accorded us so much honor for being Jews, our teens started to realize the value and power of our tribal legacy. It made each of them enormously proud to be a Jew.

Over the next few days, there was a marked change in the attitude of our young people. They peppered me with questions about the very texts that were of no interest to them several nights before. One seventeen-year-old named Sophie, whose family were members of Adat Shalom for a few years before they dropped out and who I did not know before the trip, blew me away with a comment she offered on the last night of our mission. She said: "Rabbi Sid, I really did not relate to all the Jewish stuff you did with us each night. But when you started preaching in church, using the lessons of Chanukah and Jewish history to give strength to the Haitians and they started yelling 'Hallelujah,' you got me too."

When we got back home, some of the teens started to come to Shabbat services, including Sophie. Several made presentations about their trip in our religious school. Four chose to go back to Haiti a year later as we made the service mission an annual congregational program. What motivated the teens to come was the covenantal mission—volunteering one's time to help poor people who were in need of help. Yet over the course of the week they came to understand that the work they were doing connected them to the original mission that God charged Abraham with in chapter 18 of Genesis—*laasot tzedakah umishpat*, "to extend the boundaries of righteousness and justice in the world." They now began to own their Jewish tribal identity.

What then is the formula that will help us more effectively engage next generation Jews? It will not be nostalgia or parents laying the Jewish guilt on extra heavy. Nor is "continuity" sufficient because that offers mostly *what* and not enough *why*. The *why* requires articulating the way that the Jewish tribal story contains universal, covenantal lessons.

Our experience in Haiti provided a lot of the answers to the *why* questions that are so rarely addressed by Jewish institutions. It turns out that the answers to "Why be Jewish?" are the same answers to the question "Why did we go to Haiti?"

Why?

- Because we are a people who were born in slavery and transitioned to freedom.
- Because we are a people who are reminded again and again in our liturgy and sacred texts, "oppress not the stranger for you were strangers in the land of Egypt."
- Because we are a people that has been history's perpetual minority so we have worked to make the most radical teaching of Torah become part of a global ethic of human rights—that every human being has within them the spark of the Divine and must be treated with respect and dignity.

These answers to the *why* question tell us what we Jews must do in the world. It takes Judaism to a level beyond customs, rituals and ceremonies. It motivates us to be agents for healing a broken world.

We must say to our children, not just by word but also by deed, that by virtue of being part of the tribe called "the Jewish people" we are potential carriers of that sacred covenantal message to a world that desperately needs it. This is the ticket to a renaissance of Jewish life in America.

A Tribal-Covenantal Balance

This brings me back to the challenge of being Jewish in America. We are no longer an immigrant community. The powerful lessons of the Holocaust and the founding of the State of Israel no longer come to us as firsthand stories but as history we read in books. We can know it intellectually, but does it *nogea b'lev*, does it touch the heart? Many of us are third- and fourth-generation American Jews. How do we fulfill the commandment from the *Sh'ma*, *V'shinantam l'vanecha*, "You shall teach it diligently to your children"? How do we convey that Judaism is not some relic of religious practices and superstitions handed down from

> We must be able to articulate the way the Jewish tribal story contains universal, covenantal lessons.

235

the past but a way of being in the world that allows us to live a life that honors our particular history and urges us to make the world better for all of humanity?

As Americans we vote for political candidates who are most likely able to ensure economic prosperity and national security. I want those things, too. But it is not enough. Judaism offers an additional value proposition: to help us live lives of sacred purpose. I have offered a glimpse of what that looks like by bringing you with me into Pastor Johnny's church on Sunday morning when covenantal mission and tribal identity were mutually reinforcing to a group of American Jews. I emphasize "mutually reinforcing" because as important as it is to convey to next-generation Jews the emotional energy of tribal identity, we must also be wary of its excesses. Many of us have lived through the end of the Cold War only to discover that the world is every bit as dangerous when it breaks into hundreds of religious and ethnic tribes that will stop at nothing to see their way of life and their belief system prevail. I spend much of my own life and career working to ensure that Jews, both in the Diaspora and in Israel, do not take tribal identity to that dark and evil extreme. There are still too many Jews who rejoice in their Jewish tribalism without thinking about the sacred purpose behind the tribe. If we allow our tribal loyalties to drive our individual and communal behavior unchecked, then we will be turning our back on core covenantal commitments that are central to Jewish teachings and values. Israel must find a way to ensure its own security even as it honors and upholds the rights of 20 percent of the population that are Arab/Palestinian. Jews in the Diaspora live among other faiths, cultures, and ethnic groups. There are times that the interests of one or more of those groups clash with Jewish group interests. The Jewish community must navigate those relationships and issues with sensitivity, not just because many covenantal Jews will have little patience for a Jewish community that doesn't but also because the Jewish tradition teaches us again and again that "because of the way of peace" (*mipnei darchai shalom*) we must go out of our way to compromise and seek peaceful coexistence with other peoples.[1]

I believe that the American Jewish community's best days are still ahead. We will need to let go of old institutional paradigms and embrace new forms of Jewish identification. We must create institutions that integrate the tribal with the covenantal. We must educate from the outside in, starting with that which matters to well-educated, mostly affluent, acculturated American Jews. We must create programs and settings that inspire, that give Jews of all ages a glimpse of the messianic and a sense of the holy. We will need synagogues to see "do-it-yourself" Judaism not as a threat to their existence but as a way to empower Jews to make the congregation ever more exciting and vibrant. We will need to offer a form of confident, cool, and maximalist Judaism in as many different idioms as possible.

The Jewish institutions that will be able to successfully address the next generation of American Jews will need to do one or more of the following:

- Convey the wisdom of Judaism and other spiritual paths
- Advance social justice so that Jews can fulfill the charge of the Hebrew prophets to ally with the "orphan, widow, and stranger in our midst"
- Offer true community and places where people can form rich and deep relationships
- Provide a glimpse of what it looks like to live lives of sacred purpose

Hillel said, "*Im ein ani li, mi li? Ucheshe'ani l'atzmi, mah ani*? If I am not for myself, who am I? But if I am only for myself, what do I amount to?" (*Pirke Avot* 1:14). It wasn't an either/or. It was a both/and. The first is tribal/particular. The second is covenantal/universal. I believe that if the Jewish community begins to follow the course of action set forth in this book, it may well be that the next generation of American Jews will be the first in Jewish history able to wholly embody the fullness of Hillel's dictum.

NOTES

Jewish Megatrends: Charting the Course of the American Jewish Future, by Rabbi Sidney Schwarz

1. See Peter Beinart, "The Failure of the American Jewish Establishment," *New York Review of Books*, June 10, 2010. The article generated a lot of discussion, dismay, and concern in the Jewish community.

2. Steven M. Cohen and Ari Y. Kelman, *Beyond Distancing: Young Adult American Jews and Their Alienation from Israel* (Jewish Identity Project of Reboot, Andrea and Charles Bronfman Philanthropies, 2007). Also, Steven M. Cohen and Ari Y. Kelman, *Thinking about Distancing from Israel* (Association for Social Scientific Study of Jewry, 2010). A study that challenged the Cohen/Kelman analysis was Theodore Sasson, Benjamin Phillips, Charles Kadushin, and Leonard Saxe, *Still Connected: American Jewish Attitudes about Israel* (Waltham, MA: Cohen Center for Modern Jewish Studies, Brandeis University, 2010). Ironically, the data in the Brandeis study was not very dissimilar from that found in the two Cohen/Kelman studies, but the authors offered a far more positive assessment.

3. "The Impact of Taglit-Birthright Israel: 2012 Update," Leonard Saxe, et. al., Cohen Center for Modern Jewish Studies, Brandeis University, 2012.

4. Jonathan S. Woocher, *Sacred Survival: The Civil Religion of American Jews* (Bloomington: Indiana University Press, 1986).

5. Sid Schwarz, *Finding a Spiritual Home: How a New Generation of Jews Can Transform the American Synagogue* (Woodstock, VT: Jewish Lights, 2000), see ch. 2.

6. Steven M. Cohen and Arnold M. Eisen, *The Jew Within: Self, Family and Community in America* (Bloomington: Indiana University Press, 2000).

7. This thesis is central to my book *Judaism and Justice: The Jewish Passion to Repair the World* (Woodstock, VT: Jewish Lights, 2006). See, in particular, chs. 2 and 16. In the book I also use the terms "Exodus consciousness" and "Sinai consciousness" to denote tribal and covenantal leanings, because the book has a more theological orientation and makes use of biblical references to describe the changing nature of Jewish identity.

8. Ibid. For evidence of this phenomenon, see ch. 16. The survey referenced is Steven M. Cohen, "Jewishly Engaged and Congregationally Unaffiliated: The Holy Grail of Jewish Engagement Efforts," *Workmen's Circle / Arbeter Ring*, September 19, 2012; www.bjpa.org/Publications/details.cfm?PublicationID=14338.

9. Robert D. Putman and David E. Campbell, *American Grace: How Religion Unites and Divides Us* (New York: Simon and Schuster, 2010).

10. Ibid.; see data in ch. 5.

11. Ibid.; see data in ch. 4.

12. Ibid., 127.

13. Paul Taylor and Scott Keeter, eds., *Millennials: A Portrait of Generation Next* (Washington, DC: Pew Research Center, 2010), ch. 9. See also Robert Wuthnow, *After the Baby Boomers: How Twenty- and Thirty-Somethings Are Shaping the Future of American Religion* (Princeton, NJ: Princeton University Press, 2007).

14. For some comparative data, see Wade Clark Roof, *Spiritual Marketplace: Baby Boomers and the Remaking of American Religion* (Princeton, NJ: Princeton University Press, 2001).

15. Robert D. Putnam, *Bowling Alone: The Collapse and Revival of American Community* (New York: Simon and Schuster, 2001).

16. Pew Internet and American Life Project, September 2011.

17. Eli Pariser, *The Filter Bubble: What the Internet Is Hiding from You* (New York: Penguin Press, 2011). See also Cass R. Sunstein, *Republic.com 2.0* (Princeton, NJ: Princeton University Press, 2011), which makes a similar argument.

18. Jonathan Sacks, *The Dignity of Difference: How to Avoid the Clash of Civilizations* (New York: Continuum, 2002).

19. For a fuller treatment of this trend, see Schwarz, *Judaism and Justice*, ch. 13.

20. For a survey of the trends in the Jewish community that show a clear growth in the social justice sector, see Shifra Bronznick and Didi Goldenhar, *Visioning Justice and the American Jewish Community* (New York: Nathan Cummings Foundation, 2008).

21. A January 2011 report from the United Synagogue of Conservative Judaism reported a 14 percent decline in membership units in just the previous nine years. In the northeastern United States, that decline was 30 percent. Even more ominous is that only 9 percent of the membership of Conservative synagogues is under the age of forty. By comparison, the decline in membership within the Union for Reform Judaism (URJ) is much more modest—a 7 percent decline in national membership from 1985 to 2010. Yet in 2009 the URJ had to cut its national budget by 20 percent due to the economic downturn, and a group of rabbis representing some of the largest congregations in the movement went public about their dissatisfaction with the direction and leadership of the URJ. Another national study of Conservative and Reform congregations in the United States conducted in 2010 by the Berman Jewish Policy Archive and Synagogue 3000 revealed that only 8 to 9 percent of affiliated members were between the ages of eighteen and thirty-four, while 26 and 21 percent, respectively, of Conservative and Reform congregations were over age sixty-five.

22. Jacob Berkman, "Jewish Federations Try a Sin City Adventure to Woo a New Generation of Donors," *Chronicle of Philanthropy*, March 20, 2011.

23. Eric Fleisch and Ted Sasson, "The New Philanthropy: American Jewish Giving to Israeli Organizations," Cohen Center for Modern Jewish Studies, Brandeis University, 2012.

24. I know of no comprehensive national study of such *minyanim* within synagogues, so there is no hard number to gauge the trend. From my own work with American synagogues, I would hazard a guess that there are two hundred to three hundred such groups across all denominations, with the number growing.

25. According to a 2010 study by Jumpstart, between 20–25 percent of all Jewish startups are non-minyan religious organizations; http://j.mp/njina10.

26. A full treatment of the quest to find community in small groups can be found in Robert Wuthnow's *Sharing the Journey: Support Groups and America's New Quest for Community* (New York: Free Press, 1994). See especially chs. 2 and 12.

27. See Schwarz, *Finding a Spiritual Home*, ch. 3.

28. See Tony Schwartz, *What Really Matters: Searching for Wisdom in America* (New York: Bantam Books, 1995).

29. I owe the observations about JDate to Sam Glassenberg, president of an entertainment company called Funtactix, who met his wife through JDate and who developed this idea for an ELI talk at the 2012 General Assembly of the Jewish Federations of North America. The corporate financial data comes from an investment company called Spark Networks and can be found at http://investor.spark.net/phoenix.zhtml?c=155314&p=irol-IRHome.

30. Founded by Andrew Rosen and Devin Schain, ShalomLearning is pitching their services to synagogues around the country. Another innovative model worth watching in the Jewish Journey Project (JJP). The brainchild of Rabbi Joy Levitt, the executive director of the Manhattan JCC, JJP launched a consortium school for six synagogues and two JCCs in Manhattan in the fall 2012. JJP is more fully described in Rabbi Levitt's chapter in this book. Full disclosure: I served as the project director for JJP during its planning stage and I have also provided consulting services to ShalomLearning.

31. See Schwarz, *Finding a Spiritual Home*, ch 2.

Jewish Culture: What Really Counts?, by Elise Bernhardt

1. American Academy in Jerusalem, internal program evaluation, Foundation for Jewish Culture, 2011.

2. Erik Ludwig and Aryeh Weinberg, *Following the Money: A Look at Jewish Foundation Giving* (San Francisco: Institute for Jewish and Community Research, 2012).

3. JSEP, internal program evaluation conducted by Tobin Belzer, Foundation for Jewish Culture, 2012.

Synagogues: Reimagined, by Rabbi Sharon Brous

1. Simon Rawidowicz, *Israel: The Ever-Dying People and Other Essays* [Sara F. Yoseloff Memorial Publications in Judaism and Jewish Affairs], ed. Benjamin C. I. Ravid (Madison, NJ: Fairleigh Dickinson University Press, 1986), 54.

2. Anna Greenberg, *"Grande Soy Vanilla Latte with Cinnamon, No Foam ...": Jewish Identity and Community in a Time of Unlimited Choices* (New York: Reboot, 2006).

3. Anna Greenberg, *OMG! How Generation Y Is Redefining Faith in the iPod Era* (New York: Reboot, 2005).

4. Ibid., 5.

5. Slonimer Rebbe, *Netivot Shalom, Netivei Da'at* (Awareness) 6:7.

Jewish Family Foundations: "Come Together, Right Now", by Sandy Cardin

1. Erik Ludwig and Aryeh K. Weinberg, *Following the Money: A Look at Jewish Foundation Giving* (Institute for Jewish and Community Research, 2012). ICJR defined "Jewish foundations" as foundations established by a Jewish donor. All foundations selected have made grants to Jewish causes and include both private foundations and supporting foundations under the roof of Jewish Federations.

2. *National Jewish Population Survey 2000–01: Strength, Challenge and Diversity in the American Jewish Population* (United Jewish Communities).

3. Anna Greenberg, *"Grande Soy Vanilla Latte with Cinnamon, No Foam …": Jewish Identity and Community in a Time of Unlimited Choices* (New York: Reboot, 2006); Joshua Avedon, Shawn Landres, and Felicia Herman, eds., *The Jewish Innovation Economy: An Emerging Market for Knowledge and Social Capital* (Los Angeles and New York: Jumpstart, Natan Fund, and Samuel Bronfman Foundation, 2011).

4. Birthright is a free, ten-day trip to Israel for young Jewish adults aged eighteen to twenty-six.

5. The Charles and Lynn Schusterman Family Foundation was among them, along with the Jim Joseph Foundation, Andrea and Charles Bronfman Philanthropies, Samuel Bronfman Foundation, Nathan Cummings Foundation, Jewish Life Network/Steinhardt Foundation, Wexner Foundation, and many others. Some of them even participate in an informal association known as the "Study Group" and talk amongst themselves about the Jewish future.

6. The Joshua Venture Group funds, trains, and supports social entrepreneurs working to transform the Jewish landscape.

7. Bikkurim, which supports innovative, New York–based, Jewish nonprofit projects in their early stages, is one of the few examples of a Federation—namely, the UJA-Federation of New York—being involved in funding innovation early on.

8. Sarah Bunin Benor, "Young Jewish Leaders in Los Angeles: Strengthening the Jewish People in Conventional and Unconventional Ways," in *The New Jewish Leaders: Reshaping the American Jewish Landscape*, ed. Jack Wertheimer (Waltham, MA: Brandeis University Press, 2011), 135.

9. Steve Schwager, "The Role of the Mega-Organization in the Era of Micro-Philanthropy," *Peoplehood Papers* 7 (2012): 56.

10. Ludwig and Weinberg, *Following the Money*.

11. PresenTense is an organization dedicated to energizing and inspiring the most creative minds of this generation, investing in their ideas and energy to revitalize the Jewish community.

12. Moishe House is an international organization that provides meaningful Jewish experiences to young adults in their twenties. The settings are forty-six houses in fourteen countries where young Jewish leaders create vibrant home-based communities for their peers.

13. Shaul Kelner, "In Its Own Image: Independent Philanthropy and the Cultivation of Young Jewish Leadership," in *The New Jewish Leaders: Reshaping the American Jewish Landscape*, ed. Jack Wertheimer (Waltham, MA: Brandeis University Press, 2011).

Israel and Jewish Life: A Twenty-First-Century Educational Vision, by Dr. Barry Chazan and Anne Lanski

1. S. Y. Agnon, *Only Yesterday*, trans. Barbara Harshav (Princeton, NJ: Princeton University Press, 2000).

2. Meir Shalev, *The Blue Mountain* (New York: HarperCollins, 1988).

3. Peter Beinart, "The Failure of the American Jewish Establishment," *New York Review of Books*, June 10, 2010.

4. Peter Beinart, *The Crisis of Zionism* (New York: Henry Holt and Co., 2012).

5. Steven M. Cohen and Ari Y. Kelman, *Beyond Distancing: Young American Jews and Their Alienation from Israel* (Jewish Identity Project of Reboot, Andrea and Charles Bronfman Philanthropies, 2007).

6. Theodore Sasson, Benjamin Phillips, Graham Wright, Charles Kadushin, and Leonard Saxe, "Understanding Young Adult Attachment to Israel: Period, Lifecycle, and Generational Dynamics," *Contemporary Jewry* 32, no. 1 (2012): 67–84; Leonard Saxe, "Never Mind," blog posted on July 19, 2012, http://blogs.brandeis.edu.

7. Steven M. Cohen and Samuel Abrams, "Youngest Adults Show Evidence of a Birthright Bump in Attachment to Israel Along with Decreased Relative Trust in Israel" (New York: Workmen's Circle/Arbiter Ring, 2012).

8. Leonard Saxe et al., *Jewish Futures Project: The Impact of Taglit-Birthright Israel: 2010 Update* (Waltham, MA: Cohen Center for Modern Jewish Studies, Brandeis University, 2011); Leonard Saxe et al., *Generation Birthright Israel: The Impact of an Israel Experience on Jewish Identity and Choice* (Waltham, MA: Cohen Center for Modern Jewish Studies, Brandeis University, 2009).

9. Erik H. Erikson, *Identity and the Lifecycle* (New York: Norton, 1988).

10. John Dewey, *Experience and Education* (New York: Collier Books, 1938).

11. Zohar Raviv, "Negotiating Multiple Landscapes," *The Aleph-Bet of Israel Education* (iCenter, 2011).

12. There are examples of attempts to present dual narratives, e.g., Paul Scham, Walid Salem, and Benjamin Pogrund, *Shared Histories: A Palestinian-Israeli Dialogue* (Walnut Creek, CA: Left Coast Press, 2005). A noteworthy educational case study in this area is the effort of the Israeli Ministry of Education to deal with the issue of multiple narratives within the context of a textbook encompassing the subject: *Yotzeym l'Derech Ezrachit* (*Embark on Projects: Israeli Society, State and Citizens*), www.reches.co.il/article_page.asp?id=719&scid=72. The book became the subject of diverse reactions and much discussion and was ultimately recalled to enable necessary adjustments. This case study reveals both the educational concern of the ministry to deal with complicated issues and the complicated nature of education in a reality of conflicted viewpoints and security realities. See the following for details about the discussion: www.ynet.co.il/articles/0,7340,L-4216938,00; www.haaretz.co.il/news/education/1.1687832; www.haaretz.co.il/news/education/1.1688123; http://citizenship.cet.ac.il/ItemList.aspx?SearchTag=e0d865e6-3218-4596-98b4-99861bbf7715; http://citizenship.cet.ac.il/ShowItem.aspx?ItemID=da9643c0-83c5-415e-b761-daca74d969ac&lang=HEB; www.haaretz.com/misc/article-

print-page/israel-education-ministry-fires-civics-studies-coordinator-attacked-by-right-1.456182?trailingPath=2.169%2C2.225%2C2.226%2C.

13. Steven Pinker, *The Language Instinct* (New York: HarperPerennial, 1994).

14. Lori Sagarin, "Modern Hebrew in Personal Identity Development," *The Aleph-Bet of Israel Education* (iCenter, 2011).

15. Yehuda Amichai, *Selected Poetry of Yehuda Amichai* (New York: Harper and Row, 1986).

16. Barry Chazan, *Does the Teen Israel Experience Make a Difference?* (Israel Experience, Inc., 1997); Leonard Saxe and Barry Chazan, *Ten Days of Birthright Israel: A Journey in Young Adult Identity* (Waltham, MA: Brandeis University Press, 2008); Leonard Saxe, "Jewish Identity Development: The Israel Dimension," *The Aleph-Bet of Israel Education* (iCenter, 2011).

17. Lesley Litman, "The Educator and Israel Education," *The Aleph-Bet of Israel Education* (iCenter, 2011).

18. Parker Palmer, *The Courage to Teach* (San Francisco: Jossey-Bass, 1998).

Denominationalism: History and Hopes, by Dr. David Ellenson

1. Pew Forum on Religion and Public Life, "U.S. Religious Landscape Survey," (2008), 22.

"Getting" the Next Generation: Young Adults and the Jewish Future, by Wayne L. Firestone

1. In 2005 and 2012, the international polling firm Penn Schoen Berland conducted two U.S. national student surveys (with a sample size each of six hundred students) that point to these changes among Jewish millennials. The first survey results are discussed in a Hillel published monograph, *Hillel's Journey. Distinctively Jewish, Universally Human*, by Dr. Beth Cousens (2007).

2. Penn, Schoen & Berland Associates, *2012 Hillel Study*. Washington, DC: Hillel: Foundation for Jewish Campus Life, 2012. www.hillel.org/NR/rdonlyres/AE6C133F-EB40-413F-A6FE 46C8196880F2/0/2012HillelStudy.pdf.

3. Craig Newmark, "16 People and Organizations Changing the World in 2012," web log post, *CraigConnects*. http://craigconnects.org/2011/12/changing-the-world-in-2012.html.

4. Steven D. Cohen, Ezra Kopelowitz, Jack Ukeles, and Minna Wolf, *Assessing the Impact of Senior Jewish Educators and Campus Entrepreneurs Initiative Interns on the Jewish Engagement of College Students—Two-Year Summary, 2008–2010* (Research Success Technologies, Ukeles Associates, November 2, 2010).

5. Jack Wertheimer, *Generation of Change: How Leaders in Their Twenties and Thirties Are Reshaping American Jewish Life* (Avi Chai Foundation, September 2010).

6. Wayne Firestone and Rachel L. Gildiner, "Engaging a New Generation: Hillel Innovates for the Millenials," *Journal of Jewish Communal Service* (Spring 2012): 87–96. The evaluation was based on a ten-campus pilot project funded by the Jim Joseph Foundation.

7. I want to acknowledge my participation in an empowering convening organized by the Charles and Lynn Schusterman Family Foundation in 2011, focused on creating a healthy Jewish ecosystem with effective transitions for teens and young adults.

8. Indeed, they illustrate that in many cases having too many options often deters someone from opting in because it is too daunting.

Jewish Social Justice: Looking Beyond Ourselves, by Rabbi Jill Jacobs

1. Robert P. Jones and Daniel Cox, *Chosen for What? Jewish Values in 2012* (Public Religion Research Institute, 2012).

2. Rabbi Isaac Jacob Weiss, *Minchat Yitzchak* 2:82, and Rabbi Ben Zion Meir Chai Uzziel, *Piskei Uziel b'She'elot Hazman Siman* 30.

3. For a more complete discussion of building partnerships and negotiating power relations, see Jill Jacobs, *Where Justice Dwells: A Hands-On Guide to Doing Social Justice in Your Jewish Community* (Woodstock, VT: Jewish Lights, 2011), ch. 6.

Interreligious Collaboration: American Judaism and Religious Pluralism, by Rabbi Or N. Rose

1. Robert D. Putnam and David E. Campbell, *American Grace: How Religion Divides and Unites Us* (New York: Simon and Schuster, 2010).

2. Diana Eck, "What Is Religious Pluralism?" The Pluralism Project at Harvard University, http://pluralism.org/pages/pluralism/what_is_pluralism. See also Eboo Patel, *Sacred Ground: Pluralism, Prejudice, and the Promise of America* (Boston: Beacon Press, 2012).

3. See Putnam and Campbell, *American Grace*, 560–61.

4. Ibid., 505, 550.

5. Ibid., 526–34.

6. Ibid., 574–76. Putnam and Campbell report that the Muslim community received the lowest favorability rating of any religious group in the United States in the Faith Matters surveys of 2006 and 2007.

7. To learn about the continuation of this historic meeting in India, see Roger Kamentz, *The Jew in the Lotus: A Poet's Rediscovery of Jewish Identity in Buddhist India* (New York: HarperOne, 2007, updated edition). Buddhism has, of course, attracted many American Jewish spiritual seekers over the past few decades, including some who identify as both Jewish and Buddhist, or "Jewbu." The wider phenomenon of hybrid religious identity is a subject I hope to explore in future writings.

8. Gregory Mobley, "What the Rabbi Taught the Reverend about the Baby Jesus," in *My Neighbor's Faith: Stories of Interreligious Encounter, Growth, and Transformation*, ed. Jennifer Howe Peace, Or N. Rose, and Gregory Mobley (Maryknoll, NY: Orbis Books, 2012), 38–40.

9. See Alan Brill, "Recognizing the Other: Sameness and Difference in a Jewish Theology of Other Religions," *Boston Theological Institute Magazine* 11, no. 2 (Spring 2012): 4–8.

The Federation System: Loving Humanity and the Jewish People, by Barry Shrage

1. Substantial research over the past several decades has made clear that American Jewish attitudes reflect strong support for Israel and lack of sympathy/trust in the Palestinian position; see surveys conducted by the American Jewish Committee (www.ajc. org/site/c.ijITI2PHKoG/b.846741/k.8A33/Publications__Surveys/apps/nl/newsletter3.asp) as well as the Cohen Center for Modern Jewish Studies research with both the general population and young adults in particular (see, e.g., https://bir. brandeis.edu/bitstream/handle/10192/24037/still.connected.08.25.10.3.pdf?sequence=9). With respect to recent developments, the most current data from the Cohen Center's surveys of applicants to Taglit-Birthright Israel indicate that an overwhelming majority agree that "Israel is under constant threat from hostile neighbors who seek its destruction" and only a minority agree that "Israel is guilty of violating the human rights of the Palestinian people" (Leonard Saxe, personal communication). There is a Taglit effect—alumni see the threat more strongly and are less likely to see violation of Palestinian rights—but even among non-Taglit young adults, support for Israel and fear for its survival remain strong compared to concern for Palestinian rights.

2. "One large chunk of non-Orthodox Jews cares less and less about Israel because they care less and less about Judaism"; Peter Beinart, *The Crisis of Zionism* (New York: Henry Holt and Co., 2012), 168. "Many American Jews know very little about Judaism. And it's hard to feel connected to something you don't understand. The evidence is clear that Jewish commitment stems from Jewish education, and by far the most effective purveyors of Jewish education are full-time Jewish schools"; Peter Beinart, "The Jewish Case for School Vouchers," *Wall Street Journal*, March 29, 2012.

3. Steven M. Cohen and Ari Kelman, "Beyond Distancing: Young Adult American Jews and Their Alienation from Israel," The Jewish Identity Project of Reboot, 2007.

4. See www.huffingtonpost.com/robert-j-rosenthal/generation-who-new-report_b_928426. html; www.volunteeringinamerica.gov/rankings/States/Millennial-Volunteer-Rate/2010.

5. Abraham Joshua Heschel, *Moral Grandeur and Spiritual Audacity: Essays,* ed. Susannah Heschel (New York: Farrar, Straus and Giroux, 1997), 27.

6. The critical importance of tying our communities of *Torah, tzedek,* and *chesed* to our love of the State of Israel and ultimately to our "tribal" sense of peoplehood is a very complicated and long discussion (if you don't instinctively "get it," as in my experience most Jews of every generation do!), but two books make the case in clear and wonderful language. The first is *The Dignity of Difference: How to Avoid the Clash of Civilizations* (New York: Continuum, 2002), by Rabbi Jonathan Sacks, and the second is *Imagine: John Lennon and the Jews* (CreateSpace, 2010), by Ze'ev Maghen. Maghen describes the critical connection between our love of the Jewish people and the passion that drives us to explore and love every part of our beautiful and meaningful civilization and to strive to create a Judaism of meaning. Rabbi Sacks reinforces the importance of difference and diversity among religions and cultures for the creative survival of humankind and for the Jewish people.

7. The 2005 Greater Boston Community Study, "Intermarried Families and Their Children," Katherine N. Gan, Patty Jacobson, Gil Preuss, and Barry Shrage, Combined Jewish Philanthropies, 2008; www.cjp.org/getfile.asp?id=24386.

Jewish Education: From Continuity to Meaning, by Dr. Jonathan S. Woocher

1. Jonathan S. Woocher, *Sacred Survival: The Civil Religion of American Jews* (Bloomington: Indiana University Press, 1986).

2. Cf. Seymour Fox, Israel Scheffler, and Daniel Marom, eds., *Visions of Jewish Education* (Cambridge: Cambridge University Press, 2003).

3. Peter L. Berger, *The Sacred Canopy: Elements of a Sociological Theory of Religion* (Garden City, NY: Doubleday, 1967).

4. Steven M. Cohen and Arnold M. Eisen, *The Jew Within: Self, Family, and Community in America* (Bloomington: Indiana University Press, 2000).

5. See Ron Wolfson, *Relational Judaism: Using the Power of Relationships to Transform the Jewish Community* (Woodstock, VT: Jewish Lights, 2013) and *The Spirituality of Welcoming: How to Transform Your Congregation into a Sacred Community* (Woodstock, VT: Jewish Lights, 2006); and Lawrence A. Hoffman, *Rethinking Synagogues: A New Vocabulary for Congregational Life* (Woodstock, VT: Jewish Lights, 2006).

6. Martin Buber, "Education," in *Between Man and Man* (London: Kegan Paul, 1947).

7. Franz Rosenzweig, *On Jewish Learning*, ed. Nahum N. Glatzer (New York: Schocken Books, 1955).

8. John Kania and Mark Kramer, "Collective Impact," *Stanford Social Innovation Review* 9, no. 1 (Winter 2011): 36–41.

Toward a Jewish Renaissance, by Rabbi Sidney Schwarz

1. Babylonian Talmud, *Gittin* 61a. For a fuller development on how this phrase has been applied to contemporary interactions between Jews and non-Jews, see Walter Wurzberger, "*Darchei Shalom,*" Gesher 6 (1977–8), and Ahron Soloveichik, "Jew and Jew, Jew and Non-Jew," in *Logic of the Heart, Logic of the Mind: Wisdom and Reflections on Topics of Our Times* (Jerusalem: Genesis Jerusalem Press, 1991), 69–91.

SUGGESTIONS FOR FURTHER READINGS

Anderson, Chris. *The Long Tail: How Endless Choice Is Creating Unlimited Demand.* New York: Random House Business, 2006.

Aron, Isa. *Becoming a Congregation of Learners: Learning as a Key to RevitalizingCongregational Life.* Woodstock, VT: Jewish Lights, 2000.

———. *The Self-Renewing Congregation: Organizational Strategies for Revitalizing Congregational Life.* Woodstock, VT: Jewish Lights, 2002.

Aron, Isa, Steven M. Cohen, Lawrence A. Hoffman, and Ari Y. Kelman. *Sacred Strategies: Transforming Synagogues from Functional to Visionary.* Hendon, VA: Alban Institute, 2010.

Bass, Diana Butler. *The Practicing Congregation: Imagining a New Old Church.* Herndon, VA: Alban Institute, 2004.

Bronfman, Edgar, and Beth Zasloff. *Hope, Not Fear: A Path to Jewish Renaissance.* New York: St. Martins Press, 2008.

Brown, Erica. *Inspired Jewish Leadership: Practical Approaches to Building Strong Communities.* Woodstock, Vt.: Jewish Lights, 2008.

Carroll, Jack W., and Wade Clark Roof. *Bridging Divided Worlds: Generational Cultures in Congregations.* San Francisco: Pfeiffer, 2002.

Cohen, Norman J. *Moses and the Journey to Leadership: Timeless Lessons of Effective Management from the Bible and Today's Leaders.* Woodstock, VT: Jewish Lights, 2008.

Cohen, Steven M., and Arnold Eisen. *The Jew Within: Self, Family and Community in the United States.* Bloomington, IN: Indiana University Press, 2000.

Collins, Jim. *Good to Great.* New York: HarperCollins, 2001.

Dreier, Peter, John Mollenkopf, and Todd Swanstrom. *Place Matters: Metropolitics for the Twenty-first Century.* 2nd ed. Lawrence: University Press of Kansas, 2004.

Duhigg, Charles. *The Power of Habit: Why We Do What We Do and How We Change It.* New York: Random House, 2012.

Eisen, Arnold. *Rethinking Modern Judaism: Ritual, Commandment, Community.* Chicago: University of Chicago Press, 1999.

Eizenstat, Stuart, E. *The Future of the Jews: How Global Forces Are Impacting the Jewish People, Israel, and Its Relationship with the United States.* Lanham, MD: Rowman and Littlefield, 2012.

Gillman, Neil: *Sacred Fragments: Recovering Theology for the Modern Jew.* Philadelphia: Jewish Publication Society, 1990.

Green, Arthur. *Ehyeh: A Kabbalah for Tomorrow.* Woodstock, VT: Jewish Lights, 2003.

———. *Radical Judaism: Rethinking God and Tradition.* New Haven, CT: Yale University Press, 2010.

Greenberg, Irving. *Perspectives: The Third Great Cycle of Jewish History, Voluntary Covenant, Power and Politics.* A CLAL Thesis. New York: The National Jewish Center for Learning and Leadership, 2001.

Hartman, David. *The God Who Hates Lies: Confronting and Rethinking Jewish Tradition.* Woodstock, VT: Jewish Lights, 2011.

Hartman, Donniel. *The Boundaries of Judaism.* London: Continuum, 2007.

Heath, Chip, and Dan Heath. *Switch: How to Change Things When Change Is Hard.* New York: Crown, 2010.

Heller, Zachary I., ed. *Synagogues in a Time of Change: Fragmentation and Diversity in Jewish Religious Movements.* Herndon, VA: Alban Institute, 2009.

Herberg, Will. *Protestant, Catholic and Jew: An Essay in American Religious Sociology.* Garden City, NY: Doubleday, 1955.

Herring, Hayim. *Tomorrow's Synagogue Today: Creating Vibrant Centers of Jewish Life.* Herndon, VA: Alban Institute, 2012.

Jacobs, Jill. *There Shall Be No Needy: Pursuing Social Justice through Jewish Law and Tradition.* Woodstock, VT: Jewish Lights, 2010.

———. *Where Justice Dwells: A Hands-On Guide to Doing Social Justice in Your Jewish Community.* Woodstock, VT: Jewish Lights, 2011.

Kamenetz, Rodger. *The Jew in the Lotus: A Poet's Rediscovery of Jewish Identity in Buddhist India.* New York: HarperOne, 1994.

Kaunfer, Elie. *Empowered Judaism: What Independent Minyanim Can Teach Us About Building Vibrant Communities.* Woodstock, VT: Jewish Lights, 2010.

Kurtzer, Yehuda. *Shuva: The Future of the Jewish Past.* Waltham, MA: Brandeis University Press, 2012.

Maghen, Ze'ev. *John Lennon and the Jews: A Philosophical Rampage.* New York: Bottom Books, 2011.

Polish, David. *The Eternal Dissent: A Search for Meaning in Jewish History.* London: Abelard-Schuman, 1960.

Putnam, Robert, and David Campbell. *American Grace: How Religion Divides and Unites Us.* New York: Simon and Schuster, 2010.

Putman, Robert, and Dan Cohen. *Bowling Alone: The Collapse and Revival of American Community.* New York: Simon and Schuster, 2000.

Rose, Or N., Jo Ellen Green Kaiser, and Margie Klein, eds. *Righteous Indignation: A Jewish Call for Justice.* Woodstock, VT: Jewish Lights, 2008.

Rosen, Jonathan. *The Talmud and the Internet: A Journey Between Worlds.* New York: Farrar, Strauss and Giroux, 2000.

Rushkoff, Douglas. *Nothing Sacred: The Truth About Judaism.* New York: Crown, 2003.

———. *Playing the Future: What We Can Learn from Digital Kids.* New York: Putnam, 1999.

Sacks, Jonathan. *The Dignity of Difference: How to Avoid the Clash of Civilizations.* London: Continuum, 2002.

———. *Future Tense: Jews, Judaism, and Israel in the Twenty-first Century.* New York: Random House, 2012.

———. *To Heal a Fractured World: The Ethics of Responsibility.* New York: Schocken, 2007.

———. *A Letter in a Scroll: Understanding Our Jewish Identity and Exploring the Legacy of the World's Oldest Religion.* New York: Free Press, 2000.

Schachter-Shalomi, Zalman, with Joel Segel. *Jewish with Feeling: A Guide to Meaningful Jewish Practice.* Woodstock, VT: Jewish Lights, 2013.

Schiffman, Lisa. *Generation J.* San Francisco: HarperCollins, 1999.

Schulweis, Harold. *For Those Who Can't Believe: Overcoming Obstacles to Faith.* New York: HarperCollins, 1994.

Schwarz, Sidney. *Finding a Spiritual Home: How a New Generation of Jews Can Transform the American Synagogue.* Woodstock, VT: Jewish Lights, 2000.

———. *Judaism and Justice: The Jewish Passion to Repair the World.* Woodstock, VT: Jewish Lights, 2006.

Shirky, Clay. *Here Comes Everybody: The Power of Organizing without Organizations.* New York: Penguin, 2009.

Silverstein, Alan. *Alternatives to Assimilation: The Response of Reform Judaism to American Culture 1840–1930.* Hanover, NH: University Press of New England, 1994.

Solomon, Lewis D. *Jewish Spirituality: Revitalizing Judaism for the Twenty-First Century.* Northvale, NJ: Jason Aronson, 2000.

Turkle, Sherry. *Alone Together: Why We Expect More from Technology and Less from Each Other.* New York: Basic Books, 2011.

———. *Life on the Screen: Identity in the Age of the Internet.* New York: Simon and Schuster, 1997.

Wertheimer, Jack, ed. *The New Jewish Leaders: Reshaping the American Jewish Landscape.* Waltham, MA: Brandeis University Press, 2011.

Wolfson, Ron. *Relational Judaism: Using the Power of Relationships to Transform the Jewish Community.* Woodstock, VT: Jewish Lights, 2013.

———. *The Spirituality of Welcoming: How to Transform Your Congregation into a Sacred Community.* Woodstock, VT: Jewish Lights, 2006.

Woocher, Jonathan. *Sacred Survival: The Civil Religion of American Jews.* Bloomington: Indiana University Press, 1986.

Wuthnow, Robert. *After the Baby Boomers: How Twenty- and Thirty-Somethings Are Shaping the Future of American Religion.* Princeton: Princeton University Press, 2007.

———. *Loose Connections: Joining Together in America's Fragmented Communities.* Cambridge: Harvard University Press, 1998.

About the Author

Rabbi Sid Schwarz is a social entrepreneur, an author, and a political activist. He founded and for twenty-one years led PANIM: The Institute for Jewish Leadership and Values, an organization dedicated to inspiring, training, and empowering Jewish youth to a life of leadership, activism, and service. Dr. Schwarz previously served as the executive director of the Jewish Community Council of Greater Washington D.C. where he oversaw the public affairs and community relations work for the Jewish community. He is the founding rabbi of Adat Shalom Reconstructionist Congregation in Bethesda, Maryland, where he continues to teach and lead services. Dr. Schwarz holds a PhD in Jewish history and is the author of numerous articles and two groundbreaking books, *Finding a Spiritual Home: How a New Generation of Jews Can Transform the American Synagogue* and *Judaism and Justice: The Jewish Passion to Repair the World*.

Rabbi Yitz Greenberg, founder of Clal—The National Jewish Center for Learning and Leadership and one of American Jewry's most notable leaders, has written about Sid, "Rabbi Sid Schwarz' life and career embody a unique mix of religious vision and an ability to implement that vision in the real world."

Currently, Rabbi Schwarz serves as a senior fellow at Clal, where he is involved in a program that trains rabbis to be visionary spiritual leaders. He helped to found and now co-chairs the Greater Washington Forum on Israeli Arab Issues, which explores the future of Israel as a democracy. He also helped to develop, and now directs, the Rene Cassin Fellowship Program, an international fellowship program on Judaism and human rights for Jewish young professionals with hubs in New York, London, and Jerusalem. His consulting work with synagogues and Jewish organizations around the United States included serving as the original project director for the Jewish Journey Project in Manhattan, an initiative to revolutionize supplementary Jewish education for children.

Rabbi Schwarz is the recipient of the prestigious Covenant Award for his pioneering work in the field of Jewish education and he was named by *Newsweek* one of the fifty most influential rabbis in North America.

Index

AVAILABLE FROM BETTER BOOKSTORES.
TRY YOUR BOOKSTORE FIRST.

Bible Study / Midrash

The Book of Job: Annotated & Explained
Translation and Annotation by Donald Kraus; Foreword by Dr. Marc Brettler
Clarifies for today's readers what Job is, how to overcome difficulties in the text, and what it may mean for us. Features fresh translation and probing commentary.
5½ x 8½, 256 pp, Quality PB, 978-1-59473-389-5 **$16.99**

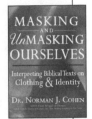

Masking and Unmasking Ourselves: Interpreting Biblical Texts on Clothing & Identity   *By Dr. Norman J. Cohen*
Presents ten Bible stories that involve clothing in an essential way, as a means of learning about the text, its characters and their interactions.
6 x 9, 240 pp, HC, 978-1-58023-461-0 **$24.99**

The Other Talmud—*The Yerushalmi*: Unlocking the Secrets of The Talmud of Israel for Judaism Today   *By Rabbi Judith Z. Abrams, PhD*
A fascinating—and stimulating—look at "the other Talmud" and the possibilities for Jewish life reflected there.   6 x 9, 256 pp, HC, 978-1-58023-463-4 **$24.99**

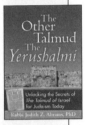

The Torah Revolution: Fourteen Truths That Changed the World
By Rabbi Reuven Hammer, PhD   A unique look at the Torah and the revolutionary teachings of Moses embedded within it that gave birth to Judaism and influenced the world.   6 x 9, 240 pp, HC, 978-1-58023-457-3 **$24.99**

Ecclesiastes: Annotated & Explained
Translation and Annotation by Rabbi Rami Shapiro; Foreword by Rev. Barbara Cawthorne Crafton
5½ x 8½, 160 pp, Quality PB, 978-1-59473-287-4 **$16.99**

Ethics of the Sages: Pirke Avot—Annotated & Explained   *Translation and Annotation by Rabbi Rami Shapiro*   5½ x 8½, 192 pp, Quality PB, 978-1-59473-207-2 **$16.99**

The Genesis of Leadership: What the Bible Teaches Us about Vision, Values and Leading Change   *By Rabbi Nathan Laufer; Foreword by Senator Joseph I. Lieberman*
6 x 9, 288 pp, Quality PB, 978-1-58023-352-1 **$18.99**

Hineini in Our Lives: Learning How to Respond to Others through 14 Biblical Texts and Personal Stories   *By Rabbi Norman J. Cohen, PhD*   6 x 9, 240 pp, Quality PB, 978-1-58023-274-6 **$16.99**

A Man's Responsibility: A Jewish Guide to Being a Son, a Partner in Marriage, a Father and a Community Leader   *By Rabbi Joseph B. Meszler*   6 x 9, 192 pp, Quality PB, 978-1-58023-435-1 **$16.99**

The Modern Men's Torah Commentary: New Insights from Jewish Men on the 54 Weekly Torah Portions   *Edited by Rabbi Jeffrey K. Salkin*
6 x 9, 368 pp, HC, 978-1-58023-395-8 **$24.99**

Moses and the Journey to Leadership: Timeless Lessons of Effective Management from the Bible and Today's Leaders   *By Rabbi Norman J. Cohen, PhD*
6 x 9, 240 pp, Quality PB, 978-1-58023-351-4 **$18.99**; HC, 978-1-58023-227-2 **$21.99**

Proverbs: Annotated & Explained
Translation and Annotation by Rabbi Rami Shapiro
5½ x 8½, 288 pp, Quality PB, 978-1-59473-310-9 **$16.99**

Righteous Gentiles in the Hebrew Bible: Ancient Role Models for Sacred Relationships
By Rabbi Jeffrey K. Salkin; Foreword by Rabbi Harold M. Schulweis;
Preface by Phyllis Tickle 6 x 9, 192 pp, Quality PB, 978-1-58023-364-4 **$18.99**

Sage Tales: Wisdom and Wonder from the Rabbis of the Talmud
By Rabbi Burton L. Visotzky 6 x 9, 256 pp, HC, 978-1-58023-456-6 **$24.99**

The Wisdom of Judaism: An Introduction to the Values of the Talmud
By Rabbi Dov Peretz Elkins 6 x 9, 192 pp, Quality PB, 978-1-58023-327-9 **$16.99**

Or phone, fax, mail or e-mail to: **JEWISH LIGHTS** Publishing
Sunset Farm Offices, Route 4 • P.O. Box 237 • Woodstock, Vermont 05091
Tel: (802) 457-4000 • Fax: (802) 457-4004 • www.jewishlights.com
Credit card orders: **(800) 962-4544** (8:30AM–5:30PM EST Monday–Friday)
Generous discounts on quantity orders. SATISFACTION GUARANTEED. Prices subject to change.

Children's Books

Around the World in One Shabbat
Jewish People Celebrate the Sabbath Together
By Durga Yael Bernhard

Takes your child on a colorful adventure to share the many ways Jewish people celebrate Shabbat around the world.
11 x 8½, 32 pp, Full-color illus., HC, 978-1-58023-433-7 **$18.99** *For ages 3–6*

It's a ... It's a ... It's a Mitzvah
By Liz Suneby and Diane Heiman; Full-color Illus. by Laurel Molk

Join Mitzvah Meerkat and friends as they introduce children to the everyday kindnesses that mark the beginning of a Jewish journey and a lifetime commitment to *tikkun olam* (repairing the world). 9 x 12, 32 pp, Full-color illus., HC, 978-1-58023-509-9 **$18.99** *For ages 3–6*

What You Will See Inside a Synagogue
By Rabbi Lawrence A. Hoffman, PhD, and Dr. Ron Wolfson; Full-color photos by Bill Aron

A colorful, fun-to-read introduction that explains the ways and whys of Jewish worship and religious life. 8½ x 10½, 32 pp, Full-color photos, Quality PB, 978-1-59473-256-0 **$8.99** *For ages 6 & up*
(A book from SkyLight Paths, Jewish Lights' sister imprint)

Because Nothing Looks Like God
By Lawrence Kushner and Karen Kushner

Real-life examples of happiness and sadness—from goodnight stories, to the hope and fear felt the first time at bat, to the closing moments of someone's life—invite parents and children to explore, together, the questions we all have about God, no matter what our age. 11 x 8½, 32 pp, Full-color illus., HC, 978-1-58023-092-6 **$18.99** *For ages 4 & up*

The Book of Miracles: A Young Person's Guide to Jewish Spiritual Awareness
Written and illus. by Lawrence Kushner

Easy-to-read, imaginatively illustrated book encourages kids' awareness of their own spirituality. Revealing the essence of Judaism in a language they can understand and enjoy. 6 x 9, 96 pp, 2-color illus., HC, 978-1-879045-78-1 **$16.95** *For ages 9–13*

In God's Hands   *By Lawrence Kushner and Gary Schmidt*

Brings new life to a traditional Jewish folktale, reminding parents and kids of all faiths and all backgrounds that each of us has the power to make the world a better place—working ordinary miracles with our everyday deeds.
9 x 12, 32 pp, Full-color illus., HC, 978-1-58023-224-1 **$16.99** *For ages 5 & up*

In Our Image: God's First Creatures
By Nancy Sohn Swartz

A playful new twist to the Genesis story, God asks all of nature to offer gifts to humankind—with a promise that the humans would care for creation in return. 9 x 12, 32 pp, Full-color illus., HC, 978-1-879045-99-6 **$16.95** *For ages 4 & up*

The Jewish Family Fun Book, 2nd Ed.
Holiday Projects, Everyday Activities, and Travel Ideas with Jewish Themes
By Danielle Dardashti and Roni Sarig

The complete sourcebook for families wanting to put a new spin on activities for Jewish holidays, holy days and the everyday. It offers dozens of easy-to-do activities that bring Jewish tradition to life for kids of all ages.
6 x 9, 304 pp, w/ 70+ b/w illus., Quality PB, 978-1-58023-333-0 **$18.99**

The Kids' Fun Book of Jewish Time   *By Emily Sper*
A unique way to introduce children to the Jewish calendar—night and day, the seven-day week, Shabbat, the Hebrew months, seasons and dates.
9 x 7½, 24 pp, Full-color illus., HC, 978-1-58023-311-8 **$16.99** *For ages 3–6*

What Makes Someone a Jew?   *By Lauren Seidman*

Reflects the changing face of American Judaism. Helps preschoolers and young readers (ages 3–6) understand that you don't have to look a certain way to be Jewish. 10 x 8½, 32 pp, Full-color photos, Quality PB, 978-1-58023-321-7 **$8.99** *For ages 3–6*

When a Grandparent Dies: A Kid's Own Remembering Workbook for
Dealing with Shiva and the Year Beyond   *By Nechama Liss-Levinson*
8 x 10, 48 pp, 2-color text, HC, 978-1-879045-44-6 **$15.95** *For ages 7–13*

Congregation Resources

A Practical Guide to Rabbinic Counseling
Edited by Rabbi Yisrael N. Levitz, PhD, and Rabbi Abraham J. Twerski, MD
Provides rabbis with the requisite knowledge and practical guidelines for some of the most common counseling situations.
6 x 9, 432 pp, HC, 978-1-58023-562-4 **$40.00**

Professional Spiritual & Pastoral Care: A Practical Clergy and Chaplain's Handbook
Edited by Rabbi Stephen B. Roberts, MBA, MHL, BCJC
An essential resource integrating the classic foundations of pastoral care with the latest approaches to spiritual care, specifically intended for professionals who work or spend time with congregants in acute care hospitals, behavioral health facilities, rehabilitation centers and long-term care facilities.
6 x 9, 480 pp, HC, 978-1-59473-312-3 **$50.00**

Reimagining Leadership in Jewish Organizations: Ten Practical Lessons to Help You Implement Change and Achieve Your Goals
By Dr. Misha Galperin
Serves as a practical guidepost for lay and professional leaders to evaluate the current paradigm with insights from the world of business, psychology and research in Jewish demographics and sociology. Supported by vignettes from the field that illustrate the successes of the lessons as well as the consequences of not implementing them.
6 x 9, 192 pp, Quality PB, 978-1-58023-492-4 **$16.99**

Empowered Judaism: What Independent Minyanim Can Teach Us about Building Vibrant Jewish Communities
By Rabbi Elie Kaunfer; Foreword by Prof. Jonathan D. Sarna
6 x 9, 224 pp, Quality PB, 978-1-58023-412-2 **$18.99**

Building a Successful Volunteer Culture: Finding Meaning in Service in the Jewish Community *By Rabbi Charles Simon; Foreword by Shelley Lindauer; Preface by Dr. Ron Wolfson*
6 x 9, 192 pp, Quality PB, 978-1-58023-408-5 **$16.99**

The Case for Jewish Peoplehood: Can We Be One?
By Dr. Erica Brown and Dr. Misha Galperin; Foreword by Rabbi Joseph Telushkin
6 x 9, 224 pp, HC, 978-1-58023-401-6 **$21.99**

Finding a Spiritual Home: How a New Generation of Jews Can Transform the American Synagogue *By Rabbi Sidney Schwarz*
6 x 9, 352 pp, Quality PB, 978-1-58023-185-5 **$19.95**

Inspired Jewish Leadership: Practical Approaches to Building Strong Communities
By Dr. Erica Brown 6 x 9, 256 pp, HC, 978-1-58023-361-3 **$27.99**

Jewish Pastoral Care, 2nd Edition: A Practical Handbook from Traditional & Contemporary Sources *Edited by Rabbi Dayle A. Friedman, MSW, MAJCS, BCC*
6 x 9, 528 pp, Quality PB, 978-1-58023-427-6 **$30.00**

Jewish Spiritual Direction: An Innovative Guide from Traditional and Contemporary Sources
Edited by Rabbi Howard A. Addison, PhD, and Barbara Eve Breitman, MSW
6 x 9, 368 pp, Quality PB, 978-1-58023-230-2 **$30.00**

Rethinking Synagogues: A New Vocabulary for Congregational Life
By Rabbi Lawrence A. Hoffman, PhD 6 x 9, 240 pp, Quality PB, 978-1-58023-248-7 **$19.99**

Spiritual Community: The Power to Restore Hope, Commitment and Joy
By Rabbi David A. Teutsch, PhD
5½ x 8½, 144 pp, HC, 978-1-58023-270-8 **$19.99**

Spiritual Boredom: Rediscovering the Wonder of Judaism By Dr. Erica Brown
6 x 9, 208 pp, HC, 978-1-58023-405-4 **$21.99**

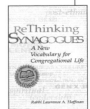

The Spirituality of Welcoming: How to Transform Your Congregation into a Sacred Community *By Dr. Ron Wolfson* 6 x 9, 224 pp, Quality PB, 978-1-58023-244-9 **$19.99**

Holidays / Holy Days

Prayers of Awe Series

An exciting new series that examines the High Holy Day liturgy to enrich the praying experience of everyone—whether experienced worshipers or guests who encounter Jewish prayer for the very first time.

We Have Sinned—Sin and Confession in Judaism: *Ashamnu* and *Al Chet*
Edited by Rabbi Lawrence A. Hoffman, PhD
A varied and fascinating look at sin, confession and pardon in Judaism, as suggested by the centrality of *Ashamnu* and *Al Chet*, two prayers that people know so well, though understand so little. 6 x 9, 304 pp, HC, 978-1-58023-612-6 **$24.99**

Who by Fire, Who by Water—*Un'taneh Tokef*
Edited by Rabbi Lawrence A. Hoffman, PhD 6 x 9, 272 pp, HC, 978-1-58023-424-5 **$24.99**

All These Vows—*Kol Nidre*
Edited by Rabbi Lawrence A. Hoffman, PhD 6 x 9, 288 pp, HC, 978-1-58023-430-6 **$24.99**

Rosh Hashanah Readings: Inspiration, Information and Contemplation
Yom Kippur Readings: Inspiration, Information and Contemplation
Edited by Rabbi Dov Peretz Elkins; Section Introductions from Arthur Green's These Are the Words
Rosh Hashanah: 6 x 9, 400 pp, Quality PB, 978-1-58023-437-5 **$19.99**
Yom Kippur: 6 x 9, 368 pp, Quality PB, 978-1-58023-438-2 **$19.99**; HC, 978-1-58023-271-5 **$24.99**

Reclaiming Judaism as a Spiritual Practice: Holy Days and Shabbat
By Rabbi Goldie Milgram 7 x 9, 272 pp, Quality PB, 978-1-58023-205-0 **$19.99**

The Sabbath Soul: Mystical Reflections on the Transformative Power of Holy Time
Selection, Translation and Commentary by Eitan Fishbane, PhD
6 x 9, 208 pp, Quality PB, 978-1-58023-459-7 **$18.99**

Shabbat, 2nd Edition: The Family Guide to Preparing for and Celebrating the Sabbath
By Dr. Ron Wolfson 7 x 9, 320 pp, Illus., Quality PB, 978-1-58023-164-0 **$19.99**

Hanukkah, 2nd Edition: The Family Guide to Spiritual Celebration
By Dr. Ron Wolfson 7 x 9, 240 pp, Illus., Quality PB, 978-1-58023-122-0 **$18.95**

Passover

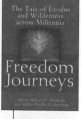

My People's Passover Haggadah
Traditional Texts, Modern Commentaries
Edited by Rabbi Lawrence A. Hoffman, PhD, and David Arnow, PhD
A diverse and exciting collection of commentaries on the traditional Passover Haggadah—in two volumes!
Vol. 1: 7 x 10, 304 pp, HC, 978-1-58023-354-5 **$24.99**
Vol. 2: 7 x 10, 320 pp, HC, 978-1-58023-346-0 **$24.99**

Freedom Journeys: The Tale of Exodus and Wilderness across Millennia
By Rabbi Arthur O. Waskow and Rabbi Phyllis O. Berman
Explores how the story of Exodus echoes in our own time, calling us to relearn and rethink the Passover story through social-justice, ecological, feminist and interfaith perspectives. 6 x 9, 288 pp, HC, 978-1-58023-445-0 **$24.99**

Leading the Passover Journey: The Seder's Meaning Revealed, the Haggadah's Story Retold *By Rabbi Nathan Laufer*
Uncovers the hidden meaning of the Seder's rituals and customs.
6 x 9, 224 pp, Quality PB, 978-1-58023-399-6 **$18.99**

Creating Lively Passover Seders, 2nd Edition: A Sourcebook of Engaging Tales, Texts & Activities *By David Arnow, PhD* 7 x 9, 464 pp, Quality PB, 978-1-58023-444-3 **$24.99**

Passover, 2nd Edition: The Family Guide to Spiritual Celebration
By Dr. Ron Wolfson with Joel Lurie Grishaver 7 x 9, 416 pp, Quality PB, 978-1-58023-174-9 **$19.95**

The Women's Passover Companion: Women's Reflections on the Festival of Freedom
Edited by Rabbi Sharon Cohen Anisfeld, Tara Mohr and Catherine Spector; Foreword by Paula E. Hyman
6 x 9, 352 pp, Quality PB, 978-1-58023-231-9 **$19.99**; HC, 978-1-58023-128-2 **$24.95**

The Women's Seder Sourcebook: Rituals & Readings for Use at the Passover Seder
Edited by Rabbi Sharon Cohen Anisfeld, Tara Mohr and Catherine Spector
6 x 9, 384 pp, Quality PB, 978-1-58023-232-6 **$19.99**

Life Cycle
Marriage / Parenting / Family / Aging

The New Jewish Baby Album: Creating and Celebrating the Beginning of a Spiritual Life—A Jewish Lights Companion
By the Editors at Jewish Lights; Foreword by Anita Diamant; Preface by Rabbi Sandy Eisenberg Sasso
A spiritual keepsake that will be treasured for generations. More than just a memory book, *shows you how—and why it's important*—to create a Jewish home and a Jewish life. 8 x 10, 64 pp, Deluxe Padded HC, Full-color illus., 978-1-58023-138-1 **$19.95**

The Jewish Pregnancy Book: A Resource for the Soul, Body & Mind during Pregnancy, Birth & the First Three Months *By Sandy Falk, MD, and Rabbi Daniel Judson, with Steven A. Rapp* Medical information, prayers and rituals for each stage of pregnancy. 7 x 10, 208 pp, b/w photos, Quality PB, 978-1-58023-178-7 **$16.95**

Celebrating Your New Jewish Daughter: Creating Jewish Ways to Welcome Baby Girls into the Covenant—New and Traditional Ceremonies *By Debra Nussbaum Cohen; Foreword by Rabbi Sandy Eisenberg Sasso* 6 x 9, 272 pp, Quality PB, 978-1-58023-090-2 **$18.95**

The New Jewish Baby Book, 2nd Edition: Names, Ceremonies & Customs—A Guide for Today's Families *By Anita Diamant* 6 x 9, 320 pp, Quality PB, 978-1-58023-251-7 **$19.99**

Parenting as a Spiritual Journey: Deepening Ordinary and Extraordinary Events into Sacred Occasions *By Rabbi Nancy Fuchs-Kreimer, PhD*
6 x 9, 224 pp, Quality PB, 978-1-58023-016-2 **$17.99**

Parenting Jewish Teens: A Guide for the Perplexed
By Joanne Doades Explores the questions and issues that shape the world in which today's Jewish teenagers live and offers constructive advice to parents.
6 x 9, 176 pp, Quality PB, 978-1-58023-305-7 **$16.99**

Judaism for Two: A Spiritual Guide for Strengthening and Celebrating Your Loving Relationship *By Rabbi Nancy Fuchs-Kreimer, PhD, and Rabbi Nancy H. Wiener, DMin; Foreword by Rabbi Elliot N. Dorff, PhD*
Addresses the ways Jewish teachings can enhance and strengthen committed relationships. 6 x 9, 224 pp, Quality PB, 978-1-58023-254-8 **$16.99**

The Creative Jewish Wedding Book, 2nd Edition: A Hands-On Guide to New & Old Traditions, Ceremonies & Celebrations *By Gabrielle Kaplan-Mayer*
9 x 9, 288 pp, b/w photos, Quality PB, 978-1-58023-398-9 **$19.99**

Divorce Is a Mitzvah: A Practical Guide to Finding Wholeness and Holiness When Your Marriage Dies *By Rabbi Perry Netter; Afterword by Rabbi Laura Geller*
6 x 9, 224 pp, Quality PB, 978-1-58023-172-5 **$16.95**

Embracing the Covenant: Converts to Judaism Talk About Why & How
By Rabbi Allan Berkowitz and Patti Moskovitz 6 x 9, 192 pp, Quality PB, 978-1-879045-50-7 **$16.95**

The Guide to Jewish Interfaith Family Life: An InterfaithFamily.com Handbook
Edited by Ronnie Friedland and Edmund Case
6 x 9, 384 pp, Quality PB, 978-1-58023-153-4 **$18.95**

A Heart of Wisdom: Making the Jewish Journey from Midlife through the Elder Years
Edited by Susan Berrin; Foreword by Rabbi Harold Kushner
6 x 9, 384 pp, Quality PB, 978-1-58023-051-3 **$18.95**

Introducing My Faith and My Community: The Jewish Outreach Institute Guide for the Christian in a Jewish Interfaith Relationship
By Rabbi Kerry M. Olitzky 6 x 9, 176 pp, Quality PB, 978-1-58023-192-3 **$16.99**

Making a Successful Jewish Interfaith Marriage: The Jewish Outreach Institute Guide to Opportunities, Challenges and Resources *By Rabbi Kerry M. Olitzky with Joan Peterson Littman*
6 x 9, 176 pp, Quality PB, 978-1-58023-170-1 **$16.95**

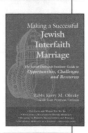

A Man's Responsibility: A Jewish Guide to Being a Son, a Partner in Marriage, a Father and a Community Leader *By Rabbi Joseph B. Meszler*
6 x 9, 192 pp, Quality PB, 978-1-58023-435-1 **$16.99**; HC, 978-1-58023-362-0 **$21.99**

So That Your Values Live On: Ethical Wills and How to Prepare Them
Edited by Rabbi Jack Riemer and Rabbi Nathaniel Stampfer
6 x 9, 272 pp, Quality PB, 978-1-879045-34-7 **$18.99**

Inspiration

God of Me: Imagining God throughout Your Lifetime
By Rabbi David Lyon Helps you cut through preconceived ideas of God and dogmas that stifle your creativity when thinking about your personal relationship with God. 6 x 9, 176 pp, Quality PB, 978-1-58023-452-8 **$16.99**

The God Upgrade: Finding Your 21st-Century Spirituality in Judaism's 5,000-Year-Old Tradition *By Rabbi Jamie Korngold; Foreword by Rabbi Harold M. Schulweis* A provocative look at how our changing God concepts have shaped every aspect of Judaism. 6 x 9, 176 pp, Quality PB, 978-1-58023-443-6 **$15.99**

The Seven Questions You're Asked in Heaven: Reviewing and Renewing Your Life on Earth *By Dr. Ron Wolfson* An intriguing and entertaining resource for living a life that matters. 6 x 9, 176 pp, Quality PB, 978-1-58023-407-8 **$16.99**

Happiness and the Human Spirit: The Spirituality of Becoming the Best You Can Be *By Rabbi Abraham J. Twerski, MD*
Shows you that true happiness is attainable once you stop looking outside yourself for the source. 6 x 9, 176 pp, Quality PB, 978-1-58023-404-7 **$16.99**; HC, 978-1-58023-343-9 **$19.99**

A Formula for Proper Living: Practical Lessons from Life and Torah
By Rabbi Abraham J. Twerski, MD 6 x 9, 144 pp, HC, 978-1-58023-402-3 **$19.99**

The Bridge to Forgiveness: Stories and Prayers for Finding God and Restoring Wholeness *By Rabbi Karyn D. Kedar* 6 x 9, 176 pp, Quality PB, 978-1-58023-451-1 **$16.99**

The Empty Chair: Finding Hope and Joy—Timeless Wisdom from a Hasidic Master, Rebbe Nachman of Breslov *Adapted by Moshe Mykoff and the Breslov Research Institute* 4 x 6, 128 pp, Deluxe PB w/ flaps, 978-1-879045-67-5 **$9.99**

The Gentle Weapon: Prayers for Everyday and Not-So-Everyday Moments— Timeless Wisdom from the Teachings of the Hasidic Master, Rebbe Nachman of Breslov *Adapted by Moshe Mykoff and S. C. Mizrahi, together with the Breslov Research Institute* 4 x 6, 144 pp, Deluxe PB w/ flaps, 978-1-58023-022-3 **$9.99**

God Whispers: Stories of the Soul, Lessons of the Heart *By Rabbi Karyn D. Kedar* 6 x 9, 176 pp, Quality PB, 978-1-58023-088-9 **$15.95**

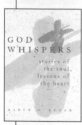

God's To-Do List: 103 Ways to Be an Angel and Do God's Work on Earth
By Dr. Ron Wolfson 6 x 9, 144 pp, Quality PB, 978-1-58023-301-9 **$16.99**

Jewish Stories from Heaven and Earth: Inspiring Tales to Nourish the Heart and Soul *Edited by Rabbi Dov Peretz Elkins* 6 x 9, 304 pp, Quality PB, 978-1-58023-363-7 **$16.99**

Life's Daily Blessings: Inspiring Reflections on Gratitude and Joy for Every Day, Based on Jewish Wisdom *By Rabbi Kerry M. Olitzky* 4½ x 6½, 368 pp, Quality PB, 978-1-58023-396-5 **$16.99**

Restful Reflections: Nighttime Inspiration to Calm the Soul, Based on Jewish Wisdom *By Rabbi Kerry M. Olitzky and Rabbi Lori Forman-Jacobi* 5 x 8, 352 pp, Quality PB, 978-1-58023-091-9 **$16.99**

Sacred Intentions: Morning Inspiration to Strengthen the Spirit, Based on Jewish Wisdom *By Rabbi Kerry M. Olitzky and Rabbi Lori Forman-Jacobi* 4½ x 6½, 448 pp, Quality PB, 978-1-58023-061-2 **$16.99**

Kabbalah / Mysticism

Jewish Mysticism and the Spiritual Life: Classical Texts, Contemporary Reflections *Edited by Dr. Lawrence Fine, Dr. Eitan Fishbane and Rabbi Or N. Rose* Inspirational and thought-provoking materials for contemplation, discussion and action. 6 x 9, 256 pp, HC, 978-1-58023-434-4 **$24.99**

Ehyeh: A Kabbalah for Tomorrow
By Rabbi Arthur Green, PhD 6 x 9, 224 pp, Quality PB, 978-1-58023-213-5 **$18.99**

The Gift of Kabbalah: Discovering the Secrets of Heaven, Renewing Your Life on Earth *By Tamar Frankiel, PhD* 6 x 9, 256 pp, Quality PB, 978-1-58023-141-1 **$16.95**

Seek My Face: A Jewish Mystical Theology *By Rabbi Arthur Green, PhD*
6 x 9, 304 pp, Quality PB, 978-1-58023-130-5 **$19.95**

Zohar: Annotated & Explained *Translation & Annotation by Dr. Daniel C. Matt; Foreword by Andrew Harvey* 5½ x 8½, 176 pp, Quality PB, 978-1-893361-51-5 **$16.99**
(A book from SkyLight Paths, Jewish Lights' sister imprint)

See also *The Way Into Jewish Mystical Tradition* in The Way Into... Series.

Spirituality / Prayer

Making Prayer Real: Leading Jewish Spiritual Voices on Why Prayer Is
Difficult and What to Do about It *By Rabbi Mike Comins*
A new and different response to the challenges of Jewish prayer, with "best prayer
practices" from Jewish spiritual leaders of all denominations.
6 x 9, 320 pp, Quality PB, 978-1-58023-417-7 **$18.99**

Witnesses to the One: The Spiritual History of the *Sh'ma*
By Rabbi Joseph B. Meszler; Foreword by Rabbi Elyse Goldstein
6 x 9, 176 pp, Quality PB, 978-1-58023-400-9 **$16.99**; HC, 978-1-58023-309-5 **$19.99**

My People's Prayer Book Series: Traditional Prayers, Modern
Commentaries *Edited by Rabbi Lawrence A. Hoffman, PhD*
Provides diverse and exciting commentary to the traditional liturgy. Will help you
find new wisdom in Jewish prayer, and bring liturgy into your life. Each book
includes Hebrew text, modern translations and commentaries from all perspec-
tives of the Jewish world.
Vol. I—The *Sh'ma* and Its Blessings
    7 x 10, 168 pp, HC, 978-1-879045-79-8 **$29.99**
Vol. 2—The *Amidah* 7 x 10, 240 pp, HC, 978-1-879045-80-4 **$24.95**
Vol. 3—*P'sukei D'zimrah* (Morning Psalms)
    7 x 10, 240 pp, HC, 978-1-879045-81-1 **$29.99**
Vol. 4—*Seder K'riat Hatorah* (The Torah Service)
    7 x 10, 264 pp, HC, 978-1-879045-82-8 **$29.99**
Vol. 5—*Birkhot Hashachar* (Morning Blessings)
    7 x 10, 240 pp, HC, 978-1-879045-83-5 **$24.95**
Vol. 6—*Tachanun* and Concluding Prayers
    7 x 10, 240 pp, HC, 978-1-879045-84-2 **$24.95**
Vol. 7   Shabbat at Home 7 x 10, 240 pp, HC, 978-1-879045-85-9 **$24.95**
Vol. 8—*Kabbalat Shabbat* (Welcoming Shabbat in the Synagogue)
    7 x 10, 240 pp, HC, 978-1-58023-121-3 **$24.99**
Vol. 9—Welcoming the Night: *Minchah* and *Ma'ariv* (Afternoon and
    Evening Prayer) 7 x 10, 272 pp, HC, 978-1-58023-262-3 **$24.99**
Vol. 10—Shabbat Morning: *Shacharit* and *Musaf* (Morning and
    Additional Services) 7 x 10, 240 pp, HC, 978-1-58023-240-1 **$29.99**

Spirituality / Lawrence Kushner

I'm God; You're Not: Observations on Organized Religion & Other Disguises of the Ego
    6 x 9, 256 pp, Quality PB, 978-1-58023-513-6 **$18.99**; HC, 978-1-58023-441-2 **$21.99**

The Book of Letters: A Mystical Hebrew Alphabet
    Popular HC Edition, 6 x 9, 80 pp, 2-color text, 978-1-879045-00-2 **$24.95**
    Collector's Limited Edition, 9 x 12, 80 pp, gold-foil-embossed pages, w/ limited-edition silkscreened
    print, 978-1-879045-04-0 **$349.00**

The Book of Miracles: A Young Person's Guide to Jewish Spiritual Awareness
    6 x 9, 96 pp, 2-color illus., HC, 978-1-879045-78-1 **$16.95** *For ages 9–13*

The Book of Words: Talking Spiritual Life, Living Spiritual Talk
    6 x 9, 160 pp, Quality PB, 978-1-58023-020-9 **$18.99**

Eyes Remade for Wonder: A Lawrence Kushner Reader *Introduction by Thomas Moore*
    6 x 9, 240 pp, Quality PB, 978-1-58023-042-1 **$18.95**

God Was in This Place & I, i Did Not Know: Finding Self, Spirituality and
    Ultimate Meaning 6 x 9, 192 pp, Quality PB, 978-1-879045-33-0 **$16.95**

Honey from the Rock: An Introduction to Jewish Mysticism
    6 x 9, 176 pp, Quality PB, 978-1-58023-073-5 **$16.95**

Invisible Lines of Connection: Sacred Stories of the Ordinary
    5½ x 8½, 160 pp, Quality PB, 978-1-879045-98-9 **$15.95**

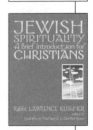

Jewish Spirituality: A Brief Introduction for Christians
    5½ x 8½, 112 pp, Quality PB, 978-1-58023-150-3 **$12.95**

The River of Light: Jewish Mystical Awareness
    6 x 9, 192 pp, Quality PB, 978-1-58023-096-4 **$16.95**

The Way Into Jewish Mystical Tradition
    6 x 9, 224 pp, Quality PB, 978-1-58023-200-5 **$18.99**; HC, 978-1-58023-029-2 **$21.95**

Theology / Philosophy / The Way Into... Series

The Way Into... series offers an accessible and highly usable "guided tour" of the Jewish faith, people, history and beliefs—in total, an introduction to Judaism that will enable you to understand and interact with the sacred texts of the Jewish tradition. Each volume is written by a leading contemporary scholar and teacher, and explores one key aspect of Judaism. The Way Into... series enables all readers to achieve a real sense of Jewish cultural literacy through guided study.

The Way Into Encountering God In Judaism
By Rabbi Neil Gillman, PhD
For everyone who wants to understand how Jews have encountered God throughout history and today.
6 x 9, 240 pp, Quality PB, 978-1-58023-199-2 **$18.99**; HC, 978-1-58023-025-4 **$21.95**
Also Available: **The Jewish Approach to God:** A Brief Introduction for Christians
By Rabbi Neil Gillman, PhD
5½ x 8¼, 192 pp, Quality PB, 978-1-58023-190-9 **$16.95**

The Way Into Jewish Mystical Tradition
By Rabbi Lawrence Kushner
Allows readers to interact directly with the sacred mystical texts of the Jewish tradition. An accessible introduction to the concepts of Jewish mysticism, their religious and spiritual significance, and how they relate to life today.
6 x 9, 224 pp, Quality PB, 978-1-58023-200-5 **$18.99**; HC, 978-1-58023-029-2 **$21.95**

The Way Into Jewish Prayer
By Rabbi Lawrence A. Hoffman, PhD
Opens the door to 3,000 years of Jewish prayer, making anyone feel at home in the Jewish way of communicating with God.
6 x 9, 208 pp, Quality PB, 978-1-58023-201-2 **$18.99**

The Way Into Jewish Prayer Teacher's Guide
By Rabbi Jennifer Ossakow Goldsmith
8½ x 11, 42 pp, PB, 978-1-58023-345-3 **$8.99**
Download a free copy at www.jewishlights.com.

The Way Into Judaism and the Environment
By Jeremy Benstein, PhD
Explores the ways in which Judaism contributes to contemporary social-environmental issues, the extent to which Judaism is part of the problem and how it can be part of the solution.
6 x 9, 288 pp, Quality PB, 978-1-58023-368-2 **$18.99**; HC, 978-1-58023-268-5 **$24.99**

The Way Into *Tikkun Olam* (Repairing the World)
By Rabbi Elliot N. Dorff, PhD
An accessible introduction to the Jewish concept of the individual's responsibility to care for others and repair the world.
6 x 9, 304 pp, Quality PB, 978-1-58023-328-6 **$18.99**

The Way Into Torah
By Rabbi Norman J. Cohen, PhD
Helps guide you in the exploration of the origins and development of Torah, explains why it should be studied and how to do it.
6 x 9, 176 pp, Quality PB, 978-1-58023-198-5 **$16.99**

The Way Into the Varieties of Jewishness
By Sylvia Barack Fishman, PhD
Explores the religious and historical understanding of what it has meant to be Jewish from ancient times to the present controversy over "Who is a Jew?"
6 x 9, 288 pp, Quality PB, 978-1-58023-367-5 **$18.99**; HC, 978-1-58023-030-8 **$24.99**

Theology / Philosophy

From Defender to Critic: The Search for a New Jewish Self
By Dr. David Hartman
A daring self-examination of Hartman's goals, which were not to strip halakha of its authority but to create a space for questioning and critique that allows for the traditionally religious Jew to act out a moral life in tune with modern experience.
6 x 9, 336 pp, HC, 978-1-58023-515-0 **$35.00**

Our Religious Brains: What Cognitive Science Reveals about Belief, Morality, Community and Our Relationship with God
By Rabbi Ralph D. Mecklenburger; Foreword by Dr. Howard Kelfer; Preface by Dr. Neil Gillman
This is a groundbreaking, accessible look at the implications of cognitive science for religion and theology, intended for laypeople.   6 x 9, 224 pp, HC, 978-1-58023-508-2 **$24.99**

The Other Talmud—The Yerushalmi: Unlocking the Secrets of The Talmud of Israel for Judaism Today   *By Rabbi Judith Z. Abrams, PhD*
A fascinating—and stimulating—look at "the other Talmud" and the possibilities for Jewish life reflected there.   6 x 9, 256 pp, HC, 978-1-58023-463-4 **$24.99**

The Way of Man: According to Hasidic Teaching
By Martin Buber; New Translation and Introduction by Rabbi Bernard H. Mehlman and Dr. Gabriel E. Padawer; Foreword by Paul Mendes-Flohr
An accessible and engaging new translation of Buber's classic work—available as an e-book only.   E-book, 978-1-58023-601-0 Digital List Price **$14.99**

The Death of Death: Resurrection and Immortality in Jewish Thought
By Rabbi Neil Gillman, PhD   6 x 9, 336 pp, Quality PB, 978-1-58023-081-0 **$18.95**

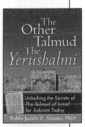

Doing Jewish Theology: God, Torah & Israel in Modern Judaism   *By Rabbi Neil Gillman, PhD*
6 x 9, 304 pp, Quality PB, 978-1-58023-439-9 **$18.99**; HC, 978-1-58023-322-4 **$24.99**

A Heart of Many Rooms: Celebrating the Many Voices within Judaism
By Dr. David Hartman   6 x 9, 352 pp, Quality PB, 978-1-58023-156-5 **$19.95**

The God Who Hates Lies: Confronting & Rethinking Jewish Tradition
By Dr. David Hartman with Charlie Buckholtz   6 x 9, 208 pp, HC, 978-1-58023-455-9 **$24.99**

Jewish Theology in Our Time: A New Generation Explores the Foundations and Future of Jewish Belief   *Edited by Rabbi Elliot J. Cosgrove, PhD; Foreword by Rabbi David J. Wolpe; Preface by Rabbi Carole B. Balin, PhD*   6 x 9, 240 pp, HC, 978-1-58023-413-9 **$24.99**

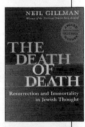

Maimonides—Essential Teachings on Jewish Faith & Ethics: The Book of Knowledge & the Thirteen Principles of Faith—Annotated & Explained
Translation and Annotation by Rabbi Marc D. Angel, PhD
5½ x 8½, 224 pp, Quality PB Original, 978-1-59473-311-6 **$18.99***

Maimonides, Spinoza and Us: Toward an Intellectually Vibrant Judaism
By Rabbi Marc D. Angel, PhD   6 x 9, 224 pp, HC, 978-1-58023-411-5 **$24.99**

A Touch of the Sacred: A Theologian's Informal Guide to Jewish Belief
By Dr. Eugene B. Borowitz and Frances W. Schwartz
6 x 9, 256 pp, Quality PB, 978-1-58023-416-0 **$16.99**; HC, 978-1-58023-337-8 **$21.99**

Traces of God: Seeing God in Torah, History and Everyday Life   *By Rabbi Neil Gillman, PhD*
6 x 9, 240 pp, Quality PB, 978-1-58023-369-9 **$16.99**

Your Word Is Fire: The Hasidic Masters on Contemplative Prayer
Edited and translated by Rabbi Arthur Green, PhD, and Barry W. Holtz
6 x 9, 160 pp, Quality PB, 978-1-879045-25-5 **$15.95**

I Am Jewish
Personal Reflections Inspired by the Last Words of Daniel Pearl
Almost 150 Jews—both famous and not—from all walks of life, from all around the world, write about many aspects of their Judaism.
Edited by Judea and Ruth Pearl   6 x 9, 304 pp, Deluxe PB w/ flaps, 978-1-58023-259-3 **$18.99**
Download a free copy of the *I Am Jewish Teacher's Guide* at www.jewishlights.com.

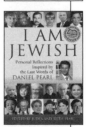

Hannah Senesh: Her Life and Diary, The First Complete Edition
By Hannah Senesh; Foreword by Marge Piercy; Preface by Eitan Senesh; Afterword by Roberta Grossman
6 x 9, 368 pp, b/w photos, Quality PB, 978-1-58023-342-2 **$19.99**

**A book from SkyLight Paths, Jewish Lights' sister imprint*

Social Justice

Where Justice Dwells
A Hands-On Guide to Doing Social Justice in Your Jewish Community
By Rabbi Jill Jacobs; Foreword by Rabbi David Saperstein
Provides ways to envision and act on your own ideals of social justice.
7 x 9, 288 pp, Quality PB Original, 978-1-58023-453-5 **$24.99**

There Shall Be No Needy
Pursuing Social Justice through Jewish Law and Tradition
By Rabbi Jill Jacobs; Foreword by Rabbi Elliot N. Dorff, PhD; Preface by Simon Greer
Confronts the most pressing issues of twenty-first-century America from a deeply
Jewish perspective. 6 x 9, 288 pp, Quality PB, 978-1-58023-425-2 **$16.99**
There Shall Be No Needy Teacher's Guide 8½ x 11, 56 pp, PB, 978-1-58023-429-0 **$8.99**

Conscience
The Duty to Obey and the Duty to Disobey
By Rabbi Harold M. Schulweis
Examines the idea of conscience and the role conscience plays in our relationships
to government, law, ethics, religion, human nature, God—and to each other.
6 x 9, 160 pp, Quality PB, 978-1-58023-419-1 **$16.99**; HC, 978-1-58023-375-0 **$19.99**

Judaism and Justice
The Jewish Passion to Repair the World
By Rabbi Sidney Schwarz; Foreword by Ruth Messinger
Explores the relationship between Judaism, social justice and the Jewish identity
of American Jews. 6 x 9, 352 pp, Quality PB, 978-1-58023-353-8 **$19.99**

Spirituality / Women's Interest

New Jewish Feminism
Probing the Past, Forging the Future
Edited by Rabbi Elyse Goldstein; Foreword by Anita Diamant
Looks at the growth and accomplishments of Jewish feminism and what they
mean for Jewish women today and tomorrow.
6 x 9, 480 pp, HC, 978-1-58023-359-0 **$24.99**

The Divine Feminine in Biblical Wisdom Literature
Selections Annotated & Explained
Translation & Annotation by Rabbi Rami Shapiro
5½ x 8½, 240 pp, Quality PB, 978-1-59473-109-9 **$16.99**
(A book from SkyLight Paths, Jewish Lights' sister imprint)

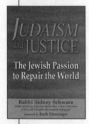

The Quotable Jewish Woman
Wisdom, Inspiration & Humor from the Mind & Heart
Edited by Elaine Bernstein Partnow
6 x 9, 496 pp, Quality PB, 978-1-58023-236-4 **$19.99**

The Women's Haftarah Commentary
New Insights from Women Rabbis on the 54 Weekly Haftarah Portions,
the 5 Megillot & Special Shabbatot
Edited by Rabbi Elyse Goldstein
Illuminates the historical significance of female portrayals in the Haftarah and the
Five Megillot. 6 x 9, 560 pp, Quality PB, 978-1-58023-371-2 **$19.99**

The Women's Torah Commentary
New Insights from Women Rabbis on the 54 Weekly Torah Portions
Edited by Rabbi Elyse Goldstein
Over fifty women rabbis offer inspiring insights on the Torah, in a week-by-week format.
6 x 9, 496 pp, Quality PB, 978-1-58023-370-5 **$19.99**; HC, 978-1-58023-076-6 **$34.95**

See Passover for *The Women's Passover Companion: Women's Reflections on
the Festival of Freedom* and *The Women's Seder Sourcebook: Rituals &
Readings for Use at the Passover Seder.*

Spirituality

The Jewish Lights Spirituality Handbook: A Guide to Understanding, Exploring & Living a Spiritual Life   *Edited by Stuart M. Matlins*
What exactly is "Jewish" about spirituality? How do I make it a part of my life? Fifty of today's foremost spiritual leaders share their ideas and experience with us.
6 x 9, 456 pp, Quality PB, 978-1-58023-093-3 **$19.99**

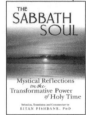

The Sabbath Soul: Mystical Reflections on the Transformative Power of Holy Time   *Selection, Translation and Commentary by Eitan Fishbane, PhD*
Explores the writings of mystical masters of Hasidism. Provides translations and interpretations of a wide range of Hasidic sources previously unavailable in English that reflect the spiritual transformation that takes place on the seventh day.
6 x 9, 208 pp, Quality PB, 978-1-58023-459-7 **$18.99**

Repentance: The Meaning and Practice of *Teshuvah*
By Dr. Louis E. Newman; Foreword by Rabbi Harold M. Schulweis; Preface by Rabbi Karyn D. Kedar
Examines both the practical and philosophical dimensions of *teshuvah*, Judaism's core religious-moral teaching on repentance, and its value for us—Jews and non-Jews alike—today. 6 x 9, 256 pp, HC, 978-1-58023-426-9 **$24.99**

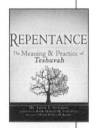

Aleph-Bet Yoga: Embodying the Hebrew Letters for Physical and Spiritual Well-Being
By Steven A. Rapp; Foreword by Tamar Frankiel, PhD, and Judy Greenfeld; Preface by Hart Lazer
7 x 10, 128 pp, b/w photos, Quality PB, Lay-flat binding, 978-1-58023-162-6 **$16.95**

A Book of Life: Embracing Judaism as a Spiritual Practice
By Rabbi Michael Strassfeld 6 x 9, 544 pp, Quality PB, 978-1-58023-247-0 **$19.99**

Bringing the Psalms to Life: How to Understand and Use the Book of Psalms
By Rabbi Daniel F. Polish, PhD 6 x 9, 208 pp, Quality PB, 978-1-58023-157-2 **$16.95**

Does the Soul Survive? A Jewish Journey to Belief in Afterlife, Past Lives & Living with Purpose   *By Rabbi Elie Kaplan Spitz; Foreword by Brian L. Weiss, MD*
6 x 9, 288 pp, Quality PB, 978-1-58023-165-7 **$16.99**

Entering the Temple of Dreams: Jewish Prayers, Movements and Meditations for the End of the Day   *By Tamar Frankiel, PhD, and Judy Greenfeld*
7 x 10, 192 pp, illus., Quality PB, 978-1-58023-079-7 **$16.95**

First Steps to a New Jewish Spirit: Reb Zalman's Guide to Recapturing the Intimacy & Ecstasy in Your Relationship with God   *By Rabbi Zalman M. Schachter-Shalomi with Donald Gropman* 6 x 9, 144 pp, Quality PB, 978-1-58023-182-4 **$16.95**

Foundations of Sephardic Spirituality: The Inner Life of Jews of the Ottoman Empire
By Rabbi Marc D. Angel, PhD 6 x 9, 224 pp, Quality PB, 978-1-58023-341-5 **$18.99**

God & the Big Bang: Discovering Harmony between Science & Spirituality
By Dr. Daniel C. Matt 6 x 9, 216 pp, Quality PB, 978-1-879045-89-7 **$18.99**

God in Our Relationships: Spirituality between People from the Teachings of Martin Buber   *By Rabbi Dennis S. Ross* 5½ x 8½, 160 pp, Quality PB, 978-1-58023-147-3 **$16.95**

Judaism, Physics and God: Searching for Sacred Metaphors in a Post-Einstein World
By Rabbi David W. Nelson 6 x 9, 352 pp, Quality PB, inc. reader's discussion guide,
978-1-58023-306-4 **$18.99**; HC, 352 pp, 978-1-58023-252-4 **$24.99**

Meaning & Mitzvah: Daily Practices for Reclaiming Judaism through Prayer, God, Torah, Hebrew, Mitzvot and Peoplehood   *By Rabbi Goldie Milgram*
7 x 9, 336 pp, Quality PB, 978-1-58023-256-2 **$19.99**

Minding the Temple of the Soul: Balancing Body, Mind, and Spirit through Traditional Jewish Prayer, Movement, and Meditation   *By Tamar Frankiel, PhD, and Judy Greenfeld*
7 x 10, 184 pp, Illus., Quality PB, 978-1-879045-64-4 **$18.99**

One God Clapping: The Spiritual Path of a Zen Rabbi   *By Rabbi Alan Lew with Sherril Jaffe*
5½ x 8½, 336 pp, Quality PB, 978-1-58023-115-2 **$16.95**

The Soul of the Story: Meetings with Remarkable People
By Rabbi David Zeller 6 x 9, 288 pp, HC, 978-1-58023-272-2 **$21.99**

Tanya, the Masterpiece of Hasidic Wisdom: Selections Annotated & Explained
Translation & Annotation by Rabbi Rami Shapiro; Foreword by Rabbi Zalman M. Schachter-Shalomi
5½ x 8½, 240 pp, Quality PB, 978-1-59473-275-1 **$16.99**

These Are the Words, 2nd Edition: A Vocabulary of Jewish Spiritual Life
By Rabbi Arthur Green, PhD 6 x 9, 320 pp, Quality PB, 978-1-58023-494-8 **$19.99**

JEWISH LIGHTS BOOKS ARE AVAILABLE FROM BETTER BOOKSTORES. TRY YOUR BOOKSTORE FIRST.

About Jewish Lights

People of all faiths and backgrounds yearn for books that attract, engage, educate, and spiritually inspire.

Our principal goal is to stimulate thought and help all people learn about who the Jewish People are, where they come from, and what the future can be made to hold. While people of our diverse Jewish heritage are the primary audience, our books speak to people in the Christian world as well and will broaden their understanding of Judaism and the roots of their own faith.

We bring to you authors who are at the forefront of spiritual thought and experience. While each has something different to say, they all say it in a voice that you can hear.

Our books are designed to welcome you and then to engage, stimulate, and inspire. We judge our success not only by whether or not our books are beautiful and commercially successful, but by whether or not they make a difference in your life.

For your information and convenience, at the back of this book we have provided a list of other Jewish Lights books you might find interesting and useful. They cover all the categories of your life:

Bar/Bat Mitzvah	Life Cycle
Bible Study / Midrash	Meditation
Children's Books	Men's Interest
Congregation Resources	Parenting
Current Events / History	Prayer / Ritual / Sacred Practice
Ecology / Environment	Social Justice
Fiction: Mystery, Science Fiction	Spirituality
Grief / Healing	Theology / Philosophy
Holidays / Holy Days	Travel
Inspiration	Twelve Steps
Kabbalah / Mysticism / Enneagram	Women's Interest

Stuart M. Matlins, Publisher

Or phone, fax, mail or e-mail to: **JEWISH LIGHTS Publishing**
Sunset Farm Offices, Route 4 • P.O. Box 237 • Woodstock, Vermont 05091
Tel: (802) 457-4000 • Fax: (802) 457-4004 • www.jewishlights.com
Credit card orders: (800) 962-4544 (8:30AM–5:30PM EST Monday–Friday)
Generous discounts on quantity orders. SATISFACTION GUARANTEED. Prices subject to change.

For more information about each book, visit our website at www.jewishlights.com